Good Schools in Poor Neighborhoods

Also of interest from the Urban Institute Press:

Examining Comprehensive School Reform, edited by Daniel K. Aladjem and Kathryn M. Borman

Reconnecting Disadvantaged Young Men, by Peter Edelman, Harry Holzer, and Paul Offner

Black Males Left Behind, edited by Ronald B. Mincy

Beyond "Bilingual" Education: New Immigrants and Public School Policies in California, by Alec Ian Gershberg, Anne Danenberg, and Patricia Sánchez

Good Schools in Poor Neighborhoods

Defying Demographics, Achieving Success

Beatriz Chu Clewell and Patricia B. Campbell with Lesley Perlman

THE URBAN INSTITUTE PRESS
Washington, D.C.

THE URBAN INSTITUTE PRESS
2100 M Street, N.W.
Washington, D.C. 20037

Library of Congress Cataloging-in-Publication Data
Clewell, Beatriz C.
  Good schools in poor neighborhoods : defying demographics, achieving success / Beatriz Chu Clewell and Patricia B. Campbell with Lesley Perlman.
    p. cm.
  Includes bibliographical references and index.
  ISBN 978-0-87766-742-1 (alk. paper)
  1. Urban schools—United States—Case studies. 2. School improvement programs—United States—Case studies. 3. Minorities—Education—United States—Case studies. I. Campbell, Patricia B. II. Perlman, Lesley. III. Title.
  LC5131.C554   2007
  371.00973'2—dc22

                                                                    2007014834

Printed in the United States of America

10 09 08 07   1 2 3 4 5

Received
NOV 2008
Acquisitions
C. U. Library

THE URBAN INSTITUTE is a nonprofit, nonpartisan policy research and educational organization established in Washington, D.C., in 1968. Its staff investigates the social, economic, and governance problems confronting the nation and evaluates the public and private means to alleviate them. The Institute disseminates its research findings through publications, its web site, the media, seminars, and forums.

Through work that ranges from broad conceptual studies to administrative and technical assistance, Institute researchers contribute to the stock of knowledge available to guide decisionmaking in the public interest.

Conclusions or opinions expressed in Institute publications are those of the authors and do not necessarily reflect the views of officers or trustees of the Institute, advisory groups, or any organizations that provide financial support to the Institute.

In memory of Beatrice (Neney) Johnson, the first and best of teachers—B.C.C.

For Seth Campbell-Mortman and all the other children going to school for the first time—P.B.C.

Contents

PART III: **What the Study Concluded**

Acknowledgments

This book is the result of the efforts of many individuals. Although we cannot name them because they must remain anonymous, we thank the staff of the schools and districts that are the subjects of our study, as well as the staff of the organizations and associations that work with these districts and schools. We are also grateful to the members of our research team at the Urban Institute who made substantive contributions to our work: Katherine Darke Schmitt, Sarah Manes, Laurie Forcier, Robert Santos, and Erin Mudd. Tom Kibler and Lesli Hoey from Campbell-Kibler Associates, Inc., provided data, insight, and support to the study.

Our colleagues, Walter Secada and Okhee Lee, and their teams of researchers contributed to our understanding of the schools and classrooms in our study. We appreciate the thoughtful feedback of the reviewers who commented on both our research report and the book manuscript. Thanks are also due to our program officer at the National Science Foundation (NSF), Bernice Anderson, for her guidance during the several phases of the study and to NSF for its support of the research.

Introduction

As educational researchers, we can recognize it the minute we enter the premises: the school that, despite its shabby exterior, is neat and clean within. Children walk happily through the hallways. Teachers are friendly and composed. We know that when we meet the principal she will be confident and efficient, with an upbeat attitude and a no-nonsense manner. Our hearts lift because we know that we have entered that anomaly that is an effective low-income, urban public school.

We remember entering one such school in New Orleans in a neighborhood notorious for its high rate of child-on-child murder. And in Philadelphia, where after getting lost and driving a rental car through appalling slum conditions for a half-hour we stepped into an oasis of calm and order. How do they do it, these schools that somehow manage to educate poor, minority children so well? What elements make a difference between the typical, defeated urban schools of newspaper fare and these bastions of educational excellence? These are the questions that drove our inquiry, that motivated us to delve into effective schools research. This book is about what we found.

Based on a three-year study comparing typical and highly effective low-income schools in urban school districts, the book is divided into three parts. Part I, "Overview and Study Methods," gives an overview of effective schools research (ESR) and describes the methods of the Urban Institute (UI) effective schools study. Chapter 1 reviews different approaches to effective schools research and discusses the recent explosion of interest in ESR and its implication for school reform. Chapter 2 outlines the conceptual model used in the UI effective schools study and describes the main data collection methods used and how the schools were matched. Part II, "What the Study Found," reports the findings of the UI effective schools study. Chapter 3 describes the context within which Cumberland City, the first district in the study, operates. It traces recent demographic and economic trends and other events affecting K–12 education, and it outlines district policies and practices. Chapter 4 summarizes the findings of a cross-case analysis of typical and highly effective schools within the district to identify factors that differentiate highly effective from typical schools in Cumberland City. The chapter presents data and vignettes from effective- and typical-school case studies to illustrate how differentiating factors play out in actual schools. Chapters 5 and 6 present similar information for the three districts that serve the Rios Calientes area.

Part III, "What the Study Concluded," discusses the study's conclusions and its broader implications and applicability to states, districts, and schools. Chapter 7 summarizes the findings from the two disparate school districts and draws some general conclusions about factors that contribute to effectiveness. These factors are shared by schools in both districts and thus may be generalizable to schools in other similar districts. The chapter also investigates the role of the district in enhancing or inhibiting school effectiveness by contrasting the effect of these two very different school districts on school effectiveness. Finally, the chapter raises provocative questions and speculations that merit further examination and exploration, concluding with implications for school-, district-, and state-level policy that emerge from study findings.

As educational researchers, we know that while resources and socio-economic factors play a role in student achievement, they are not the sole determinants of student success. Poor, urban schools *can* make a difference—and some of them do.

PART I
Overview and
Study Methods

1

Defeated by Demographics
Are Poor, Urban Schools Doomed to Failure?

The minority-white achievement gap has been the focus of national attention for decades (Jencks et al. 1972; Jencks and Phillips 1998). While there is evidence that the black-white score gap narrowed substantially in the 1970s and '80s, racial disparities remain very large (Grissmer, Flanagan, and Williamson 1998; Hedges and Nowell 1998; Perie, Grigg, and Dion 2005). Schools that educate minority students—more specifically, African American and Latino students—are being called upon through legislation to narrow the gap.[1] And the onus for attaining this goal is on the urban schools that educate the vast majority of these students (U.S. Department of Education, National Center for Education Statistics 2003).[2]

As noted in a recent report from the Council of the Great City Schools, "The movement to reform education in the U.S. is fundamentally about improving America's urban public schools" (Casserly 2005, 1). It is also in these schools that the battle for U.S. economic preeminence is being fought. With the increasing presence of African American and Latino adults in the workforce, the nation will become more dependent on their contributions to maintain its ascendancy in the global economy.

This book addresses the important question of whether schools that serve poor minority students can rise to the challenge of improving the educational attainment of these students and narrowing the achievement gap. It identifies and describes characteristics of highly effective urban elementary schools serving low-income minority students. Using an effective schools research (ESR) approach, the book compares *highly effective* urban schools, where students score high on standardized tests, with *typical* urban schools, where students score average or below-average on the same tests. The goal of the approach is to determine the characteristics, policies, practices, and activities that differentiate highly effective schools from typical ones.

This chapter provides an overview of effective schools research and links the resurgence of interest in this type of research to the recent school reform movements. The chapter also introduces the Urban Institute effective schools study and shows how it differs from other recent effective schools studies.

Effective Schools Research: A Response to Coleman and Jencks

The national thinking about whether education can effectively narrow the achievement gap has evolved considerably since the sociologist James Coleman and his colleagues (1966) concluded that schools have very little effect on student learning. Effective schools research has done much to counter the chilling effect of such studies on initiatives to improve poor urban schools.

A Brief History of the Effective Schools Research Movement

Effective schools research emerged as a reaction to the conclusions of Coleman and others that schools have little influence on student achievement independent of family background variables such as socioeconomic status (Coleman et al. 1966; Jencks et al. 1972). In the 1970s, Ron Edmonds and other researchers challenged these conclusions by suggesting an alternative approach to studying school effects: to identify schools serving similar students but differing significantly in student achievement and to examine, through such in-depth research methods as case studies, what makes these schools different (Brookover et al. 1979; Edmonds 1979; Klitgaard and Hall 1975). The researchers' rationale was that although schools may have similar contexts, they vary in practice and achieve different outcomes with similar populations.

Researchers in the 1970s felt that looking at outcomes for students across a large number of schools obscured the effects of individual schools. And, many in the educational research community considered the findings of Coleman and Jencks dangerous from a philosophical viewpoint. Researchers feared that acceptance of these findings could result in rampant indifference to school reform: why reform schools if no amount of change or investment was going to make a difference in students' lives?

The first "effective schools" studies focused on highly effective schools for the urban poor. Later, these studies were expanded to identify characteristics of effective schools for other student groups, such as middle-class students and students in rural and remote areas (Young 1997).

What Works? Characteristics of Effective Schools

The search for characteristics of effective schools began with the five "correlates" of school effectiveness established by Edmonds and colleagues: strong administrative leadership, high expectations for children's achievement, an orderly atmosphere conducive to learning, emphasis on basic skill acquisition, and frequent monitoring of pupil progress (Edmonds 1979). Since then, successive studies have added to or revised the list of effective schools characteristics. Nonetheless, researchers have marveled at the consistent findings of effective schools studies. In the words of Rosenholtz, "It strains the limits of credibility that different studies, conducted by different investigators in different urban areas, could produce strikingly similar findings by chance" (1985, 353). Purkey and Smith summarize common findings across studies as "high staff expectations and morale, a considerable degree of control by staff over instructional and training decisions in the school, clear leadership from the principal or other instructional figure, clear goals for the school, and a sense of order in the school" (1983, 438).

Later research has revised these categories. Zigarelli (1996) identifies the most frequently cited variables from several ESR studies and collapses them into six factors: employment of quality teachers, teacher participation and satisfaction, principal leadership and involvement, a culture of academic achievement, positive relations with the central school administration, and high parental involvement. Using the National Education Longitudinal Study of 1988[3] data to assess the effects of these variables on student achievement, Zigarelli finds no evidence that certain other school variables influence student achievement, including teacher empowerment and autonomy, continuing teacher education, principal management responsibilities, or warm relations between the school and the administration. In a more recent review of the research on school-level factors, Marzano (2003) identifies and ranks five basic categories into which these factors fall: (1) a guaranteed and viable curriculum, (2) challenging goals and effective feedback, (3) parental and community involvement, (4) a safe and orderly environment, and (5) collegiality and professionalism.

As many researchers have noted, results from effective schools research do not provide specific instructions for developing more effective schools (Creemers et al. 2001; Sammons, Hillman, and Mortimore 1995). Despite this caveat, this research is a valuable resource for those concerned with school improvement as long as the tenets are not applied mechanically and the schools' contexts are always kept in mind.

Classrooms, Schools, or Districts?

Until recently, effective schools research has focused on either school-level or classroom-level effects, perhaps because these two research areas emerged separately. In fact, after reviewing studies in the two areas with a combined total of 328 references (Brophy and Good 1986; Good and Brophy 1986), Teddlie (1994) finds that only 3 percent of the studies consider both school- and classroom-level effects. Most teacher effectiveness studies focus only on processes that occur within classrooms (to the exclusion of anything that might be happening schoolwide), whereas most school effectiveness studies involve practices that occur throughout the school, with little emphasis on teaching behaviors within individual classrooms (Teddlie 1994).

Nevertheless, the prevalent trend in effective schools research is the study of school-level effects. As Purkey and Smith (1983) explain, the school "forms the immediate environment in which the classroom functions. The quality of the process at the classroom level will be enhanced or diminished by the quality of activity at the level above it" (428).

The Louisiana School Effectiveness Study is one of the few studies that addresses both the school and classroom levels and uses both quantitative and qualitative techniques (Teddlie and Stringfield 1993). In this study, classrooms in the more effective schools exhibit higher student time on task, more frequent introduction of new material, encouragement of independent practice, high expectations, positive reinforcement, firm discipline, a friendly environment, display of student work, and pleasant classrooms (Reynolds et al. 2002).

It is only recently, with the advent of the systemic reform movement, that effective schools research has considered the district as a unit of analysis. A recent study compares urban school districts that are improving rapidly with other urban districts that are making less progress (Snipes, Doolittle, and Herlihy 2002). The research, which uses case study methodology, finds that the "effective" districts share nine common approaches to reform:

1. focus on student achievement and specific goals;
2. development of concrete accountability systems;
3. focus on the lowest-performing schools;
4. adoption or development of districtwide curricula and instructional approaches;
5. support for districtwide strategies at the central office level;
6. a role for the central office in guiding, supporting, and improving instruction at the building level;
7. commitment to data-driven decisionmaking and instruction;
8. initiation of reforms at the elementary grade levels; and
9. provision of intensive instruction in reading and math to middle- and high-school students.

District-level studies, nevertheless, continue to be rare, with several researchers agreeing with Marzano that "the school (as opposed to the district) is the proper focus for reform" (2003, 10).[4]

From Characteristics to Practices: A Growing Trend?

A recent trend in effective schools research focuses on *practices* rather than *characteristics* that differentiate effective from typical or ineffective schools. A possible explanation for this development is the emergence of the school reform movement with its increased emphasis on applying research to practice. Research that identifies effective practices can be applied more readily than studies that describe effective characteristics.

In one recent ESR study, Reynolds and Teddlie (2000) identify *processes* of school effectiveness: effective leadership, effective teaching, developing and maintaining a pervasive focus on learning, producing a positive school culture, creating high and appropriate expectations for all, emphasizing student responsibilities and rights, monitoring progress at all levels, developing staff skills at the school site, and involving parents productively and appropriately.

Most recently, a large-scale survey of California elementary schools looks at factors that might explain the gap in academic performance within a group of 500 schools with similar demographic characteristics.[5] Four clusters of practices are most strongly correlated with higher scores: "(1) prioritizing student achievement; (2) implementing a coherent, standards-based instructional program; (3) using assessment data to improve student achievement and instruction; and (4) ensuring the availability of instructional resources" (Williams, Kirst, and Haertel 2005, 6).

Another recently released study of "best practices" reviews studies during the past six years of more than 250 schools across the nation to identify those that consistently outperform demographically similar schools for three consecutive years on state exams. The researchers chose 140 schools in 20 states that met their criteria and compared educational practices in these high-performing schools with those of similar average-performing schools in the same states (National Center for Educational Accountability 2006).

ESR Methodologies: Case Studies, Outlier Studies, or Program Evaluations?

Effective schools research employs varied methodologies, the most prevalent of which—case studies and outlier studies—have been criticized by researchers as having inherent weaknesses. In an extensive review of ESR studies, Purkey and Smith (1983) divide these studies into four groups: outlier studies, case studies, program evaluation studies, and other studies. The researchers identify common weaknesses in the first two types of study examined, concluding that the program evaluation studies they have reviewed are methodologically stronger than either outlier studies or case studies. Both outlier studies and case studies, Purkey and Smith find, share similar weaknesses: small and unrepresentative samples; the possibility of errors in identifying effectiveness; achievement data aggregated at the school level; inappropriate comparisons, if any; and the use of subjective criteria to judge school effectiveness. They note, nevertheless, that the common findings across all the studies they have reviewed are "remarkably consistent" (437). Similarly, Rosenholtz (1985) cites common methodological problems found in an analysis of ESR studies,[6] yet she also comments that all the studies "produce common findings with remarkable consistency" (353).

Because outlier studies, in contrast to high-cost, large-scale data gathering efforts that focus on norms and trends, use their scarce resources to carefully observe and describe desirable practices within a school, these studies can be useful and enlightening. Outlier studies have produced many of the most frequently cited findings from the school effectiveness literature. Despite their flaws, these studies are likely to remain a dominant methodology in the research on school effects (Stringfield 1994).

Outlier Studies: When the Exception Disproves the Rule

Outlier studies, an outgrowth of effective schools research, contrast unusually effective schools with ineffective or average schools that have similar demographic characteristics. The ESR literature contains dozens of examples of outlier studies.[7] Writing about the sampling designs that characterize outlier studies, Stringfield (1994) describes the strengths and limitations of four basic designs: studies of positive outliers only; studies contrasting positive and negative outliers; studies comparing positive outliers and typical schools; and studies of positive outliers, typical schools, and negative outliers.

Each study type has its drawbacks. Positive outlier studies, which document only exemplary cases, lack a comparison group that could confirm that "effective" characteristics identified by the research are indeed unique to these positive outliers. Studies contrasting positive and negative outliers confine the research to extreme cases, increasing the cost of conducting research or reducing the number of cases. Another drawback identified by Stringfield (1994) and others (Purkey and Smith 1983; Rowan, Bossert, and Dwyer 1983; Rosenholtz 1985) is that these studies do not study the average or typical schools that stand to benefit the most from the example of effective schools. Studies that compare positive outliers and typical schools seem to have overcome some disadvantages of the previous two types, but they may not provide the maximum opportunity for differentiation. Studies that examine positive outliers, typical schools, and negative outliers allow researchers to discriminate at three points along the school effects continuum, but they also demand the most resources. Stringfield, writing in 1994, states that he has been unable to identify examples of the latter two types of outlier studies in the U.S. literature. Ten years later, the authors of this book, too, can say that when they initiated their research, they were also unable to locate examples of these types of studies.

School Reform and Effective Schools Studies

Forty years have elapsed since the renowned sociologist James S. Coleman and his colleagues (1966) threw cold water on education reform. Jencks and his associates dealt a second blow to education reform a few years later with the pronouncement that "school quality has little effect on achievement or on economic success" (1972, book jacket). Nonetheless, U.S. public schools today are being asked to narrow the so-called achievement gap between minority and white students.

Although researchers are still pondering the effect of family background on children's performance in school,[8] something has happened along the way to renew public belief in schools as instruments of economic and social mobility. In recent years, there has been a veritable explosion of interest in education reform, culminating in the enactment of one of the most ambitious attempts to legislate school reform: the No Child Left Behind Act. What happened in the four decades since the Coleman report to rekindle hope and interest in schools as places where low-income minority children can achieve at the level of their middle-class white counterparts? One contributor to the resurgence of hope in public schools is the effective schools research movement described earlier.

The focus on education reform that has marked the previous 20 years has stimulated interest in this research, which advances the tenet that schools serving low-income minority students *can* effectively educate these students. The math reform movement that inspired the National Council of Teachers of Mathematics' development of standards for mathematics education (1991) also launched the standards movement that still drives many state-level reform efforts today. That same year, an influential book chapter by Smith and O'Day (1991) laid out the concept of *systemic school reform,* later described by the authors as content-driven school reform that provides "a clear and continuing vision, structure, and system of support [for schools that] could enhance the stability and coherence they need to be effective" (O'Day and Smith 1993, 269). Although Smith and O'Day emphasized state systemic reform, their prescriptions included the role of the district and schools in influencing reform. In 1995, the American Association for the Advancement of

Science and the National Academy of Sciences released science standards that would influence the teaching of science in many of the nation's schools. Inherent in all these standards-based reform movements is the belief that all children have the right to high-quality education and that all children can reach high achievement levels.

The standards movement continues to grow as state after state strives to develop and implement appropriate standards and align these with curriculum and assessment. How has this climate of standards and reform affected effective schools research? By accepting the possibility that education reform can and does work, the standards movement has renewed the legitimacy and credibility of this stream of research. Since 2000, "effective schools" studies have sprouted like mushrooms during a rainy fall. These studies vary widely in their quality, scope, and focus. Some identify characteristics and practices of effective districts,[9] while others enumerate successful elements of schools.[10] Many cite the same attributes of effectiveness. All, however, are based on the belief that it is possible for districts or schools serving poor urban students to provide these students with a good education.

In the 1990s, the National Science Foundation (NSF) launched the multimillion dollar Systemic Initiative that encompassed statewide and districtwide reform in K–12 mathematics and science education. This initiative embodied many principles of the systemic school reform movement (O'Day and Smith 1993). A component of NSF's Systemic Initiative, the Urban Systemic Initiatives (USI) program, began in 1994. It was described by NSF as a "comprehensive and systemic effort to stimulate fundamental, sweeping, and sustained improvement in the quality and level of K–12 science, mathematics, and technology (SMT) education" (Williams 1998, 7). The initiative involved 22 cities with the largest numbers of school-age children living in poverty. In their charge to provide high-quality, rigorous mathematics and science for all students, the USIs were guided by six drivers for achieving educational system reform (chapter 2 in this volume lists and describes the drivers). These drivers were designed to facilitate the USI districts' transition to standards-based instruction for all students through the establishment of curriculum, professional development, assessment, and other systems to support instruction. Some USI sites have reported impressive student outcomes that include gains in state and local assessment results, while others have been less successful. These mixed results make USI sites ideally suited for effective schools research—especially research on outliers.

About This Study

The study on which this book is based uses an *effective schools outlier study* approach to identify school-level characteristics, policies, and practices of highly effective urban elementary schools serving low-income minority students. Highly effective schools (where students scored high on standardized tests) are compared to typical schools (where students scored average or below-average on standardized tests) with similar demographic characteristics in the same school districts. The purpose of the study is to determine the characteristics, policies, practices, and activities that differentiate the highly effective schools from their typical counterparts. School districts chosen for the study were part of an NSF-funded math/science improvement initiative.

The Urban Institute effective schools study differs in three very important ways from the most recent books and reports on effective schools.

First, *it compares highly effective schools to typical schools that are closely matched demographically and in the same districts.* Many recent studies have looked only at groups of good schools and have generalized from them about the characteristics of effective schools. These common characteristics, however, may not be unique to good schools. Since comparisons have not been made to typical or less-effective schools, it is impossible to tell. Other studies have examined effective schools across various settings and locations. Since the UI effective schools study looks at both highly effective and typical schools in the same districts and with the same school-level demographic characteristics, operating under the same union contracts and other district constraints, the differences found should be those that actually differentiate between the two types of schools.

Second, *the study is both quantitative and qualitative.* Another distinction between recent publications and this study is that data in many of the former tend to be either quantitative or qualitative. This study's findings are derived from several quantitative and qualitative measures including attendance and achievement data, surveys, interviews, focus groups, and material reviews. While quantitative data can help researchers focus in on *what* is different and even the degree of difference, qualitative data provide insight into *how* these differences manifest in the school setting. Each type of data supports the other.

Third, *the study sets the findings within the context of each district setting.* This study's work is set within the economic, social, and policy context of each school district. The two very different contexts in which the schools operate—a growing southwestern border area and a northeastern city with a declining population—enrich the study and increase the generalizability of the cross-district results.

Chapter 2 details the goals, structure, and methodology of the study. It presents the conceptual model that drives the research, defines the study components, and describes data collection and analysis methods.

2

Highly Effective versus Typical Schools

How the Exception Contradicts the Rule

The study on which this book is based uses an effective schools outlier study approach to identify various traits of highly effective urban elementary schools serving low-income minority students. Highly effective schools (where students score high on standardized tests) are compared against typical schools (where students score average or below-average on standardized tests) with similar demographic characteristics in the same school districts. The school districts examined are part of an NSF-funded math/science improvement initiative; as such, all were implementing systemic reform of their mathematics and science instruction at the time of the study. Four school districts were selected for the study, three of which share many characteristics and are treated as one site. From each of the two sites, five highly effective and three typical elementary schools were selected to be studied.

The Urban Institute (UI) effective schools study has two primary research goals. It seeks to identify the characteristics, policies, practices, and activities that differentiate highly effective schools from comparable schools with poorer results. It also examines how the description of such activities, policies, and practices of exemplary elementary schools can inform systemic reform efforts in mathematics and science education in other schools, especially schools that enroll poor minority students.

The study uses an input-output conceptual model to identify characteristics of highly effective schools within the context of districts that are implementing school reform. The model looks within the "black box" of what takes place at the school level to study the differences between highly effective and typical schools. The study uses the outlier approach, which compares schools that have average or below-average student achievement outcomes with schools—matched in demographic characteristics—that have much higher outcomes. It addresses the question: given a group of schools with similar demographic makeup, why do some perform better than others?

Various sources were used to collect data including principal and teacher surveys; site visits; district administrator and principal interviews; teacher interviews and focus groups; and parent and student focus groups. Additional data were collected from state, district, and school web sites.

Research Questions and Conceptual Model

The outlier design for this project includes two comparison groups, one of highly effective or exemplary schools and the other of typical schools. By choosing an outlier study design involving a comparison of effective and typical schools, this study's researchers hoped to avoid the pitfalls of using a positive outlier–only design or a positive and negative outlier design.[1] The funding for this study was not enough to allow researchers to implement a positive outlier–typical schools–negative outlier design and retain a reasonable number of cases.

Two research questions guided this study. First, what characteristics, activities, policies, and practices of the most effective elementary schools in a district differentiate them from typical elementary schools there? Second, how can identifying the most effective activities, policies, and practices of exemplary elementary schools inform systemic reform efforts in mathematics and science education in other schools, especially schools that enroll poor minority students?

Interest in "what works best" for minority students in the context of high-achieving schools serving low-income students is very high. A recent report that presents survey findings of 366 schools in 21 states seeks to identify common elements shared by high-poverty schools that foster unusually high academic performance (Education Trust 1999). An article in *Education Week* published in May 1999 discusses the presence of high-poverty schools among top-scoring schools in Kentucky (White 1999). While praising this achievement, the article goes on to note that while the gap between low-income and wealthy students has been closing, a similar closing of the gap has not occurred between African American and white students. The districts (and schools) in the UI effective schools study serve large enrollments of low-income minority students—African American in one case and Latino in the other.

The conceptual framework that guides this research takes a school effectiveness model and incorporates drivers developed by the National Science Foundation to produce a model of school effectiveness for schools striving toward systemic reform in mathematics and science education. The school effectiveness model was developed and used by Heneveld and Craig (1995) to study primary and secondary schools in Madagascar. Heneveld and Craig based their model on school effectiveness and school improvement research, much of it conducted in industrialized countries.

In the Heneveld and Craig model, factors that determine school effectiveness are based on the notion of schools as a complex network of social systems that form a single social entity and the belief that the complex interactions among various factors making up an effective school influence student achievement. Heneveld and Craig identify 16 school effectiveness factors most commonly cited by the research literature and divide them into five main categories: supporting inputs (support from parents/community, the education system, and material support), enabling conditions (effective leadership, capable teaching force, flexibility and autonomy, and high level of time in school), school culture and climate (high expectations, positive teacher attitudes, order and discipline, organized curriculum, rewards and incentives), and the teaching/learning process (high learning time, variety in teaching strategies, frequent homework, frequent student assessment and feedback); these four categories are all influenced by the final group—the cultural, political, and economic context of the surrounding school environment.[2] The supporting inputs flow into each school, where the enabling conditions, school climate, and teaching/learning process combine to produce student outcomes.

To guide the systemic reform of mathematics and science education, NSF identified six critical developments that drive systemic change. NSF dubbed these developments "the drivers" of systemic reform:

1. implementation of comprehensive, standards-based curricula as represented in instructional practice;
2. development of coherent, consistent policies that support provision of high-quality mathematics and science education for each

student; excellent preparation, continuing education, and support for each mathematics and science teacher; and administrative support for all persons who work to improve achievement among students served by the system;

3. convergence of all resources that are designed for or that reasonably can be used to support science and mathematics education into a focused and unitary program to constantly upgrade, renew, and improve the educational program in mathematics and science for all students;

4. broad-based support from parents, policymakers, institutions of higher education, business and industry, foundations, and other segments of the community for the goals and collective value of the program;

5. accumulation of a broad and deep array of evidence that the program is enhancing student achievement; and

6. improvement in the achievement of all students, including those historically underserved.

The first four drivers identify changes in the system that are necessary to achieve reform, while the last two refer to student achievement outcomes (Anderson et al. 1998).

In the model for the UI effective schools study, the first four NSF process drivers are the supporting inputs into the general factors that affect school effectiveness at the school level, transforming these factors so they characterize effective systemic reform efforts in mathematics and science (figure 2.1). The supporting inputs flow into the schools, where the enabling conditions and the school climate combine to produce student outcomes. Driver 5, which calls for "a broad and deep array of evidence," is part of an accountability and evaluation system (an enabling conditions variable) that forms a feedback loop with the school climate variables. Driver 6, "the achievement of all students, including those historically underserved," is an outcome variable represented by two student outcomes: increases in student achievement in mathematics and science and increased gains for underrepresented groups. Those two outcomes are the focus of this research. In this framework, student characteristics are also inputs, with race or ethnicity, gender, and socioeconomic status interacting with the school-level variables to produce student outcomes.

The study hypothesizes that effective schools will demonstrate a higher level of implementation of the process drivers and, consequently,

Figure 2.1. Conceptual Framework: Factors that Determine the Effectiveness of Systemic Reform in Elementary Math and Science Education

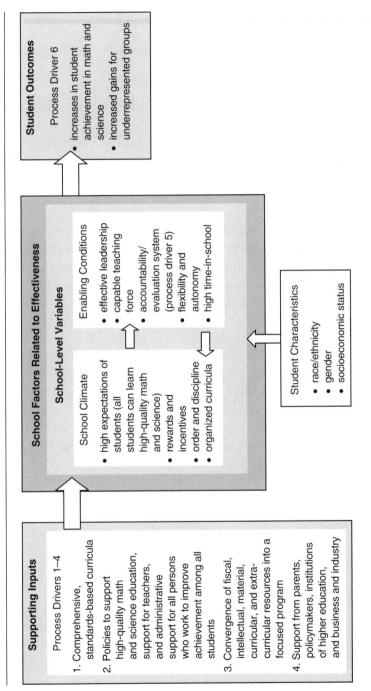

Source: Adapted from Heneveld and Craig (1995), figure 1.

are more likely to possess school-level characteristics related to success than typical schools. Effective schools are defined as those that show more evidence of success in achieving the two student outcomes.

Study Components: District and School Selection

This section describes how the highly effective schools in the Urban Institute effective schools study were selected and matched with typical schools. It also describes the characteristics of the schools themselves.

District Selection

The study targeted two sites, the Cumberland City school district and a collaboration of three districts in and around Rios Calientes.[3] These districts were selected because they served predominately low-income minority students; had strong mathematics education reform efforts; adhered to elementary grade standards in mathematics, science, and language arts; and gave standardized tests to 4th grade students in mathematics and language arts. One major difference between the two sites was the Cumberland City district served a predominately African American student population while the three Rios Calientes districts served a predominately Latino student population.

All four districts have used standardized criterion-referenced tests to evaluate 4th grade students in mathematics and language arts over several years. The Cumberland City school district also tests 4th grade students in science. In the Cumberland City school district, 4th grade student achievement is measured with the Stanford Achievement Test–9th Edition (SAT9): Intermediate I, while in the three Rios Calientes districts (Cesar Chavez, Omar Torrijos, and Simon Bolivar), student achievement is measured with the State Assessment of Academic Skills (SAAS).

The Tests

The SAAS and SAT9 are aligned to different standards: the SAAS to its state standards, and the SAT9 to national standards including those established by the National Council of Teachers of Mathematics. On examination as part of the UI effective schools study, the tests' standards are found to overlap significantly. For example, 74 percent of the SAT9 math objectives are, at least somewhat, covered by the SAAS math objectives, while 83 percent of the SAAS math objectives are, at least somewhat, covered by the SAT9 math objectives.

The scoring categories used by the two tests are also similar. SAAS scores are broken into three levels: academically recognized (95 percent or better), proficient (85 percent or better), and pass (70 percent or better). The SAT9 has comparable categories:

- *advanced:* superior performance beyond grade-level mastery;
- *proficient:* solid academic performance, indicating that students are prepared for the next grade; and
- *basic:* partial mastery of the knowledge and skills that are fundamental for satisfactory work.[4]

In addition, the SAT9 has a fourth category—*below basic,* less than partial mastery—that appears comparable to failing the SAAS.

Selection of Sample Schools

The UI effective schools study sample comprised eight schools from each district. To emphasize what schools were doing "right," while still allowing for adequate comparison data, researchers decided to oversample the highly effective schools. Study researchers sampled five highly effective schools from Cumberland City and five from the Rios Calientes districts. These schools were matched with three typical schools from each area.

Cumberland City School District

Since the effective schools study emphasized math and science, study researchers defined a highly effective school as one where the vast majority of students were demonstrating at least a basic level of performance in these areas, while a significant minority were achieving at higher levels. Since test scores can be volatile, schools needed to either have students scoring at high levels for four years or have scores that had been increasing over that four-year period to be selected.

The nine criteria used to select the five highly effective Cumberland elementary schools were as follows:

- a majority of students from underrepresented minority groups;
- a majority of low-income students, as defined by the district. The district definition is based on guidelines for eligibility for welfare and is more stringent than the common definition of eligibility for free or reduced-price lunches;
- 90 percent or more students tested using the SAT9 during the 1998–99 school year;
- 66 percent or more of the 4th graders taking the 1999 SAT9 math test scoring basic or higher;
- 30 percent or more of the 4th graders taking the 1999 SAT9 math test scoring academically proficient or higher;
- 66 percent or more of the 4th graders taking the 1999 SAT9 science test scoring basic or higher;
- 30 percent or more of the 4th graders taking the 1999 SAT9 science test scoring academically proficient or higher;
- student math and science scores at the 4th grade level either increasing or being consistently high over the 1996, 1997, 1998, and 1999 SAT9s; and
- among schools meeting the above criteria, those with the highest share of 4th grade students scoring basic or higher on the 1999 SAT9 reading test.

Typical schools were matched with the highly effective schools on the following criteria:

- location in the same district administrative unit, called a cluster, as a highly effective school to ensure that the schools were in the same geographic region of the city and had similar access to professional development services;
- approximately the same percentage of low-income students;
- approximately the same student racial and ethnic breakdown; and
- to the degree possible, a similar school size.

Based on data provided by the Cumberland City school district, researchers selected five highly effective schools: Andrew Jackson, James Monroe, John Adams, Thomas Jefferson, and John Tyler (table 2.1). The director of the NSF-funded math/science improvement effort and the

Table 2.1. Demographic and Achievement Variables of Cumberland City Highly Effective Schools

| School | Enrollment | Low-income (%)[a] | Race/Ethnicity (%) | | | 1999 SAT9 Achievement (%) | | | | |
			African American	Latino	White	Math basic or above	Math proficient or above	Science basic or above	Science proficient or above	Reading basic or above
Andrew Jackson	645	54	99	0	0	65.8	41.8	78.5	43.0	75.9
James Monroe	466	49	56	17	26	86.8	61.8	89.7	35.3	70.6
John Adams	820	58	25	75	0	68.9	49.1	58.5	37.7	67.9
Thomas Jefferson	834	56	72	11	16	73.4	35.5	87.9	33.9	80.6
John Tyler	385	64	19	79	1	86.2	34.5	63.8	24.1	65.5

Source: Cumberland City school district.

Note: The five schools listed, along with one back-up school, came closest to reaching all criteria of the school study.

a. Low-income is based on the Cumberland City school district definition. In all the selected schools, at least 85 percent of students were eligible for free or reduced-price lunches.

Table 2.2. Demographic Variables of Cumberland City Typical Schools

			Race/Ethnicity		
School	Enrollment	Low-income (%)[a]	African American	Latino	White
George Washington	647	51	62	25	11
James Madison	557	57	98	1	1
Martin Van Buren	1,398	63	23	71	5

Source: Cumberland City school district.

a. Low-income is based on the Cumberland City school district definition. In all the selected schools, at least 85 percent of students were eligible for free or reduced-price lunches.

Figure 2.2. Relative Locations of Cumberland City Highly Effective and Typical Schools

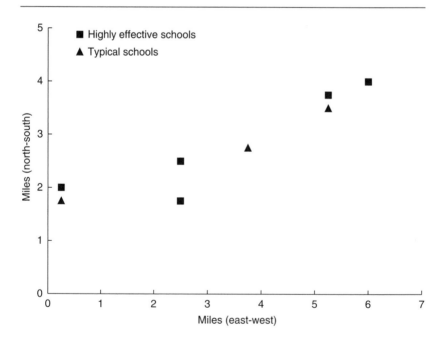

district director of research reviewed the names of the suggested highly effective schools. Both agreed that the selected schools were highly effective, and no changes were made.

Three typical schools were then selected: George Washington, James Madison, and Martin Van Buren (table 2.2). George Washington was in the same cluster as highly effective schools James Monroe and Thomas Jefferson. James Madison was in the same cluster as Andrew Jackson, and Martin Van Buren was in the same cluster as John Adams. The highly effective and typical schools were also geographically close to each other (figure 2.2).

While race/ethnicity, income levels, and cluster location were similar for the typical and highly effective schools, it was not possible to match school sizes. For the 1998–99 school year, highly effective schools ranged in size from 385 to 834 students for an average size of 630, while typical schools ranged from 557 to 1,398 students for a average size of 867.

As table 2.3 indicates, the percentages of Cumberland City School District students achieving at the basic and proficient levels in the selected highly effective schools were higher than those in all schools with comparable percentages of low-income students. The highly effective schools' percentages were also higher than the percentages for all district elementary schools.

In 2000, SAT9 test scores plummeted at Andrew Jackson, and they remained very low in 2001. As a result, Andrew Jackson moved from a highly effective school to a formerly effective school (table 2.4).

Table 2.3. Cumberland City Student 1999 SAT9 Achievement (percent)

Comparison group	Math basic or above	Math proficient or above	Science basic or above	Science proficient or above	Reading basic or above
4th graders in selected highly effective schools	77	42	76	31	72
4th graders in all district schools with > 49 percent low-income students	43	11	48	9	50
All district 4th graders	52	17	56	14	60

Source: Cumberland City school district.

Table 2.4. Andrew Jackson Students Scoring Proficient or Above on SAT9 (percent)

	1996	1997	1998	1999	2000	2001
Math	15	26	28	42	4	5
Science	6	21	12	43	3	0
Reading	6	23	29	38	10	7

Source: Cumberland City school district.

Rios Calientes–Area Districts

There were several differences in the criteria used to select highly effective schools in the three Rios Calientes–area districts. The low-income measure used in Rios Calientes was eligibility for free and reduced-price lunches, and an additional criterion of having a significant minority of limited English proficient students was added. Since no science test was given, that criterion was eliminated; however, higher percentages of students were required to have earned pass and proficient levels in math for a school to be selected as highly effective. The eight criteria used to select the five highly effective Rios Calientes elementary schools were as follows:

- a majority of students from underrepresented minority groups;
- a majority of low-income students, as defined by eligibility for free and reduced-price lunches;
- 30 percent or more limited English proficient (LEP) students;
- 90 percent or more students tested using the SAAS during the 1998–99 school year;
- 90 percent or more of the 4th graders taking the 1999 SAAS math passing the test;
- 50 percent or more of the 4th graders taking the 1999 SAAS math test scoring proficient or higher;
- 4th grade student math scores either increasing over time or being consistently high compared with the top 10 matched schools in the state (as defined by Just4Kids.org) on the 1997, 1998, and 1999 administrations of the SAAS; and
- among schools meeting the above criteria, those with the highest share of 4th grade students passing the 1999 administration of the SAAS language arts test.

In addition, at least one highly effective school had to be located in each participating district.

Based on data provided by the state education agency and Just4Kids.org, researchers created a list of all possible highly effective schools. That list was given to the research director and staff from each of the three districts. The final selection was made based on staff input. Five highly effective schools were selected: Diego Rivera, Frida Kahlo, Carlos Fuentes, Sor Juana Ines de la Cruz, and Luis Barragan (tables 2.5 and 2.6).

Three typical schools were then selected: Rosario Castellanos, Rufino Tamayo, and Octavio Paz (table 2.7). As shown in tables 2.5 and 2.7, the race/ethnicity and low-income levels of the highly effective and typical schools were similar. In addition, Octavio Paz was in the same district as Sor Juana Ines de la Cruz, while Rufino Tamayo and Rosario Castellanos were in the same district as Diego Rivera, Frida Kahlo, and Carlos Fuentes. Although the schools were in three different districts, they were relatively close to each other, especially the five schools in the Bolivar district (figure 2.3).

Highly effective schools had a broader range of school sizes, with enrollments varying from 474 to 1,040 students with an average size of 660, while typical schools ranged from 638 to 720 students with an average size of 672.

The analysis of differences between the achievement levels of Rios Calientes highly effective schools and other schools found less variation in the percentages of students achieving at different levels of proficiency than was found in Cumberland City. This is in part because the Rios Calientes districts used free and reduced-price lunch eligibility as their definition of low income. Under that criterion, 88 percent of the area schools qualified as low income (table 2.8).

Study Components: District- and School-Level Data

The UI effective schools study examined eight schools within the Cumberland City school district and eight schools within the three districts that made up the Rios Calientes site.[5] At each site, five schools were designated as highly effective, while three were selected as typical or average.

Although the study focused on school-level variables, district-level data were collected to provide context for the findings. Both quantitative and qualitative data were collected via surveys, focus groups, and interviews at both the district and school levels.

text continues on page 32

Table 2.5. Demographic Variables of Rios Calientes–Area Highly Effective Schools

School	District	Enrollment	Race/Ethnicity (%)			Low-income[a] (%)	LEP (%)
			African American	Latino	White		
Diego Rivera	Simon Bolivar	474	2	94	3	81	53
Frida Kahlo	Simon Bolivar	512	1	96	2	89	35
Carlos Fuentes	Simon Bolivar	711	2	94	4	85	36
Sor Juana Ines de la Cruz	Cesar Chavez	564	2	76	19	60	44
Luis Barragan	Omar Torrijos	1,040	2	77	20	47	29

Sources: Rios Calientes school districts.

LEP = Limited English proficient.

a. Defined as eligibility for free or reduced-price lunches.

Table 2.6. Achievement Variables of Rios Calientes–Area Highly Effective Schools

		Students at School at Least Three Years[a] (%)			All Students (%)	
School	District	Math pass	Math proficient	Math academic recognition	Math pass	Reading pass
Diego Rivera	Simon Bolivar	96.9	65.6	50.0	86.7	87.1
Frida Kahlo	Simon Bolivar	92.0	55.6	30.6	91.9	94.6
Carlos Fuentes	Simon Bolivar	97.8	58.7	21.7	100.0	100.0
Sor Juana Ines de la Cruz	Cesar Chavez	98.1	51.9	36.5	94.0	98.5
Luis Barragan	Omar Torrijos	95.2	60.6	38.5	95.5	91.7

Sources: For students at school at least three years, http://www.Just4Kids.org; for all students, state data.

a. Using available state data, passing rates were available for all 4th grade students. However, percentages of students passing at the proficient and academically recognized level were only available from Just4Kids.org. These data are reported only for students who have been in the same school for three or more years. There were other differences between state and Just4Kids data in the number of students included based on special education status.

Table 2.7. Demographic Variables of Rios Calientes–Area Typical Schools

School	District	Enrollment	Race/Ethnicity (%)			Low-income[a] (%)	LEP (%)
			African American	Latino	White		
Rosario Castellanos	Simon Bolivar	658	0	95	4	86	37
Rufino Tamayo	Simon Bolivar	720	1	95	3	96	36
Octavio Paz	Cesar Chavez	638	14	63	18	70	22

Sources: Rios Calientes school districts.

LEP = Limited English proficient.

a. Defined as eligibility for free or reduced-price lunches.

Figure 2.3. Relative Locations of Rios Calientes–Area Highly Effective and Typical Schools

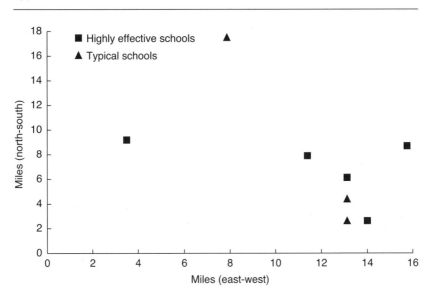

Table 2.8. Rios Calientes–Area Student 1999 SAAS Achievement (percent)

Comparison group	Math pass	Math proficient	Math academically recognized	Reading pass
4th graders in selected highly effective schools	95	61	38	95
4th graders in all schools in the three districts with > 49 percent low-income students[a]	87	44	23	86
All 4th graders in the three districts	87	45	24	87

Source: http://www.Just4Kids.org.

a. 88 percent of all schools in the area met this criterion.

District-Level Data Collection

Data were collected in the Cumberland City district and in three districts in Rios Calientes.

To collect information about the Cumberland City school district, researchers conducted 30- to 60-minute in-person interviews with district personnel. Interviewees included the chief academic officer, assistant superintendents, directors of various district offices related to math and science instruction, math and science specialists, the chief information officer, and the director of accountability and assessment. These interviews focused on district policies, with a particular focus on the interviewee areas of expertise such as teacher hiring and firing, curriculum, professional development, assessment and accountability, math and science improvement efforts, community partnerships, and parent involvement. In all, 13 Cumberland City district staff were interviewed.

Researchers also conducted in-person interviews with three nondistrict Cumberland City employees who worked with the district in its science and math reform efforts. These interviews focused on the roles that they and their organizations played in the district.

Cluster leaders from three of the four clusters in which the selected schools were located were interviewed by telephone for 30 to 45 minutes each. Cluster leader interviews focused on the roles of the cluster and the cluster leader as well as on professional development opportunities and community support and involvement.

In addition, researchers collected documentation from the district, including district elementary-level content standards, district assessment plans, SAT9 reports, state reports on district performance, copies of district policies, and evaluation reports and annual reports of various programs operating within the district.

To collect information about the three Rios Calientes districts, researchers conducted 30- to 60-minute in-person interviews with the following district personnel in each district: the superintendent/chief academic officer; directors of research, evaluation, and assessment; and science and mathematics specialists. These interviews focused on district policies, with a particular focus on the interviewee areas of expertise such as teacher hiring and firing, curriculum, professional development, assessment and accountability, math and science improvement efforts, community partnerships, and parent involvement. In all, 13 Rios Calientes district staff were interviewed.

Researchers also conducted in-person interviews with staff members of the NSF-funded math/science improvement effort in Rios Calientes who were responsible for its implementation. Six staff members were interviewed, including the director, assistant director, parent coordinator, and the math and science coordinators. The interviews tapped these staff members' knowledge of math and science policy and practice in the three districts.

In addition, various documentation was collected including district-level evaluation reports, the district and campus planning and decisionmaking resource guide, and program evaluation reports.

School-Level Data Collection

Since this study focused on the characteristics of individual schools, most research efforts focused on school-level data. Researchers collected data through teacher and principal surveys, principal interviews, teacher interviews and focus groups, parent and student focus groups, and site visits.

Teacher Surveys

The teacher survey sought answers to two questions. One, how do the characteristics, activities, policies, and practices of the elementary schools in the study reflect the NSF drivers and school-level effectiveness variables? Two, does the presence of these characteristics, activities, policies, and practices differentiate highly effective from typical elementary schools? The content of the survey grew out of several areas: a review of the literature on highly effective schools; a survey of NSF Systemic Initiative principal investigators about research areas that would be of greatest use of them (Campbell, Harris, and Webb 1998); the NSF drivers; an examination of teacher surveys used by such institutions as the Council of Chief State School Officers, the University of Florida, Systemic Research, Ohio State Systemic Initiative, and the Education Development Center; and discussions with staff members from the participating districts.

The UI effective schools researchers developed a draft 12-page teacher survey that covered the following areas:

- teacher demographic characteristics and educational backgrounds;
- educational leadership and professional development experiences;

- school and class information including teachers' reasons for coming to or staying at the school, control over curriculum, control over schedule, control over pedagogy, and student behavior;
- math/science curriculum;
- student assessment;
- parent involvement; and
- educational philosophy/classroom practice.

The draft version of the survey was piloted at two schools in each site, neither of which was part of the larger study. Five Cumberland City teachers and 12 Rios Calientes teachers completed the draft survey. Based on their feedback, revisions were made as needed.

Surveys were administered to all teachers in the eight selected Cumberland City schools and the eight selected Rios Calientes–area schools. In Cumberland City, 235 of 288 teachers completed the survey, for an overall response rate of 82 percent. The response rate for highly effective schools ranged from 58 to 100 percent for an overall highly effective school response rate of 83 percent (138). The response rate for typical schools ranged from 74 to 96 percent for an overall typical school response rate of 80 percent (97).

Survey administration in the Rios Calientes schools netted an overall response rate of 95 percent, with surveys received from 278 of 293 possible teachers. The response rate for highly effective schools ranged from 91 to 96 percent for an overall highly effective school response rate of 94 percent (176). The response rate for typical schools ranged from 93 to 100 percent for an overall typical school response rate of 96 percent (102).

Principal Surveys

The principal survey was designed to provide data to help answer the same two questions as the teacher survey. One, how do the characteristics, activities, policies, and practices of the elementary schools in the study reflect the NSF drivers and school-level effectiveness variables? Two, does the presence of these characteristics, activities, policies, and practices differentiate highly effective from typical elementary schools?

The content of the principal surveys grew out of a review of the literature on highly effective schools and an examination of principal surveys administered by other effective-schools studies. Based on this review, study researchers developed a 15-page principal survey that covered the following areas:

- principal demographic characteristics and educational backgrounds;
- administrative leadership;
- school academic goals;
- expectations for students;
- order and discipline;
- rewards and incentives;
- monitoring of student progress;
- opportunities for student participation;
- teacher efficacy;
- academic learning time;
- school climate;
- curriculum;
- community support and involvement; and
- effective teaching.

The draft version of the survey was piloted by a Cumberland City elementary school principal and six Rios Calientes elementary school principals, none of whom were part of the larger study. Based on their feedback, revisions were made as needed. Surveys were then distributed to the eight Cumberland City and eight Rios Calientes–area principals, all of whom completed the surveys. When returning the surveys, principals attached, upon request, several supplementary documents, such as the school's written statement of academic goals, homework policies, the discipline code, the instrument used in supervising teachers, and other relevant materials.

Interviews and Focus Groups

Interview protocols were developed to guide interviews with the principals, parent coordinators, math and science coordinators, small learning community coordinators, and custodians. Separate protocols were developed for each interviewee type.

Protocols to guide focus groups of teachers, parents, and students were also developed. There were separate protocols for each focus group type.

Site Visits

One-day site visits were scheduled at each Cumberland City District school in spring 2001. Researchers arranged focus groups with samples of teachers, students, and parents as well as interviews with the principal, the custodian, and a sample of other administrators including parent coordinators and small learning community coordinators. In six schools, one researcher spent a day conducting the interviews or focus groups; in the remaining two schools, two researchers spent the day conducting the interviews or focus groups. Table 2.9 provides an overview of the interviews and focus groups conducted by school.

As with the Cumberland City site, Rios Calientes District principals facilitated one-day site visits to each school by two researchers in spring 2001. These site visitors collected data via interviews with the principals, parent coordinators, and math and science coordinators in each school (only two schools had math and science coordinators). Researchers also conducted focus groups with teachers, parents, and students in each school. Interviews with parents were conducted in both English and Spanish. Table 2.10 gives an overview of the data collected for each school.

Data Analysis

After teacher survey data were entered into a database, researchers used Statistical Package for the Social Sciences (SPSS) to generate descriptive statistics comparing teachers in highly effective schools with teachers in typical schools. Using descriptive statistics, researchers also compared Cumberland City District teachers in highly effective schools to their counterparts in typical schools and Rios Calientes–area teachers in highly effective schools to their counterparts in typical schools. Where appropriate, researchers used two-way analysis of variance, *t*-tests, and chi square analyses.

Principal survey data were also entered into a database. Using SPSS, descriptive statistics were used first to compare Cumberland City District principals in highly effective schools with principals in typical schools and Rios Calientes–area principals in highly effective schools with principals in typical schools. Because of the small sample sizes, inferential statistics were not used. Based on the areas of difference found in the

Table 2.9. Cumberland City District Data Collection Respondents

School	Surveys		Interviews				Focus Groups		
	Classroom teachers	Principals	Principals	SLC coordinators	Parent coordinators	Custodians	Teachers	Students	Parents
Adams	34	1	1	3	0	1	7	9	2
Tyler	20	1	1	2	0	1	5	4	6
Jackson	15	1	0	0	2	1	4	6	3
Jefferson	28	1	1	1	0	1	6	5	3
Madison	20	1	1	2	1	1	3	6	2
Monroe	19	1	1	1	1	1	3	6	3
Van Buren	48	1	1	4	1	1	5	6	1
Washington	24	1	1	2	1	1	5	6	2

Source: Urban Institute effective schools study.

Table 2.10. Rios Calientes–Area Districts Data Collection Respondents

School	Surveys		Interviews				Focus Groups		
	Classroom teachers	Principals	Principals	Math coordinators	Science coordinators	Parent coordinators	Teachers	Students	Parents
Barragan	46	1	1	0	0	1	6	10	6
Castellanos	38	1	1	1	1	1	4	8	4
de la Cruz	32	1	1	1	1	0	4	4	5
Fuentes	35	1	1	0	0	1	6	4	7
Kahlo	32	1	1	0	0	1	4	8	10
Paz	29	1	1	0	0	1	5	6	4
Rivera	31	1	1	0	0	1	5	8	4
Tamayo	35	1	1[a]	0	0	1	8	5	5

Source: Urban Institute effective schools study.

a. Both the principal and assistant principal (via separate interviews) contributed to the principal interview.

teacher and principal surveys, questions were developed for the school principal, teacher, parent, student, and custodian focus groups and interviews.

Interviews and focus group results were written up and coded based on survey categories and results from the search of the literature. Researchers developed a template for the case studies and wrote case studies for each of the 16 schools. Cross–case study analysis was done for the eight Cumberland City District schools and the eight Rios Calientes–area schools. To provide context for each district, researchers collected data from various sources including the U.S. Census, the Core of Common Data, Chambers of Commerce, Federal Reserve Bank, U.S. Bureau of Economic Analysis, State Workforce Commission, State Bureau of Labor, Economic Reports, and regional economic, development, and planning commission data.

Conclusion

Because it is generally assumed that urban schools enrolling low-income, disadvantaged students will do poorly, studies that focus on schools serving low-income, disadvantaged students well are particularly valuable and intriguing. As shown in the following chapters, finding what makes these highly effective schools effective can contribute substantially to the knowledge base about what works in educating low-income students.

PART II
What the Study Found

3

Cumberland City
Coping with Population Change

This chapter examines the context in which the Cumberland City school district operates, including the city that it serves. It describes recent demographic and economic trends and other events that affect K–12 education, including a declining population and a workforce that is largely white-collar and drawn from the surrounding areas rather than from the city. The chapter also looks at the district's recent history, conflicts among the various stakeholders, and changes in district administrative structures, practices, and policies.

About Cumberland City

Located in the northeast with a population of 1.5 million, Cumberland City is one of the largest cities in the United States.[1] Between 1990 and 2000, its population decreased 4.3 percent. The city's population is expected to decrease another 9 percent between 1990 and 2025, while the population in the area surrounding the city is expected to grow 13 percent. Cumberland City's population is racially mixed: forty-five percent of the residents are white, 43 percent are African American, 8.5 percent are Latino, and 4.5 percent are Asian.

According to the Federal Reserve Bank, the private industries providing the largest share of employment in the Cumberland metropolitan area are education, health care, and social services (22 percent of total employment); professional and business services (12 percent); manufacturing (12 percent); and retail trade (12 percent). There are 11 colleges and universities within Cumberland City, while the surrounding area has more than 80 colleges and universities. About 60 percent of the workforce is white-collar, 19 percent is blue-collar, and 21 percent is in the service industry. From 1989 to 1999, jobs grew 7 percent in the Cumberland area, but this increase was primarily the result of 30 percent job growth in the service sector.

Median household income in Cumberland City is lower than both the state and national median incomes. Unemployment in 1990 and 2000 was over 6 percent, higher than the national and state figures. Based on the federal government's definition of low income, Cumberland City has a poverty rate of 22.9 percent, twice that of its state (11 percent).

About the Cumberland City School District

In many ways, the Cumberland City school district differs from the city it serves. Cumberland City's population is decreasing, while the school district's enrollment is increasing. The number of Cumberland public-school students decreased between 1987 and 1990 but has since increased to over 200,000. Almost a quarter of Cumberland City's school-age children are not attending public schools. According to the U.S. Census, 76.3 percent of elementary enrollments in Cumberland City were in public schools and 23.7 percent were in private schools. A slightly higher percentage of secondary school students attended public schools (78.8 percent), with 21.2 percent attending private schools.

Currently, Cumberland City has 264 schools, including 174 elementary schools. This represents three fewer schools than in 1999, when the study commenced. The demographic breakdown of the students attending public schools in Cumberland City differs from that of the overall population of the city. In the city, about half the population is white (45 percent) and half is African American (43 percent); in the schools, most students are African American (65 percent) with approximately equal numbers of white (16 percent) and Latino (13 percent) students. About 5 percent of students are Asian and 0.2 percent are Native American. Public-school teachers in Cumberland City are more likely to be white (62 percent) and less likely to be African American (36 percent) or Latino (1 percent) than the student population or the population of the city.

Students in the public schools are predominately low income, with 89 percent of district students eligible for free or reduced-price lunches. The school district has a more stringent definition of low income based on guidelines for eligibility for welfare. Based on that definition, 42 percent of the Cumberland City students were classified as low income in 1999.

Overall student achievement in Cumberland City public schools is low. As table 3.1 indicates, over a five-year period, 5th graders in Cumberland City public schools placed well below the state average in math and reading. The state average, based on the statewide System of Schools Assessment 1995–96 scores, places 25 percent of all students in each quartile. In Cumberland City, most students scored in the bottom quartile.

In 2000, the entire district was placed on the state educational empowerment list. Districts and individual schools are placed on the list if a combined average of 50 percent or more of their students score in the bottom quartile (as defined by statewide scores in 1996) in math and reading on the SSA.

Administrative Structure

On December 1, 1999, when the UI effective schools study commenced, a superintendent who reported to an elected school board led the district.

Table 3.1. Cumberland Fifth Grade Student Scores on System of Schools Assessment Test (percent)

	Math				Reading			
Year	Top quartile	High middle quartile	Low middle quartile	Bottom quartile	Top quartile	High middle quartile	Low middle quartile	Bottom quartile
1996	5	9	20	66	5	9	20	66
1997	4	9	22	65	5	10	23	62
1998	4	9	22	66	5	10	21	65
1999	3	9	24	64	4	10	22	64
2000	5	10	23	61	6	11	23	59

Source: Cumberland City school district.

Note: Changes in the test in 2001 made comparisons of earlier scores to more recent scores invalid.

At that point, the district was divided into 22 clusters, each composed of a public high school and its nearby feeder elementary and middle schools. Cluster leaders served in many ways as regional superintendents, with principals of each school in the cluster reporting to the cluster leader.

A major role of the clusters was to coordinate resources and services to member schools. Within each cluster, under its teaching and learning network, was a cadre of master teachers, including a coordinator, several facilitators, and in-school teacher leaders. Master teacher activities included in-class peer coaching, small learning community and school council support, whole-school professional development, cluster-based content work, and facilitation of pre-K–12 articulation. Each cluster also had a family resource network that connected children and families to health and social services. The cluster system was dismantled in 2001 in response to a $250 million district budget deficit.

Each school in the district had a school council that acted as a site-based decisionmaking body. Each council included an administrator (usually the principal) and representatives of the parents, teachers, and noninstructional staff. The council also included student members at the secondary school level. Council responsibilities included making the community aware of the initiatives within the schools; reviewing the school improvement plan, budget, and discipline policy; and making recommendations.

Each school was also broken down into small learning communities (SLCs), independent units of no more than 400 students, with a corresponding cadre of teachers. The SLCs were led by small learning community coordinators (SLC coordinators), teacher leaders who maintained some teaching responsibilities while supporting other teachers in their SLCs.

In 1995, the district received a five-year grant from the National Science Foundation (NSF) to facilitate mathematics and science education improvement efforts. Based on the district's performance, the grant was renewed and expanded. These grants provided resources districtwide to improve math and science education.

During 2000 and 2001, the years over which the data were collected, the district experienced a great deal of upheaval:

- the replacement of the elected school board with a school board appointed by the mayor;
- a district suit against the state alleging a disproportionately lower number of tax dollars were being returned to the city for education;

- the passage of the Education Empowerment Act, which allowed state takeover of Cumberland City schools;
- the superintendent's resignation;
- a threatened teacher strike;
- a threatened state district takeover;
- a $250 million school budget deficit;
- the replacement of a management structure of a board-appointed superintendent with a board-appointed chief executive officer, chief academic officer, chief operating officer, and chief financial officer;
- the replacement of the cluster system with eight academic areas;
- the replacement of the appointed school board with a school reform commission composed of five members, three appointed by the governor and two appointed by the mayor of Cumberland City;
- the resignation of the chief executive officer; and
- the approval of a plan for the privatization of some district schools (which took place after the data were collected).

Curriculum and Textbooks

In September 1997, the Board of Education of the Cumberland City School District approved a series of academic content standards and cross-cutting competencies that included between 5 and 14 broad pre-K–12 standards for 11 subject areas:

- English and language arts,
- mathematics,
- science,
- social studies,
- world languages,
- health,
- physical education,
- dance,
- music,
- theater, and
- visual arts.

The standards were partly based on theories of constructivism, which involves an understanding of the content and processes of learning. In constructivism students are seen as bringing multiple intelligences and previous knowledge into the classroom and as learning by constructing knowledge through a variety of meaningful activities. Curriculum frameworks were developed from the standards and, along with the standards, were to be the basis for the development and selection of new curricula for the district. During the UI effective schools study data collection, there was a transition in instructional leadership and philosophy. In 1999, the state adopted its own academic content standards and compelled all districts to align with the state assessment system. At that time, the third edition of the district's curriculum frameworks was adjusted to align with the state academic standards. District administrators saw these state-mandated standards and assessments as significantly less progressive than the district's own standards.

At the elementary school level, there was a district language arts curriculum, *Balanced Literacy,* but no mandated districtwide curriculum in science or mathematics. Some schools made mathematics and science curricula decisions as a whole; others left the decisions to individual teachers. While there was no list of accepted mathematics or science curricula, if schools wanted to access resources from the NSF-funded math and science improvement effort, they had to select math or science curricula that had been approved by district administrators involved in the math/science improvement efforts. To increase the amount of hands-on science teaching, programs and activity kits were recommended at grades K–5 instead of a textbook series. Inquiry-based math curricula were also recommended. District math coordinators reported that *Everyday Mathematics* was the most widely used elementary mathematics curriculum but that other curricula were being used, including *Math in Context, Mathland, Mimosa, Connected Math,* and *Mathscape.* Teachers in the eight schools studied reported using a broader list of curricula that included less inquiry-based curricula such as *Saxon Math.* One administrator indicated that the teachers' union encouraged the use of *Saxon Math* over the use of more inquiry-based curricula.

Teachers and administrators agreed that, across the district, they were paying less attention to mathematics and science than to reading and language arts education. According to the then chief education officer, science and math were the district's weakest areas. Other staff felt that there was more emphasis on math, particularly math at the elementary level, than there was on science and that science was "rather left out." The NSF-funded effort was, administrators said, the "only district curriculum effort in math and science."[2]

Professional Development

The goal of the school district's professional development system was to enable every teacher, administrator, and staff member to develop the knowledge, skills, and behaviors required to create learning settings that enable all students to meet the standards and cross-cutting competencies. The belief, according to the district administrators, was that "professional development should be intensive and sustained, and should involve observing good practice, practicing good practice, being coached in good practice, reflecting on good practice, and repeating the process." Professional development was seen as "never ending." Even then, as one administrator commented, "There is never enough professional development; we never catch up because we are always losing teachers."

At the time of the study, new teachers were required to undergo a month of professional development. Other district teachers were mandated to receive 20 hours of professional development annually, although the 2000 District/Cumberland City Federation of Teachers' contract required at least 28 hours of professional development annually. In addition, the state mandated all teachers have 180 contact hours of professional development or six college credits every five years. All other professional development was voluntary.

The content of the annual professional development was based on each school's improvement plan, with the content of 10 hours decided by each school's principal and 10 hours decided by a school committee of teachers, administrators, parents, and staff. By the requirements of the 2000 District/Cumberland City Federation of Teachers' contract, each school had to set up a professional development committee to conduct a needs assessment for planning professional development activities in the following school year.

Professional development came from various sources. In each cluster, between two and five cluster facilitators went to the schools for professional development. Individual clusters and schools could contract district staff, partners from outside the district, or others including university staff or publishers to conduct the professional development. However, one outside partner reported that the district increasingly wanted to offer the bulk of its professional development in-house. Some district administrators felt that the major push for professional development came from district offices, not individual schools, while others felt the push came from principals.

Professional development offerings were diverse and included, at the district level, summer and fall content institutes, cultural inclusion institutes, and "voices in dialogue" discussion series. In addition, professional development was a major thrust of the NSF-funded math and science improvement efforts, including doing pre-K–12 math articulation to move toward a unified math curriculum. Staff or others funded by the NSF math and science improvement effort provided the districtwide professional development. District administrators explained that the NSF-funded math and science improvement effort was the math and science arm of the district, not a separate program.

There were quite a few differences in the professional development programs each cluster offered. For example, the cluster that included the George Washington, James Monroe, and Thomas Jefferson schools focused on the early grades and early literacy, in great part because of a grant they had received. The cluster that included the John Tyler School focused on K–16, including K–12 articulation, school-to-career programs, education for employment, job readiness, work-based learning, and service-learning coordination. The cluster that included the Martin Van Buren and John Adams schools focused on implementing classroom management, supporting parents, and addressing students with behavioral and mental disorders.

Some differences in the professional development offered by the clusters, district administrators felt, resulted from the quality and interest of the cluster leadership. District administrators explained that where there was a strong leader, "everyone was on the same page, things went smoothly, and over a hundred teachers would show up for professional development, jumping up for materials." In other clusters, "no one knew what was going on, and there was no communication. Teachers didn't know about professional development opportunities and didn't show up."

School Accountability

At the time of the study data collection, the school performance index (SPI) was at the core of school accountability. The SPI was a weighted academic rating based on the percentage of students scoring on the reading, math, and science sections of the SAT9 at advanced, proficient, basic, and below-basic levels III, II, and I as well as the percentage of students not tested,[3] student and staff attendance, and student promotion.

The SAT9 was at the core of the district's accountability system. SAT9 tests in reading, mathematics, and science were administered in grades 3, 4, 7, 8, 10, and 11. A writing assessment was given in grades 6, 9, and 11, but the results were not incorporated into the school accountability structure. The state mandated that students take the SSA in reading and mathematics in grades 5, 8, and 11, but at the time of this study, these results were not included in the district's assessment system. Each school was required to have a school improvement plan designed to positively affect its performance index, and the cluster was mandated to assist each school in implementing the plan.

Among the accountability data schools received from the district were

- quarterly attendance;
- school performance indices broken out by SLC;
- SAT9 school- and grade-level summary scores reported by
  - gender, broken down further by race/ethnicity and income level;
  - students who have exited English for speakers of other languages (ESOL) programs; and
  - students in bilingual programs;
- SAT9 scores by class; and
- SAT9 individual student scores broken out by skill area tested.

Teacher Employment and Accountability

In 1996, the district employed approximately 12,000 teachers at an average salary of $46,659, compared with a state average of $47,147. The state certified teachers. Initial state teacher certification required

- completion of state-approved teacher education (including student teaching/internship) with at least a bachelor's degree,
- Praxis I and II assessments, and
- application materials documenting that all certificate requirements had been met.

For teachers who did not meet initial certification criteria, the state offered one-year emergency certifications to those with bachelor's degrees from a state-approved college or university.

State and district policies and union agreements controlled teacher recruitment and retention. The Cumberland City Federation of Teachers, an affiliate of the American Federation of Teachers, represented the teachers. They were hired by the district and placed on an eligibility list, giving schools little choice in their selection. Teacher assignment was based on teacher seniority. In addition, seniority provisions in the teachers' union contract enabled teachers to apply for transfers to other schools in the district with vacancies after just two years of service in the original school. The Cumberland City Education Fund found that Cumberland City teachers used this provision to transfer out of high-poverty schools to schools with more advantaged and higher-achieving student bodies, a practice that allowed, as district staff commented, "low-performing schools to serve as a farm system for stronger schools." During the UI effective schools study, the district had a pilot program where up to 25 schools could select their own teachers. A school had to have 75 percent teacher agreement before it could participate. Only 13 schools, none of them part of this study, signed up to participate.

Filling teacher positions was a major problem for the district. One way the district sought to recruit teachers was by offering signing bonuses. Teachers with math or science backgrounds were given larger bonuses, and teachers with math or science backgrounds willing to go to schools in special need, even larger ones. The district also recruited math and science teachers from India through a contractor.

Teacher performance was rated on a standardized district observation form used by principals, assistant principals, and other administrators. Teachers were rated in four areas—personality, preparation, technique, and pupil reaction—on a scale of 1 (no evidence) to 4 (positive and sustained presence or use). Sample criteria included

- "Teacher deals with diversity issues in ways that promote the acceptance, participation, and achievement of students from diverse backgrounds."
- "Students actively participate in lesson/activity in ways that are conducive to learning."[4]

Principal Employment and Accountability

Principals were also represented by a union, the Association of School Administrators, an affiliate of the Teamsters. The principals' contract stated that the Board of Education has "the sole right to hire, discipline or discharge for cause, lay off, transfer, and assign administrators." Principals reported to cluster leaders who had the responsibility to both train the principals and evaluate their performance, based in part on district criteria. While parents were not part of the official evaluation process, some principals had been removed because of parent concerns.

Student Assessment

At the time of the study, a new Cumberland City School District assessment system was being implemented that included districtwide tests (the SAT9), projects, citywide midterms and finals at the secondary school level, and citywide reading levels in grades K–4. As indicated earlier, SAT9 tests were administered in grades 2, 3, 4, 7, 8, 10, and 11, and SSA tests were administered in grades 5, 8, and 11. At the elementary school level, the district had requirements for student promotion, but schools could add their own criteria. In 2000, 4th grade students needed to pass English, math, and science to be promoted. Their SAT9 scores were averaged into their English, math, and science grades, with advanced equaling an A, proficient a B, basic a C, below basic III a D, and below basic II or lower an F.[5] In addition, students had to score at least "basic" on writing and on a citizenship project. For 12th graders, the 2000 graduation requirements included 21.5 course credits and passing grades on districtwide final exams in English, math, and science. Graduating seniors needed to pass English, math, and science and, as with 4th graders, their SAT9 scores were considered as part of their grades. Students also had to score at least "basic" on interdisciplinary and citizenship projects. At the time of the UI effective schools study, the Cumberland City school district was increasing its graduation and promotion requirements.

Student Discipline

The Cumberland City school district did not have a districtwide student disciplinary policy. Individual schools developed their own policies. There were board policies dealing with civility, acceptable behavior, and "consistency in terms of consequences." In addition, schools could choose to have an accommodation room where misbehaving students could be temporarily assigned during the school day.

Class Size

Teacher contracts in Cumberland stipulated a class size no larger than 30 students in grades K–2 and no larger than 33 for the higher elementary grades. Fourth grade classroom observations in Cumberland found class sizes ranging from 21 to 39 students, with an average of 28.

Ability Grouping and Inclusion

Cross-grade heterogeneous grouping was required by the Cumberland City school district. No school could have a class of high- or of low-achieving students; each class had to be mixed in terms of student academic levels. There was no district policy about ability grouping within classes, although the district-mandated language arts curriculum (*Balanced Literacy*) used homogeneous grouping in the selection of reading groups. By policy, special education students were mainstreamed in regular classes, although there were some special education classes, including a class at Thomas Jefferson School for autistic students, that drew students from throughout the district.

Parent Involvement

Principals made schoolwide decisions about the degree of access parents could have to the school, including open-door policies. It was also a board policy that each school had a school council that included at least five parents. Welfare reform, especially the work requirement, "put a dent in traditional parent involvement" throughout the district. At the time of the study, the district was "working on ways to get parent input without their physical presence." It was board policy that parent involvement be built into principals' performance evaluations. These evaluations were done by cluster leaders and were used, at least in part, to determine principals' raises.

Partnerships

The district was involved in a number of partnerships with local colleges and universities. The Center for Community Partnerships of the President's Office in one local university organized partnerships and collaborations that involved the district all over the city. In addition, at the time of the study, the district was working with three private universities to design courses that combined content and methods. They had previously worked in these areas with three other colleges. There was some administrator concern that colleges and universities tended to move too slowly for urban districts and that they were not preparing teachers to teach standards-based math. Among other district partners were the local science center and the Cumberland City Education Fund as well as, in the words of one administrator, "anyone in the city with an NSF grant."

Under the former superintendent, each cluster had set up a resource board that included business partners. At the time of the UI study, 12 clusters had resource boards. However, a representative of one of the district's outside partners commented on the lack of corporate involvement in education reform, professional development, and in the schools themselves, feeling that corporate involvement had decreased since the NSF-funded math and science improvement grant had been implemented.

Conclusion

Like so many other urban areas in the United States, Cumberland City is losing population and is becoming the type of place where the people who work there are not the people who live there. Almost half the city's population is white, yet less than 20 percent of the district's public-school students are white. And, the district went through many challenges, reorganizations, and transitions during the study period, to put it mildly.

4

What Makes Some Cumberland City Schools Highly Effective?

Between 1999 and 2001, the Cumberland City school district went through a difficult time. Despite these citywide difficulties, the UI effective schools study reveals major differences between the four highly effective schools, the three typical schools, and the formerly effective school. The differences cluster in five educational areas: principal leadership, the teaching force, instruction, student behavior and discipline, and parent-school relationships.

All eight Cumberland City principals participating in this study see themselves as instructional leaders. However, only in the four highly effective schools do teachers and others agree with that assessment. In the typical and formerly effective schools, staff see their principals as delegators, supporters, or uninvolved, but not as leaders. Compared with the typical-school principals, highly effective school principals are more visible in the school, more responsive to their teachers and the community, more involved with teacher professional development, and more likely to work around the rules to get and keep good teachers. Highly effective principals also come to their positions with more administrative experience and more education.

Teachers in the highly effective schools differ from teachers in the typical and formerly effective schools as well. Teachers at highly effective schools are more likely to possess such characteristics of teacher quality as state certification, participation in postgraduate education, and number of college-level math and science courses. Teachers in highly effective schools are also more likely to be experienced teachers and less likely to be new to their school. In addition, teachers in the highly effective schools have higher attendance, are willing to go beyond the duties of their contract, and are more likely to take responsibility for their students' learning. Although professional development opportunities are similar across schools, teachers at highly effective schools receive more professional development. Similarly, while teachers in general report receiving support, the support provided to teachers in highly effective schools appears stronger and more effective.

Highly effective–school teachers spend more time working on mathematics with their students, have higher expectations for their students' mathematics learning, and have students who appear more involved with and more positive about their academic learning. Another instructional difference is related to educational philosophy. Three of the four highly effective schools have explicit educational philosophies, while none of the others do.

Unlike the typical and formerly effective schools, highly effective schools have structured, consistent, and clear discipline policies. Teachers from the highly effective schools speak of the role effective planning and appropriate lessons play in discipline and mention their own responsibilities, not just for the behavior of their own students, but also for the behavior of other students.

There are differences in schools' relationships with parents as well. Parents of students in the highly effective schools are welcome in the schools any time; parents in the typical and formerly effective schools have to make appointments to come into their schools. Unsurprisingly, relationships between parents and the schools are much more positive in the highly effective schools than they are in the other schools. In one typical school and in the formerly effective school, the school-parents relationships often reflect open warfare.

The rest of this chapter expands on these results, using stories and statistics from case studies and surveys completed during the UI effective schools study to illustrate differences between the highly effective schools and the typical or formerly effective schools.[1]

Principal Leadership

Principal leadership in the highly effective schools manifests itself in several ways. Highly effective principals are instructional leaders. They are also highly visible and responsive to teacher and school needs. Principals at highly effective schools are also involved in teacher hiring and have extensive experience and educational backgrounds.[2]

Instructional Leadership

Principals in urban elementary schools have many responsibilities: they are instructional leaders, managers, decisionmakers, disciplinarians, and even role models. The principals of the eight schools in this study fill these roles to differing degrees using varied leadership styles. There are, however, commonalities among the principals in the highly effective schools in areas that lead to stronger student achievement. Among the most important of these is the principal's role as an instructional leader.

All eight principals see themselves as instructional leaders. However, only teachers and other staff from the four highly effective schools agree. At highly effective Thomas Jefferson, the teachers, administrators, and the principal herself all see Sally Pierce as a strong, instructional leader who is heavily involved with curriculum and with professional development. Similarly, Margaret Riley, principal at highly effective school John Tyler, is seen as and sees herself as an instructional leader. She is very visible and involved, and stays informed about what is happening in the classrooms. As one teacher explains, "She likes to know what's going on."

James Monroe principal Julie Simmons is a highly visible, hands-on leader. She is very involved in supervising teachers, determining the curriculum, and deciding time spent on academic tasks. As a principal of a highly effective school, she is aware of what goes on in the classroom, although she does not get to observe as much as she would like. In highly effective John Adams, principal George Lindsey is a strong leader, seen by himself and others as an instructional leader and manager who is supportive and highly visible in the school and in the classrooms. As one teacher explains, Mr. Lindsey sets "the feeling for the school and pushes the academics."

The situation at the three typical schools and the formerly effective school is quite different. Teachers and others do not see their principals as instructional leaders, and neither teachers nor the principals themselves speak of the principal as a visible presence in the school.

At the formerly effective school, Andrew Jackson, principal Elizabeth Cuomo rates herself as an instructional leader who is very involved in supervising teachers and determining the curriculum. The comments of one teacher, however, reflect teachers' general feelings about her:

"[Ms. Cuomo] doesn't affect me at all. She doesn't pay attention . . . doesn't come into my room at all. She is so busy with parents and parent complaints and with paperwork [that she] doesn't come in the classroom." In addition, parents interviewed for this study blame Ms. Cuomo for what is going wrong in the school.

At typical school George Washington, principal Raymond Stanley feels he is an instructional leader because he puts teachers "on the pathway to use their skills to do what they have to do." However, Mr. Stanley says his overall role in the supervision of instruction is "making sure that the teachers adhere to the district policies and procedures." Neither the interviewed teachers nor the SLC coordinators feel that Mr. Stanley is an instructional leader.

Teachers and the SLC coordinators describe Martin Van Buren principal Tamara Jones's role as that of a "delegator" or "facilitator," with one SLC coordinator commenting that the principal "is very good at delegating; she likes her SLC coordinators to be autonomous, and we make the decisions." The teachers interviewed at this typical school agree that "in urban education, you don't have an instructional leader" and that in reality, the principal deals with "cleanliness, ordering materials, [and] paperwork issues," in the words of one teacher. Ms. Jones appears removed from the day-to-day instruction, discipline, and other student-centered activities of the school. One teacher goes so far as to describe her as an example of when "teachers who can't teach become administrators."

At the final typical school, principal Marietta Nichols sees herself as an instructional leader, but there is little indication that she actively stays informed about what happens in the James Madison classrooms. It is the math and science teachers, she says, who "go to the classroom to decide how math and science is taught." Although the teachers say Ms. Nichols supports their ideas and is willing to give those ideas a try, they also say she does not really push them.

Highly effective schools' principals appear to take a more active approach to professional development as well. All four highly effective–school principals say that they have either attended professional development sessions or have learned about professional development sessions in other ways so they could make better decisions about professional development for their teachers. None of the typical- or formerly effective–school principals report doing this.

Principal ratings of their involvement in instructional issues reflect their teachers' comments. Principals in highly effective schools rate themselves as much more involved in determining the curriculum (4.0 versus 2.7 on a scale of 1 [not involved] to 4 [very involved]) and in determining the time spent on academic tasks (3.8 versus 2.7) than the principals in typical and formerly effective schools do. In yet another indicator of instructional leadership, three highly effective–school principals and one typical-school principal (Marietta Nichols from James Madison) directly supervise teachers.

Visibility

Highly effective–school principals are more visible and involved in the various aspects of the school than are principals of the typical or formerly effective schools. While three of the four highly effective–school principals speak of going into every classroom as often as possible, none of the typical-school principals or the principal of the formerly effective school do. John Adams's principal George Lindsey says he visits every classroom at least four times a week. Margaret Riley, John Tyler's principal, explains that she stops

> in classes for few minutes. It makes a big difference if the class is actively engaged compared to those just sitting there. I look at off-task versus on-task. I walk through the school yard and lunch room to let people know I am watching and am happy when they are doing it right.

Although James Monroe principal Julie Simmons finds being visible in the school is not always easy, she says,

> I always believed the IBM policy about being visible and managing by walking around. If you are visible and making daily rounds and in classrooms and available for parents, you know what is going on around. Does it always happen the way I want? No, because of the demands of paperwork. But it is important to be around.

Responsiveness

Highly effective–school principals also appear more responsive to teachers and school needs than do principals in typical schools. For example, the Thomas Jefferson principal changed the math curriculum based on teacher wishes. John Tyler principal Margaret Riley, who is white, is learning Spanish to communicate better with her predominantly Latino school population and is seen by interviewed parents as understanding African American and Latino issues. Teachers at the other two highly effective schools and at typical school Martin Van Buren describe their principals as supportive of teachers. There is no mention of the two other typical-school principals, or of the formerly effective–school principal, as responsive or supportive. Instead, it was noted that George Washington principal Raymond Stanley took no steps to relieve a difficult situation where SLC coordinators were unable to leave their own classes to support teachers.

Involvement in Teacher Hiring

According to district policy, teacher hiring and assignment in Cumberland City is totally outside principal and teacher control. It is a district function based on seniority and covered under the union contract. The three typical-school principals agree that they are not involved in teacher hiring. The situation is more ambiguous in the highly effective schools, where two of the four principals actively work to shape their teaching forces.

Although by contract Mr. Lindsey cannot recruit teachers, he has no problem filling positions at highly effective John Adams. One way he does this is through internships. He currently has several interns at the school who he wants to stay on after they receive their certifications.

Julie Simmons, principal of highly effective James Monroe, actively recruits teachers. She goes to the district office and speaks to the new teachers to see if she can recruit them for her school. She also tries to recruit student teachers from a local college but is not always successful because, as she explains, "I have very little control. I can write a letter [or] call downtown but it is all on seniority." Helping these principals in their efforts to recruit or grow their own teachers, 75 percent of the James Monroe and John Adams teachers have supervised student teachers, compared with 40 percent of teachers in the typical schools.

The other two highly effective schools shape their teaching force by "encouraging" some teachers to leave. While teachers and principals have no official say in teacher hiring and firing, John Tyler principal Margaret Riley explains, "You can decide which positions to cut, and if there is someone who is not very good, who is at the bottom of the seniority list, you can put a lot of pressure on them to leave." Principal Sally Pierce from Thomas Jefferson feels there is nothing she can do in terms of teacher recruitment. Her teachers, however, report that if new teachers do not fit into the school's strong teacher support network, they do not stay. As one teacher explains, "We end up needing each other to keep sane. People who can't work that way leave. . . . If they can't accept us, they leave."

Experience and Educational Background

The backgrounds of the principals in highly effective schools differ from the backgrounds of principals in typical schools and the formerly effective school. Before coming to their current schools, the highly effective–school principals all had previous experience in school administration, either as principals or assistant principals. The three typical-school principals and the formerly effective school principal, in contrast, are holding their first educational administrative jobs.

Three highly effective principals are relatively new to their schools, with two following well-loved principals and one following an unpopular principal. The fourth highly effective principal has been in the job for seven years. One typical principal is also new to the job, while the other two have been principals for six years at the time of the study. There is some question about the length of time the formerly effective principal has served as principal. While she says she has been the principal for four years, official records and teacher comments indicate she has been principal for only a year.

There are differences in principals' educational backgrounds as well. The highly effective–school principals are highly educated; two have doctorates, one has two master's degrees, and one has a master's degree with a number of post-master's graduate credits. Typical-school principals tend to be less educated. Martin Van Buren's principal has a law degree, while the other two typical-school principals and the principal of Andrew Jackson have master's degrees in education.

The Teaching Force

Although teachers in Cumberland City schools are assigned to schools based on seniority, teachers in highly effective schools differ from other teachers in many ways. Highly effective teachers are better qualified, more experienced, and more likely to participate in professional development programs. They also display more commitment to their schools, more responsibility for student achievement and behavior, and more support for their colleagues.

Qualifications

Demographically, the teachers in all eight schools are similar. They are overwhelmingly female (85 percent) and predominately white (59 percent) with an average age of 40. Most were raised in and live in the area (75 percent), although less than 5 percent of them live close to their schools. While 18 percent of teachers have elementary school–age children of their own, less than 5 percent have their own children in the school where they teach.

While they are demographically similar, teachers in highly effective schools differ from their counterparts in qualifications. At least 85 percent of the teachers at each highly effective school are fully certified, a level reached by only one typical school. In addition, teachers in highly effective schools are significantly more likely to have earned degrees beyond bachelor's degrees (64 percent versus 44 percent). In all the highly effective schools, but in only one typical school, 50 percent or more of the teachers have master's degrees (figure 4.1). In contrast, teachers in typi-

Figure 4.1. Teacher Certification and Graduate Education at Cumberland City Schools

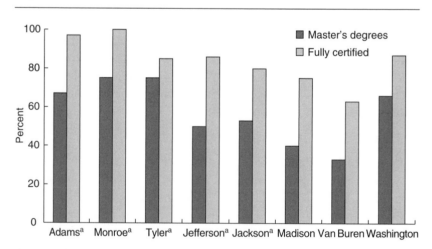

Source: UI effective schools teacher survey.

a. highly effective school. Andrew Jackson, the formerly effective school, started the study as highly effective.

cal schools are 2.5 times more likely than teachers in highly effective schools to have emergency certifications (22 percent versus 9 percent).[3]

The content knowledge of math and science teachers also varies. Teachers in highly effective schools have taken significantly more undergraduate- or graduate-level math courses (3.6 versus 2.6) and science courses (4.8 versus 3.6) than teachers in typical schools have. Teachers in highly effective schools are also almost twice as likely to have either taken a math content course or studied math in depth in the previous 12 months (22 percent versus 12 percent).

Experience

In general, teachers with three or fewer years of experience are seen as "inexperienced." Those with two or fewer years at a school are seen as "new to the school" (*Education Week* 2003). Using these definitions, teachers in highly effective schools are significantly more likely to be experienced and significantly less likely to be new to their schools. Eighty-three percent of the teachers in highly effective schools have been teaching for over three years, as have 70 percent of the teachers in the typical schools. The share of experienced teachers in the four highly effective schools ranges from 80 to 100 percent, while in the typical schools it ranges from 65 to 75 percent. Only 52 percent of teachers in the formerly effective school are experienced.

Twenty-eight percent of teachers in the highly effective schools and 41 percent of teachers in the typical schools are new to their schools, a significant difference. The proportion of teachers new to the school ranges from 3 to 46 percent at the highly effective schools, while at the typical schools it ranges from 40 to 42 percent. Forty percent of the teachers in the formerly effective school are new to the school (figure 4.2).

In the typical schools, teacher inexperience is seen as a problem. Teachers at Martin Van Buren speak of teacher turnover as a contributing cause of students' bad behavior. James Madison principal Marietta Nichols says she feels hindered in her efforts by teacher inexperience: "Everyone's so new . . . they need a lot of assistance." A teacher in that school echoes the principal's concern about the high turnover: "We have a lot of inexperienced teachers [that] leads to poor instruction." And inexperience is not reserved for new teachers: "We get transfers from other buildings, so even though they may have years of experience, there was also a weakness there."

Figure 4.2. Teacher Experience at Cumberland City Schools

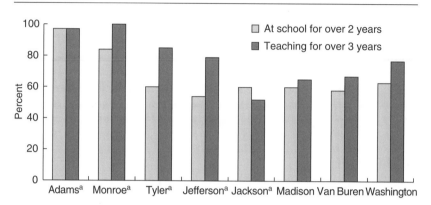

Source: UI effective schools teacher survey.

a. highly effective school. Andrew Jackson, the formerly effective school, started the study as highly effective.

Professional Development

From a policy perspective, highly effective and typical schools have several professional development similarities. All teachers are required by the district to receive 20 hours of professional development annually, and professional development opportunities are similar for teachers in highly effective and typical schools within the same cluster. All schools, except the formerly effective school Andrew Jackson, "bank time" to increase the hours available for professional development.[4]

Most teachers feel professional development improves their instruction, although individual teacher comments about the quality of professional development are mixed. In the words of one teacher at highly effective school Thomas Jefferson, "Teachers get a different level of professional development depending on your need." At highly effective John Adams, a teacher feels, "[Professional development] didn't go deeply enough. I felt lost and had to seek out information myself." Typical-school teachers have similar responses. "Some professional development is useful and beneficial and some a waste," according to a Martin Van Buren teacher. A James Madison teacher agrees: "Some [professional development] is redundant; some you can get good ideas."

Although opportunities are the same and attitudes toward professional development similarly varied, teachers in highly effective schools are much more likely to participate in professional development. Most dramatically, principals in highly effective schools report that 84 percent of their teachers have spent at least 10 hours in math-related professional development in the past year, while principals in typical schools report that is the case for only 29 percent of their teachers. Science-related staff development shows a similar pattern. Highly effective–school principals say that, on average, 71 percent of their teachers have 10 or more hours of science-related professional development; for typical schools, the average is 20 percent. Not only do teachers from highly effective schools participate in significantly more math content professional development than do teachers from typical schools, they also are significantly more likely to study math assessment methods (31 percent versus 16 percent) and to read national math standards (39 percent versus 26 percent).

Commitment

There is an old saying that the first step to success is showing up. Teachers at highly effective schools show up more. On average, two-thirds of the teachers from the highly effective schools have attendance rates of at least 95 percent (a district goal), compared with less than half the teachers in the typical schools. The percentage of teachers with attendance rates of 95 percent or higher at the highly effective schools ranges from 66 to 75 percent, while at the typical schools the range is 18 to 64 percent (figure 4.3). The percentage at formerly effective school Andrew Jackson is 45 percent. The day she was interviewed, an Andrew Jackson parent pointed out that in a school with 26 teachers, "today there are 12 teachers out and no subs."

High teacher attendance sends a message, as a parent from highly effective John Tyler notes: "Attendance of the teachers keeps me here. The school doesn't have a problem with subs. The teacher is there and is an example for the children." According to this parent, since the teacher is never absent, the kids are trying not to be absent as well.

Committed teachers are also likely to go above and beyond the duties their contracts specify. Instances of teachers doing this were reported in three of the four highly effective schools. John Tyler teachers spend nonschool time helping with bake sales, car washes, food sales, and plant sales to get money for student trips and other special events like graduation.

Figure 4.3. Shares of Cumberland City Teachers with Attendance Rates of 95 Percent or Higher

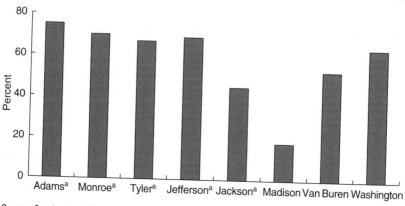

Source: Cumberland City school district.

a. highly effective school. Andrew Jackson, the formerly effective school, started the study as highly effective.

They even supervise the school yard because there is no crossing guard. At James Monroe, teachers volunteer for a cadre that meets before and after school to create policies and go over guidelines. Teachers also help in the lunchroom without being asked. John Adams teachers volunteered for recess duty under a special project, although they stopped once the project was over. Currently one John Adams staff member performs lunchroom and recess duties voluntarily, even though it is against the contract.

Such volunteerism among teachers is not reported in any of the typical schools or in the formerly effective school.

Responsibility

During the interviews, educators were asked "What does the phrase 'all children can learn' mean to you?" Respondents from the four highly effective schools speak of their responsibility in children's learning. They mention actively reaching students at their level, engaging students, and modifying instruction for students at their own level. In addition to explicitly stating that the teacher's responsibility is to go to the student's level to jumpstart learning, teachers from the four highly effective schools describe using data to change the way they teach, teaching the students a culture of learning, developing strategies for different subjects and skill levels, and challenging higher-level students when they are bored.

Teachers in highly effective James Madison speak of giving children, as one teacher describes it, "the right combination of tools and circumstances." A second teacher expands on this statement, saying that if "the slowest children . . . are given what is necessary to make up for what they don't have, they will learn." The principal concurs: "You need to understand that they learn differently, at different paces with different abilities and strengths, and you have to find it for each child."

Principal John Lindsey at highly effective John Adams believes that "all means all, that every child can and will learn given the proper supports." One teacher explains that this belief is

> part of a philosophy. You are taking kids from where they are at, taking them from a low level and modifying instruction. This may not happen overnight or over a couple of weeks, but you do see growth and learning. You understand that it can happen.

At highly effective Thomas Jefferson, teachers feel responsible for student success. As two teachers explain: "You have to find a way to get through to students using different avenues;" "You have to find a way to engage [students] in what needs to be taught so you can teach them, so they will have success." The principal agrees, feeling "staff wrack their brains to come up with different things" to support student success.

At highly effective John Tyler, teachers and the principal all speak of students' potential to learn, given the right conditions and environment, and two teachers speak specifically of their responsibility to find what works for each child. Principal Margaret Riley is very clear that it is the educator's responsibility to figure out what might be blocking students. "You need to figure out how to jumpstart learning."

Teachers from the typical schools do not speak of their own responsibilities in ensuring that all children can learn, although two typical-school principals do feel it is a teacher responsibility. At Martin Van Buren, Tamara Jones's response to "all children can learn" emphasizes the teachers' role in making this happen, while the teacher responses do not. James Madison principal Marietta Nichols speaks of adapting teaching to meet the students' needs and different paces rather than just keeping them interested: "It's our responsibility to find out how they can learn and meet their needs." When asked what "all children can learn" means, one James

Madison teacher explains it means "that all are included; we don't leave anybody out. That there is something somewhere that interests a child to make them stretch." Unfortunately, no teachers speak of it being explicitly their responsibility.

Typical school George Washington's principal and teacher responses to the phrase "all children can learn" focus on different strategies and levels at which students can learn. Individual teachers say, "Given the right setup, all kids can learn" and "I think teachers today are using all different strategies . . . modalities [to help students learn]." No teachers, however, speak of children's learning as their own responsibility.

The Andrew Jackson teachers feel the phrase "all children can learn" means, as individual teachers say, "Every [student] can do something" and that while students can all learn, "they don't all do it at the same time and the same way."

Support

Teachers in all eight schools report receiving support from others in their school or small learning community, including receiving and giving advice and sharing resources regularly. The way in which teachers describe their school community and the support they receive, however, differs.

Teachers at highly effective Thomas Jefferson come together as a community to, as two teachers explain, "make a nice place" and "value ourselves as professionals, as humans." The support also goes into academic areas, where one teacher says they keep up with "what others are using to see if could work for us." As another teacher explains, just because she "had success in the past doesn't mean it will be successful next year," so she has to keep learning.

At James Monroe, a second highly effective school, teachers also come together, particularly to support colleagues who are struggling. As one teacher explains, "Everyone works together. Teamwork, that is why James Monroe School is successful. You can't do it without each other."

At highly effective John Adams, one teacher especially appreciates the supportive environment: "[This] is probably the best school. . . . Other schools aren't as friendly, not such a friendly atmosphere. There's camaraderie, togetherness, everybody gets along."

Teachers from the typical schools speak of support but did not see it as comprehensive. At Martin Van Buren, teachers mention they get support from their SLC, though according to one teacher, they "really don't talk too much outside the SLC." Similarly, according to Principal Marietta

Nichols, James Madison teachers "share strategies and support, [but] it's not happening as much as it should." James Madison teachers help each other out by using "time out in others' rooms" for disruptive students and assist each other through "mini counseling."

Teachers at the typical and formerly effective schools feel they have some support, but that it is limited. One new Andrew Jackson teacher speaks of having an outstanding mentor. Without the mentor, this teacher "would have left already, I would have walked out. That's how tough it is in the beginning. The mentor is my support—not that I get a lot of [other] support." At George Washington, interviewed teachers have few comments about teacher community, other than one teacher who says, "We support each other." Since teachers are often unable to leave their classrooms, SLC coordinators have to work to facilitate communication among teachers.

Instruction

There are several instructional similarities between teachers in highly effective schools and those in typical schools. All teachers use *Balanced Literacy,* the district-mandated curriculum, for language arts. Teachers in both highly effective and typical schools use a similar range of math curricula including some that are approved by the NSF-funded math/science improvement effort and some that are not. *Mathland, Connected Math,* and *Heath Mathematics* are the curricula most often used.

There are no differences in teacher ratings of how well they are able to implement such instructional practices as inquiry-based teaching, basic skills development, and multiple learning styles. Too, most teachers group students by ability level in class, primarily for reading. All teachers give homework in math and language arts and most give homework in science and social studies, although highly effective teachers are slightly more likely to give homework in social studies (95 percent versus 88 percent) and science (91 percent versus 87 percent).

Instructional Philosophies

One of the bigger instructional differences is in instructional philosophy. The instructional philosophies of the schools vary, but three of the four highly effective schools have explicit instructional philosophies. John Adams is a "Success for All"[5] school and among the earliest implementers of the bilingual version, "Exito Para Todos." James Monroe follows the Accelerated Schools model,[6] while John Tyler uses a hands-on inquiry approach. The remaining highly effective school, the three typical schools, and the formerly effective school do not have specific schoolwide instructional philosophies.

Amount and Level of Instruction

There are other instructional differences between the highly effective and typical schools, particularly in mathematics. Teachers in highly effective schools spend more time teaching mathematics each week (4.3 hours versus 3.9 hours) than do teachers in typical schools. They also have higher expectations for student learning than do teachers in typical schools.

Teachers were asked the highest level at which they cover such math topics as number operations and quantitative reasoning, geometry and spatial reasoning, and measurement. Sixty-six percent of teachers in highly effective schools and only 36 percent of teachers in typical schools report covering at least half their math topics at analysis levels or higher, a significant difference. In highly effective schools, the percentage of teachers covering most math topics at higher levels ranges from 46 to 90 percent while at typical schools, the range is from 25 to 48 percent.

Science instruction does not differ significantly. Teachers in both highly effective and typical schools spend about two hours a week teaching science. Half the teachers teaching science in highly effective schools teach the majority of their topics at analysis and higher levels, compared with just over a third of those teaching science in typical schools.

There are major differences in student responses about what they are learning. Highly effective–school students go into more detail about their subjects. For example, although most students in both groups say they are learning math, 66 percent of students in highly effective schools say they are learning fractions, compared with 22 percent of the typical-school students, a significant difference. And students from highly effective schools do not simply say they are learning fractions; they describe learning about adding, subtracting, multiplying, and dividing fractions. Similarly, these students speak not just of learning geometry but of learning about circumferences and π.

Sixty-three percent of the highly effective–school students say they are learning language arts, compared with 17 percent of the typical-school students, another significant difference. Only students in highly effective schools go into detail about the language arts they are learning, speaking about reading books about specific subjects, studying grammar (main ideas, key words, and paragraphs), learning spelling words, and reading in two languages. The following examples from each of the four highly effective schools highlight both the variety of things students feel they are learning and the level of detail they provide.

> "Math, using new calculators for fractions, adding fractions in groups, renaming a fraction and simplifying," which students say is "easy because we learned it already." They want to learn how to do "hard fractions like the 6th, 7th, and 8th graders do" along with computers and "how to type without looking."—James Monroe

> "Math, including decimals, fractions, times tables, division, and counting by 10s." Students also say they are learning "spelling, how to say big words, that English has a lot of words, and how to read in two languages." Other things they are learning include "how to do things on your own without help," "how to share," and "how to help people when they are down."—John Adams

> Students say, "Our teacher teaches us big stuff not baby stuff." The "big stuff" they are learning includes dodecahedrons, "fractions and about denominators being different," and "about Africa and Brazil—the people, the pollution, the things they do. People from Brazil and Africa came to visit and talk." Students are disappointed they are not learning "algebra and big stuff like in high school."—John Tyler

> Fractions, adding and dividing, circumferences, algebra, π, circles, the solar system, and that "pollution is screwing the earth, something will happen if people keep polluting, there is a big hole in the ozone, ice caps are melting." Students are also learning about Daniel Boone and the wilderness and are reading fairy tales and about famous people and things that happen in the real world.—Thomas Jefferson

With the exception of typical school James Madison, students in the formerly effective and typical schools report learning far fewer things and provide less detail about what they are learning.

> Fractions, addition, subtraction, and division, bigger spelling words, all 43 presidents.—Andrew Jackson

> Math, reading, science, and social studies . . . algebra, and geometry. —George Washington

> Reading and spelling, math (including fractions), science, and social studies.—Martin Van Buren

> History, math, and language arts. Germs, gas, dry ice, and orangutans and their habitats. Students also say they are learning about the Harlem

Renaissance, China, the Greeks, and the pyramids, as well as long division, algebra, and decimals. In language arts, they are learning about paragraphs and doing "a lot" of reading.—James Madison

Academics play a big role in what typical school students do not like about school. Student dislikes from typical Martin Van Buren all involve academic areas including "math because it's frustrating and kind of difficult," "social studies because it's boring and all they talk about is history," and "reading because it's boring and because all you do is sit there and listen to silence and stare at words for fifteen minutes." In comparison, the only thing students from highly effective John Adams do not like about their school is the lunchroom.

When students from the typical and formerly effective schools are asked what they do not like about school, 23 (79 percent) of the 29 student responses cover academic areas including math, social studies, language arts, reading, and music. Only 2 (8 percent) of the 26 responses from highly effective school students mention academic areas as what they do not like about school, a significant difference.

Assessment

There are few differences between teachers in highly effective and typical schools in terms of how they use standardized test results and teacher assessment data. Teachers in highly effective schools, however, are more likely to systematically observe students at least daily (58 percent versus 34 percent) and use performance assessments (33 percent versus 14 percent) and extended response items (28 percent versus 12 percent) daily.

Student Behavior and Discipline

Seven of the eight schools report some problems with student behavior. Highly effective schools, however, are more likely to have clear, consistent disciplinary policies, and teachers in the highly effective schools are more likely to see themselves as responsible for the behavior of not just their students but other students as well.

Policies

Since Cumberland City does not have a districtwide student disciplinary policy, individual schools develop their own policies, including whether they have an accommodation room where misbehaving students can be assigned temporarily during the school day. All the typical schools and all but one highly effective school choose to have an accommodation room.

There are major differences between the discipline policies and practices of highly effective and typical schools. The highly effective schools tend to have more structured, enforced, and clear discipline policies than do the typical schools. Teachers comment that they know and understand the policies and that the students do as well. In one highly effective school, teachers have created a code of conduct with explicit strategies for dealing with misbehavior that they feel everyone understands and is implementing. In a second highly effective school, the behavioral standards are highly structured and the students are held accountable for their behavior. In the two other highly effective schools, policies are not as structured, but teachers and administrators are active and involved; principals are involved in all discipline procedures, and teachers say most discipline issues are taken care of in the classroom.

Unlike other schools, highly effective John Adams does not have a special accommodation room for disruptive students. Rather, the accommodation policy includes having a private conference with the student. If the conference does not work, the next step of the policy is to contact the parent. Subsequent steps include a plan with the SLC coordinator, a plan with the counselor, and finally a comprehensive support process, the district's individual plan for special-needs students. Under this principal, teachers say, "the behavioral standards have become more structured; kids are being held more accountable." The principal feels that to have good discipline,

> we have to have support for the kids. Children act up because they have a need. I have had individuals who felt children should be transferred and isolated because of disciplinary incidents. But I don't believe that. I believe in progressive discipline, not to transfer a child after the first incident.

An SLC coordinator at John Adams agrees, saying, "One big thing we do—we are able to listen to somebody when children need to be listened to."

The discipline policy at highly effective James Monroe is clear, and teachers and parents are aware of it. The school has a "time out" or accommodation room and uses classroom time out and lunch detentions for discipline, as well as "behavior modification with more difficult cases." The teachers have created a code of conduct with explicit strategies to deal with the misbehavior, and everyone understands the code of conduct and strategies. The principal appears more concerned about student behavior issues than do the teachers and the students. Her original plan to deal with student misbehavior by dramatically increasing out-of-school suspensions decreased student achievement and, probably, student promotion. When she realized the plan had negative effects, she dropped it. With teacher assistance, other strategies have been developed to deal with student behavior, including in-school suspension where students can keep up on their work.

At highly effective John Tyler, teachers do not see discipline as a problem overall. They feel that there might be individual cases of bad behavior in each classroom, but in general it is pretty good. Teachers credit the grandparents club and the interns for helping to maintain discipline. The principal plays a role in discipline as well: as one teacher explains, "Most of the time the principal is involved with any discipline problems. She doesn't tolerate any discipline problems with kids." The school has an accommodation room, which the students do not like. Students accept that sometimes they have to go because "You did something bad and you have to do your time."

Thomas Jefferson, the fourth highly effective school, has an accommodation room where teachers can send misbehaving students, but it does not appear to be widely used. Interviewed teachers say that when there are discipline problems, unless it is a dire emergency, teachers do not call for outside help and do not take kids to the office. Instead, they go to other teachers who know the kids. Teachers feel the discipline policy is pretty well enforced but not particularly effective.

In the three typical schools, discipline procedures are described as unstructured, unclear, subjective, and inconsistently applied. For example, James Madison has disciplinary policies in effect, but interviewed teachers comment that there is "not a whole lot of structured discipline." George Washington has an extensive disciplinary procedure, but one teacher feels the enforcement of the discipline code is biased, saying it's "very subjective . . . based on the time of day . . . the teacher." In addition, teachers say the George Washington accommodation room does not work. Students "kind of enjoy" going to the accommodation room. Martin Van Buren students do not see going to the accommodation room as a punishment either. In fact, some students ask to be sent there. As with George Washington teachers, Martin Van Buren teachers feel the enforcement of the discipline code is, as one teacher explains, "not consistent . . . it really depends on the teacher," and that the consistency depends "on the mood of the day."

The formerly effective school, Andrew Jackson, has discipline polices in place. However, parents feel that the school rules are not clear for parents and students and that they do not know what "will be tolerated and what won't," in the words of one parent. Two parents feel that if the school "sticks to the rules then the parents will too—if the school gets lax, then parents will too." And they feel the school is lax, pointing out that while Andrew Jackson is a uniform school, the students do not have to wear their uniforms.

Student Behavior

People in each school describe a range of student behavior. Only at highly effective John Tyler, however, are students described in very positive ways, such as "creative" and "really great" students who "love to help." At the other extreme, teachers in two of the three typical schools and in the formerly effective school describe students as "needy," "lacking self-control," and "lacking social skills." There are other differences as well. Teachers in highly effective schools are significantly more likely to feel that three-quarters or more of their students are familiar with classroom routines and make transitions between activities smoothly (61 percent versus 43 percent). They are also more likely to feel that students making transitions in and out of the classroom do not waste time, are ready to work, and rarely have to be reminded of what they are supposed to be doing (27 percent versus 15 percent).

Shared Responsibility

While the differences in policies and attitudes are great, even greater are the differences in perceptions of responsibility for students and for student behavior. Across most schools, staff discuss the problems of poor urban America and how they affect student behavior. At highly effective Thomas Jefferson, the custodian reflects the views of other staff: "Kids don't have anyone at home. Teachers are the only ones they can look up to with any kind of respect."

At typical school James Monroe, staff are concerned about the lack of social skills in students. One teacher explains: "We have every social ill in this neighborhood, crack vials, condoms in the schoolyard. In our curriculum, we don't address what they need, the morals they aren't getting at home." Another teacher echoes this sentiment, saying there are children who have "never been taught what is disrespectful." The principal adds that teachers "just want to teach, but for many of my students, the social needs have to be addressed first."

The difference between the highly effective and typical schools is not in the experiences and problems that students bring to school. In fact, the teachers in the highly effective schools are significantly more likely to have students with learning disabilities (58 percent versus 42 percent) in their classes and somewhat more likely to have students with emotional disabilities (43 percent versus 34 percent). The difference is in what educators themselves do to affect student behavior in their schools. Teachers and administrators in two highly effective schools speak of the role of effective planning and appropriate lessons in controlling student behavior. Keeping students engaged and interacting with the teacher and with one another is a disciplinary strategy teachers find works for even the most difficult students.

At highly effective John Adams, teachers focus on getting students to take ownership of their behavior, using time outs, behavior modification, and a focus on positive reinforcement. One teacher comments, "All teachers hold their students accountable; there are consequences for the student from the teacher for their behavior." Some teachers use "incentives to try to promote the behavior of students doing the right thing, to promote and reward the good citizen." "Very effective planning and very appropriate lessons" contribute, teachers feel, to good discipline and cements the teacher as the one in charge of the classroom.

Principal Margaret Riley does not see highly effective John Tyler as having major behavioral problems. She believes this is "first because the teachers in classroom use a lot of strategies and maybe because of *Balanced Literacy*—kids are more active."

Teachers at typical schools James Madison and Martin Van Buren see teacher inexperience and low student academic skills as contributing factors to student behaviors. Unlike some of the highly effective schools, however, they do not see these factors as things over which they have control.

At Martin Van Buren, teachers have various explanations for student behavior problems, none of which they feel are under teacher control. They speak of a lack of social skills and lack of respect for authority figures—that, as one teacher explains, the "laws of the neighborhood are a lot different than the school." Teachers feel that some students not only do not learn social skills at home, but that parents will tell their children to fight and hit. As a result, in the words of one teacher, students learn the "cycle of abuse . . . and that's how they deal with frustration and anger." Along with the culture, teachers ascribe student behavior problems to staff turnover, attendance and tardiness, unmedicated emotional disturbances, and student frustration if their academic level is low in a particular area.

Teachers in typical school James Madison agree with one teacher's comment that some students "haven't gotten past the learning-to-read stage, much less at the reading-to-learn stage," especially in the upper grades, causing frustration and aggravation for students. This issue becomes all the more pronounced when "60–65 percent students have learning problems," as another teacher explains. One teacher who does not "have too many problems" feels that the behavior problems are related to the amount of time teachers have been at the school, adding that the more experienced teachers have fewer behavioral problems.

At the third typical school, George Washington, nothing is said about any school factors affecting student behavior. Teachers there see the causes of student behavior as, in one teacher's words, a "lack of self-control and discipline. A lot of them are very impulsive." Principal Raymond Stanley attributes discipline problems to "a whole litany of things," including the environment, society, and lack of respect for adults.

In the highly effective schools, teachers feel responsibility not only for the students in their class, but for other students as well. For these teachers, this means knowing all the students at their grade level and correcting a misbehaving student, regardless of whether that student is in their class.

At highly effective John Tyler, the sense of shared responsibility for all the children is great. Principal Margaret Riley explains that, "Teachers all see each other as competent in behavior management and work together to maintain order within the school as a whole. Teacher A knows that teacher B doesn't want a student to do that, so she will correct another teacher's child." In addition, Riley feels that "the community helps. Parents expect children to behave and have respect for the school." Parents take responsibility for other people's children as well. At school events, "parents take up for other students whose mothers can't come."

Other highly effective schools display similar attitudes. At James Monroe, all teachers play an integral role in the discipline. If there is an emergency and a teacher calls, then every free teacher goes to that room.

The John Adams philosophy, as a SLC coordinator explains, is "the way to achieve success is for everyone to be responsible and to raise the bar for effectiveness." At Thomas Jefferson, "we've come together out of necessity," one teacher says. "We needed each other really badly. One floor is always willing to help another. It works across floors as well as within floors."

This is not the case in the typical schools or the formerly effective school. In George Washington and Martin Van Buren, not only are teachers not taking responsibility for students other than their own, but the principals feel the teachers need to take more responsibility for student discipline within their own classrooms.

George Washington teachers seem to take very little ownership of the school, feeling that you need effective parents to have effective schools. Teachers also do not indicate a feeling of responsibility for all children in the school, and it is unclear how much responsibility they feel toward their own students. Principal Raymond Stanley is concerned that teachers are not dealing with their own disruptive students; he wants them to deal with minor student infractions themselves and to address students' needs "before it becomes a problem." Martin Van Buren principal Tamara Jones is similarly concerned that teachers "abdicate" their power when they send the children to the administration for discipline and feels the teachers need to "take ownership of what's going on in the classroom."

Unlike the visits to other schools, the visits to formerly effective school Andrew Jackson showed a school seemingly out of control. Students were running, teachers were yelling, and one student was lying down in a dirty stairwell crying. Adults stepped over him; no one appeared to be responsible.

Parent-School Involvement

Parent involvement tends to be difficult in Cumberland City. School officials feel welfare reform, especially the work requirement, has "put a dent in traditional parent involvement." There are few statistical differences in the amount of parent involvement between the highly effective and typical schools. Only about a quarter of the teachers in both highly effective and typical schools report that they have had some contact with all parents of their students. There are some differences, however, in the type of parent involvement. Teachers in highly effective schools are more likely to contact parents when a child does something well (88 percent versus 74 percent) and are more likely to hold classroom open houses (68 percent versus 50 percent).

The major difference between highly effective and typical schools is in parent-school relationships, including parent access to the school. The four highly effective schools all have "open door" policies, where parents are welcome at the school any time. When parents want to come to the school, they just come. All that is required is that they check in at the office. The policy at the typical schools and the formerly effective school is quite different. Before parents are allowed in the school, they have to make appointments.

This difference in policies reflects very different parent-school relationships between the highly effective and typical schools. At the highly effective schools, parents are seen as part of the school community and are welcomed and, perhaps more important, respected.

According to John Adams's principal, "If you want community involvement, then [parents] should be able to come whenever they want and [there should be] people there who speak the language." Mr. Lindsey continues, "We don't put a show on. Parents are welcome to visit any class at any time." Teachers agree, saying, "Parents have an opportunity to see what it is like in the classrooms." The principal credits the high involvement of parents to the

> nonthreatening environment. . . . [Parent involvement] is high because people feel comfortable. From principal to building engineer, parents can talk to anyone. There are no appointments for parents. They come in and I talk to them.

John Tyler principal Margaret Riley "is really gung-ho on getting parents involved in any way." As Dr. Riley explains, "A lot of people in community feel 'it is my school—I went here.' They are real comfortable here, like to be a part of something." Parents agree: "The school is nice here. The parents are always here." John Tyler's staff are connected to the community in other ways as well. As the custodian explains, "You get to know people—the 92-year-old lady across the street, I talk to her. I talk to the guy at the store." The custodian also has an assistant who is doing court-ordered community service, and the John Tyler staff are trying to keep him away from the gangs.

Parents at highly effective Thomas Jefferson are pleased with parent-school relationships. While the principal is not of the community, they feel she is involved with the community, seeing her as "the only principal who comes to the neighborhood." They also praise the way parents on the school council are treated:

> Whatever the topic is, once you sit at the table—all hats are the same. You're someone who will express your views. Just because you are the principal doesn't mean you can overrule the group. When parents first came on board we had our insecurities, but now I can express how I felt.

There are, parents feel, barriers to getting parents involved, including parent fears. But they feel they are working things out, "slowly chipping away the barriers [to greater parent involvement]."

At highly effective James Monroe, administrators feel that "there is a gelling of the staff, community, and parents." While there are a few parents they cannot reach, administrators feel the parents support them. Parents and the home-school coordinator are concerned about reduced parent involvement. They feel the major reason is parents' participation in "welfare to work" with its mandatory minimum of 20 hours of work a week. To better reach working parents, the school is adding night meetings for parents and a parent homework help line because "a lot of parents don't understand the homework and are kind of shy. If they don't know how to do the work, they can't and don't help."

The situation is much different in the other schools. In the formerly effective school and one typical school, there is close to open warfare between the schools and the parents.

Parents at formerly effective school Andrew Jackson are upset about what they feel is happening in the school. They blame the principal—as one parent states, "if the head don't work the body don't." The parents feel the principal does not have time to sit down and hear what anyone has to say and, in the words of a second parent, "If you talk to her [she talks to you] like you are a child." Andrew Jackson's school/community coordinator is also concerned. The school has fewer outreach programs for parents than before, but "if we had a principal who would support us, we would have more," according to the coordinator.

George Washington principal Raymond Stanley feels he has "to be more of a people person. . . . Parents can't be fearful of you." Staff in this typical school agree. Individuals comment that "working well with the community" is one of Mr. Stanley's strengths and that he is "a really good people person, good at giving advice on how to handle the parents." Yet there is great tension between the community and the school. A big part of the community relations liaison's role is to "calm [the parents] down before they meet the principal or teachers. . . . I try to keep the peace between the teachers and the parents." There is, Mr. Stanley says, a "lack of trust . . . among parents and teacher, teachers and teachers, kids and teachers. Parents don't want to talk to the teachers because the teachers made them feel ignorant." Teachers, for their part, don't want what they say in meetings to get back to the community. Tensions are at such a level that some teachers will not let parents come into their classrooms, and some parents have had the telephone company block the school's telephone number from ringing in their homes. Others parents use caller ID and will not answer the phone when the school calls.

School-parent relationships are more mixed in the other two typical schools. James Madison principal Marietta Nichols feels that parent involvement is good, "I think because they trust us. I have very few negative parents." But teachers' feelings are mixed. One teacher sees "some of my parents daily. All of them are available by phone; some are on speed dial." Yet a second teacher explains, "My parents are not supportive at all. I've had parents that haven't picked up report cards from last year, even for a student that is on the honor roll." Other teachers say they do not see parents getting involved at James Madison because, as individual teachers say "a lot of them know how the kids are—they just don't want to deal with their kids" or "some parents have that fear about school because they've had a bad experience."

Martin Van Buren staff disagree about the degree of parent involvement. Principal Tamara Jones says there is almost no parent involvement, while the teachers and the parent coordinator say there is a lot of involvement, especially with parent-teacher conferences. In the teacher survey, over half the teachers (55 percent) say that the majority of parents attended parent-teacher conferences during 1999–2000, and 38 percent of teachers say that at least one-quarter of their students' parents contacted them about their child during 1999–2000.

In Summary

These highly effective and typical schools served the same minority children in the same low-income neighborhoods. Their principals and teachers belong to the same unions and are subject to the same district rules and regulations. Their salary scales are the same, as are the resources the state, district, and clusters provide them. Yet, working together, the highly effective schools are able to create communities where children are learning. Strong principals who are real instructional leaders, teachers who are responsible not only for the behavior and learning of their own students but for other students as well, and an atmosphere where parents are respected all come together to make up a working formula. At Cumberland City, some things *do* make a difference.

5

Rios Calientes
Responding to NAFTA

The Rios Calientes area has undergone dramatic changes recently as
a result of the North American Free Trade Agreement (NAFTA) and
the city's close proximity to the Mexico–U.S. border. The presence of a
large maquiladora economy just across the border in Mexico has stimulated economic growth in the city and accelerated changes in the employment structure. The creation of high-technology jobs has increased
demands for a labor force skilled in information technology processing
and services and, therefore, the need for residents of Rios Calientes to
upgrade their educations and skills. Workforce development is thus a
major priority in the area, and academic institutions have been working
closely with the community to improve education. This has increased
pressure on the area's schools to produce graduates qualified to enter two-
and four-year programs at local colleges and universities. This chapter
describes the three Rios Calientes districts' responses to this pressure (as
well as to the directives of a demanding state-driven school reform effort).[1]

According to Census 2000, Rios Calientes is the fifth-largest city in its
state and among the 25 largest cities in the country. Montecito, across the
border in Mexico, is the largest city in the state of Chihuahua and the
fifth-largest city in Mexico. Census 2000 figures indicate that the population of the county that includes Rios Calientes increased 15 percent (by
88,000 people) from 1990 to 2000. Within the city limits, the increase was
about 9.5 percent, but outside the city limits, the increase was 52 percent,

85

Table 5.1. General Demographic Characteristics for Rios Calientes County, 2001

	Number	Percent
Total population	679,622	100.0
Persons below poverty (1999)		23.8
Language other than English spoken at home		73.3
Male		48.2
Female		51.8
Median age (years)	31.1	—
Under 18 years	174,935	32.0
White		73.9
Black or African American		3.1
American Indian and Alaska Native		0.8
Asian		1.0
Hispanic or Latino origin[a]		78.2

Source: U.S. Census Bureau, Census 2000.

a. These people may also be counted as white.

exceeding the national population rate of increase of 13.2 percent. Population projections estimate that by 2010, Rios Calientes's city population will surpass 700,000 and the Metropolitan Statistical Area (MSA) population will reach 900,000;[2] by 2025, the MSA population will reach 1.01 million.

As table 5.1 shows, the population of Rios Calientes is largely Latino, and one-third of the total population is under age 18. The poverty at the county level (23.8 percent) is high compared with the state average of 15.4 percent.

Politics and the Economy of Rios Calientes

Rios Calientes was founded over four centuries ago as an outpost for traders and missionaries in the west. Today, Rios Calientes and the Mexican city of Montecito make up the largest metropolitan area on the U.S.–Mexico border, with the two downtown areas within walking distance. Montecito greatly influences the area's economy, and the area serves as an integrated international trade region. Because of Rios Calientes's proximity to Mexico, businesses are able to capitalize on NAFTA, the maquiladora industry, and other prospects for business collaboration in Central and South America. International trade has made the local economy relatively stable. Globalization and information technology have also accelerated economic structural change. As information technology demands a labor force skilled in processing and services, Rios Calientes has started to emphasize the creation of high-technology jobs.

Income

Personal income in the Rios Calientes MSA for the next 10 years is expected to grow 5.8 percent.[3] As the hub of the border economy, the city attracts people from nearby counties, including some in New Mexico and Mexico, who come to Rios Calientes for employment.[4] Residents enjoy a relatively low cost of living compared with other cities in the United States. In the fourth quarter of 2000, the cost of living index for Rios Calientes was 93.5 percent of the national average. At $17,216, the county's per capita income is lower than the state average of $26,834, and the number of persons per household (3.18) is also higher than the state average of 2.74. Homeownership, however, is comparable to the state's average (63.8 percent).[5]

Employment and the Labor Market

New industries, a retrained labor force, a robust economy, and investment in education and infrastructure are all contributing to alleviating area unemployment. Area unemployment has been slowly declining since 1990, reaching 8.2 percent for 2000. Starting in the 1990s, Rios Calientes evolved from a low-skilled, manufacturing-based economy to a more service-oriented economy. Despite the decline in manufacturing, specifically apparel, Rios Calientes experienced a net gain of more than 42,000 jobs over the 1990s. The city is in a unique situation, moreover, because the manufacturing sectors related to maquiladora activity in Montecito are growing, and services and services-related employment in Rios Calientes benefit from the economic interchanges generated by daily flows of trade and people between the two cities.

Manufacturing employment, which accounted for 20 percent of the city's employment in 1994, fell 4.2 percent from 1990 to 1999, but the service sector grew 38 percent over that time (making up 20 percent of the MSA workforce in 2000). By 1999, 74 percent of the city's basic industries were either service or service-related. With an expanded border region economy and the need for services to support the population, the service sector has seen an increase in health care, professional, and business services. With help from NAFTA, Rios Calientes has a strong trade sector (24 percent). The city also has healthy public utilities, construction and mining, and finance, insurance, and real estate sectors.

The government sector, which includes the public school system, increasingly employs a large portion of the workforce. The growing number of public-school enrollments has forced local school districts to increase their workforce. Of the top ten government-sector employers, five are education-related: the Chavez School District (8,500 employees), the Bolivar Independent School District (8,200 employees), Rios Calientes Community College (3,700 employees), the State University at Rios Calientes (3,700 employees), and the Torrijos Independent School District (2,800 employees). A military installation at Fort Benign also has a notable impact on the local economy and in 1999 added about $983 million to Rios Calientes's economy. The military-related population is about 21 percent of the area population.

Maquiladoras

Maquiladoras are twin-plant manufacturing facilities that allow foreign businesses to import duty-free raw materials and other commodities for use in fabricating goods at competitive production costs. The finished products are exported and are subject only to a value-added tariff. Maquiladoras operate under a special Mexican customs program that allows complete foreign ownership of these production facilities. Maquiladoras in Montecito (312 plants in 2001) provide about one-fifth of Mexico's overall maquila employment. Montecito has the largest maquiladora employment concentration of any Mexican city, with more than 200,000 workers. Major plants in Montecito include Philips Consumer Electronics, General Motors, Allied Signal, and the Ford Motor Company.

Several important trends related to maquiladoras are significantly affecting the economy of the Rios Calientes area. First, a growing percentage of the employment maquiladoras generate has been in technical and administrative positions instead of direct labor, suggesting that maquiladoras are becoming more sophisticated and that maquiladora workers' skills are increasing. Second, growing numbers of companies have sprung up in Rios Calientes to service the Mexican maquiladora industry. Although these manufacturing subsector companies may employ fewer workers, they demand more highly skilled labor, and thus wages are higher. Further, manufacturing activity in Montecito positively affects employment in transportation, business, and legal services in Rios Calientes. Business service employment, which includes personnel services as well as computer and data services, grew 75 percent from 1990 to 1999. In addition to the impact that maquiladoras have on employment patterns, they have helped create a customer base of Montecito residents. Not only are Montecito residents coming to Rios Calientes for retail shopping, they are also increasingly relying on the financial and health services their neighbor provides.

Workforce Development

To meet the changing employment requirements, the local workforce in Rios Calientes needs to change as well. A report about the future of the border region concludes that local residents must develop the higher skills needed for jobs that pay higher wages. With a growing college-age population and more than 52,000 additional Rios Calientes residents by 2010 (a 54 percent increase from 1997), the State Higher Education Coordinating Board estimates that by 2010 about 8,000 additional students will attend either the State University at Rios Calientes or Rios Calientes Community College.

Workforce development is a major priority in Rios Calientes, and academic institutions have been working closely with the community to improve education. In addition to limited funds and resources, the border setting presents other challenges (including the higher cost of bilingual education and the concentration of poverty in the area) to local schools. As a result, recent state funding reforms have addressed the challenge of educating Rios Calientes's youth. Recognizing the unique situation of the border region as well as the economic potential in the future, the state legislature approved the Border Initiative in 1989. This effort provided additional funding for border universities with the hopes of achieving parity with other state institutions. The initiative increased educational funding to the area and allowed universities to improve course offerings, add new academic programs, hire more faculty members, construct new buildings, and renovate old ones. But what of the K–12 institutions that feed the higher education system in Rios Calientes?

The Rios Calientes Educational System

Rios Calientes County has nine school districts, three of which serve the city. A large percentage of K–12 students from Montecito also attends school in Rios Calientes. By 2010, enrollment in city schools is expected to increase by 20,000 students, from 154,823 to 173,700. Districts are contributing to workforce development to meet the region's specific needs. All three districts feature programs to prepare students for careers in information technology. For example, programs at each district train students for careers as computer network specialists and microcomputer technicians.

Higher education institutions in the area are also working to meet the workforce demands with degree programs targeted at local needs. The State University at Rios Calientes (SURC), Neighboring State University, Rios Calientes Community College, and the University of the Sierra Nevada are the major institutions of higher education in the region that draw local students. Many research programs at these schools operate in conjunction with institutions in Montecito, focusing on issues specific to the border region.

SURC, the largest Mexican-American-majority university in the United States, is a comprehensive university offering 61 bachelor's, 58 master's, and 10 doctoral degrees. Two-thirds of SURC's more than 16,000 students are Mexican-American, and 9 percent are Mexican nationals, many of whom commute to the campus from Montecito. As a major public research university, SURC receives funds from the National Science Foundation, the National Institutes of Health, the U.S. Department of Energy, the Environmental Protection Agency, and the U.S. Department of Education.

In an effort to meet the demand for information technology (IT) workers, area institutions are emphasizing IT skills in their curricula. SURC, for example, is meeting the demand by offering bachelor's and master's degree programs in computer science and, jointly with the Department of Electrical and Computer Engineering, a doctoral program in computer engineering. The Rios Calientes Community College offers an associate's degree in computer information systems. The college also offers several certificate programs, including office technology, computer operations, basic computer skills, and office information systems. Several proprietary and trade schools in the area also offer a range of computer training courses, from basic computer skills to certification programs.

The State Education Agency (SEA) plays a major role in setting education policy. Though districts and schools have a certain amount of flexibility within these areas, the state sets policies on textbooks and curriculum, class size and teacher-to-student ratios, instructional hours, assessment and reporting, and professional development. The education policies described in this section are those in effect during the data collection and site visit phases of the study (2000–01).

The state determines a foundation curriculum, with essential skills identified for each content area. The state then provides a list of approved text materials that meet the requirements for the essential skills. Districts must maintain an average ratio of not less than one teacher per 20 students in average daily attendance; for grades K–4, the class size is limited to no more than 22 students. The school day lasts at least seven hours, and there are at least 180 instructional days in the school year. There are required assessments in 3rd, 5th, and 8th grades for which students must demonstrate satisfactory performance to progress to the next grade. Districts must provide written notice of a student's performance to parents at least once every 12 weeks; if students consistently perform unsatisfactorily, written notice must go home every three weeks. For staff development, there are no requirements for hours in training, but teachers must receive training in certain areas (such as gifted and talented education) and it must be predominantly school-based and related to achieving the school performance goals.

The state standards were created to clarify instructional objectives for each grade level and subject. They were implemented in 1993 and revised in 1997. The key component is the standards for student performance. All students, with few exceptions, must demonstrate proficiency in each essential element the standards specify. Proficiency is demonstrated through assessments, primarily the State Assessment of Academic Skills, which is a criterion-referenced assessment closely aligned with the state standards. It was first implemented in 1990.

Districts and schools are assessed based on their performance levels; the highest performing are exempt from specific regulations and requirements. Schools in the state are rated as "exemplary," "recognized," "acceptable," or "low-performing." Though the standards have changed slightly over the years, the ratings are generally based on student performance by content area on the SAAS and average dropout rates. A secondary set of indicators may also be used, including attendance, advanced placement course completion, and college testing results.

The Three Rios Calientes School Districts

Not only is there a large Mexican population living in the Rios Calientes area, many students come from across the border. According to one district superintendent who was interviewed, the city is essentially divided into three parts based on demographics and location: the northeast part is characterized by a sizable, steadily growing population of former military personnel; the northwest is affluent, diverse, and growing quickly; and the south central area, also called the "segundo barrio," is nearly 100 percent Latino and low income but generally stable in terms of growth, with pockets of rapid expansion.

Rios Calientes's regional education center serves an important role in the area public education system. Established by the State Board of Education, the 20 regional education service centers throughout the state are not regulatory arms of the SEA, and school participation in service centers is voluntary. The centers help school districts improve student performance in each region, enable school districts to operate more efficiently and economically, and implement initiatives assigned by the legislature or the commissioner. The regional education service center serving Rios Calientes offers almost 100 different programs and services to area schools, including some specific to mathematics for both students and teachers.

Three school districts serve the Rios Calientes area: Cesar Chavez Independent School District, Omar Torrijos Independent School District, and Simon Bolivar Independent School District. This chapter refers to these districts as Chavez, Torrijos, and Bolivar, respectively.[6]

Cesar Chavez Independent School District

Chavez is the largest school district in the Rios Calientes area and serves the city of Rios Calientes; it is one of the five largest districts in the state, with an enrollment of 62,451 students in 2000–01. The district has 77 regular pre-K–12 schools, 5 special schools, and 5 other campuses and programs. There are 10 high schools, 14 junior high schools, 1 combined elementary-secondary school, 54 elementary schools, and 4 alternative schools. The school district also offers districtwide programs, including the Center for Career and Technology Education, which offers half-day classes in career and technology education for interested students. Martinez Magnet School,[7] housed within one of the high schools, offers health education classes for students interested in pursing health careers. Chavez has 57 acceptable, 17 recognized, five exemplary, and no low-performing schools.

Demographics

Of the 62,451 students in 2000–01, most were Latino (77.3 percent), few were white (16.5 percent), and even fewer were African American (4.8 percent). A very large percentage crossed the border every day from Montecito to attend school in the Chavez district. About one-third (31.7 percent) were LEP, and a large percentage (66.9 percent) were considered economically disadvantaged. The attendance rate was 95.3 percent, and there were few disciplinary placements (2.1 percent).

Governance Structure

The superintendent, who is responsible to the seven-member school board for the administration of the Chavez district, oversees five associate superintendents. Three are regional associate superintendents: one each for the northwest, northeast, and south central regions. The remaining two oversee facilities, maintenance, and support; and curriculum, instruction, and assessment, respectively. Working under these associate superintendents are managers and executive directors.

Curriculum

District staff agree that the state dictates the curriculum and that it is based on the state standards. There is some flexibility, however, in how the schools choose their instructional approaches. Schools can select how they wish to deliver the curriculum. According to a staff member,

> The state only says, "These are the [state standards]. This is what you're supposed to teach." But the district, through the Curriculum and Instruction Department, is in charge of writing the curriculum guides and guiding instructional practice.[8]

Textbooks and Supplemental Materials

The district follows the state-mandated procedure for textbook adoption. For supplemental materials, schools may use any materials they wish as long as the materials are aligned with the state standards. The district has created a resource for the schools to use in the teaching of science, called an "extended reading with science." Staff have taken a reading book, the adopted science book, and American Institute of Mathematical Sciences activities and integrated all three, incorporating math as well. This approach facilitates science instruction, especially for teachers in the elementary grades who are, in the words of one district staff member, "mostly reading specialists."

Instructional Policies

The state determines the number of hours of instructional time provided to students in a day and a year, but there is flexibility in terms of how many hours students must devote to each subject. Schools decide these schedules, but they must be approved by the district (through a districtwide planning committee and then the regional associate superintendent). Block scheduling is a school-level decision.

When asked about district policies for ability grouping, a district staff member responds, "We are not allowed to have that. There are heterogeneous mixtures and each teacher must meet the needs of whatever kinds of students there are in the classroom." One staff member describes the mainstreaming of special education students as having occurred "big time" in the district. The majority of students in the district are bilingual, and the district offers bilingual, monolingual, and dual-language classes.[9]

Student Assessment

District staff report that the state hands down the student assessment policy. During the site visit, the district was preparing to add a science assessment to the SAAS.

Monitoring and Reporting Student Progress

The district requires progress reports to parents every three weeks and report cards every six weeks, which is more frequently than the 12-week intervals the state mandates. The state sends SAAS scores to the district and the district sends them to the schools, which in turn send them to individual parents. Scores are also disseminated to teachers. The state makes SAAS scores available on the Internet so the media have immediate access to them. The district responds to media requests, and its Research and Evaluation Office prepares reports comparing past years' results with current results.

Graduation Requirements

Like the other two districts in this study, Chavez requires four years of math and four years of science for a student to graduate.

Professional Development

Although the district has a professional development center, it mainly focuses on new teachers, custodial employees, bus drivers, and support staff. The staff development personnel at the district put together a booklet that they distribute every spring and fall announcing the activities and trainings that will be offered. Professional development seems to focus mostly on curriculum and instructional issues. One district employee states that teachers receive training through the state university, which is the local university, while another mentions that a local private, nonprofit organization provides professional development.

Parental Involvement

Title I and other federal compensatory programs have parental involvement requirements. The district requires parental representation on campus planning and district planning committees. The parent-teacher association is considered a district-level parent activity.

Resources

The major federal resources the district receives are Title I schoolwide funds. Chavez also receives some state bilingual funding. The district receives funding and resources through all the entitlements, special education funding, Eisenhower funds, Innovative Schools funding, Title VI, local education organizations, and E-rate.

Teacher Shortage and Teacher Hiring

The district reports a teacher shortage in math, science, bilingual, and special education areas. Although there have been major recruitment efforts to hire teachers from out of state, staff reported that those efforts are being abandoned. According to one staff member, "We have a university here but they don't produce enough bilingual teachers for our schools." Most teachers in the district are produced by two area university programs. A small percentage comes from the nearby military base.

The district has an alternative certification program not only through SURC but also through its regional service center. Staff admit that the district has had to issue emergency certifications to allow individuals without certifications to teach in shortage areas. In terms of hiring, teaching applicants must be screened by the district's human resources department, which then sends a list of screened applicants to the principals who have reported vacancies. Interviews are conducted at the campus level, and the final decision to hire is made at that level.

Principal Recruitment and Hiring

Most principals are hired from within the district employees, usually assistant principals. Principal hiring is done through a committee at the regional level, overseen by the associate superintendent for that region. Candidates for the position interview with the campus improvement team, made up of teachers and parents at the school where the vacancy must be filled.

Partnerships

District staff state that individual schools establish most partnerships independently.

Omar Torrijos Independent School District

The Torrijos Independent School District serves two neighboring towns and a portion of Rios Calientes. Torrijos implements a year-round multi-track schedule. The rapidly growing district expects 56,700 students to attend its schools by 2010, up from 26,711 in 2000–01. Students in the Torrijos district can earn the following certificates: certified nursing assistant, cosmetology, security service, Cisco certification, A+ certification, and Microsoft certification. Torrijos also has a four-year Health Profession Academy and a pharmacy technician certification program. There are 12 acceptable, 9 recognized, 1 exemplary, and no low-performing schools in the district, which includes 3 high schools, 5 junior high schools, 14 elementary schools, and 1 alternative school.

Demographics

Of the 26,711 students the district served in 2000–01, most were Latino (91 percent), with very few white (7 percent) and even fewer African American students (1 percent). Well over half (68.1 percent) were considered economically disadvantaged as defined by eligibility for free or reduced-price lunches. The average attendance rate was 95.3 percent.

Governance Structure

The superintendent reports to the board of trustees. Under the superintendent are five assistant superintendents—one each supervising instructional services, personnel services, student services, financial/business services, and physical plant/operational services. Under each assistant superintendent are two to five directors who are the links to the schools. About a year before the site visit, the superintendent appointed an area executive director to oversee each of the three feeder patterns. This person is a liaison from the principals to the superintendent and works with the principals in their feeder-school pattern to ensure that principals implement the curriculum, that instructional programs have continuity from elementary to middle to high school, and that activities among the feeder pattern schools are coordinated. District staff mention that the principals are encouraged to work with the area executive director to propose programs for their individual schools that the superintendent would then approve.

District staff point out that 10 years ago Torrijos decided to be more site-based and to relinquish a great deal of control over procedures, policies, and programs to individual schools. The district made the campuses and their school improvement teams responsible for evaluating their needs and determining the programs that best meet these needs. A staff member comments, "The district's role is to advise and to let [the schools] know what's out there, but they have the responsibility and authority to decide what's best for their school."

Curriculum

The curriculum in Torrijos is based on the state standards, as are curricula all across the state. Several district staff express a belief that, essentially, the schools are following national math and science standards because the state standards are based on those standards. District staff feel that there are differences among schools in terms of how the curriculum is "delivered," and that these differences depend on the instructional leadership the principals provide.

Textbooks and Supplemental Materials

The district follows the state-imposed procedures for textbook adoption. As is the case with the other two districts in the study, principals and teachers may purchase supplemental materials for use as additional instructional materials.

Instructional Policies

The instructional policy at the district level is "pretty open-ended as far as how subjects ought to be taught," according to staff. State law specifies the subject areas and content according to grade level, but no state or district policy determines the time that should be devoted to instruction of each subject. "That's left up to the flexibility of the campus and the teachers to decide what's best for the students," observes one district staff member.

Student Assessment

The district complies with the state requirements concerning SAAS administration as the main vehicle for student assessment. At the school level, according to district staff, teachers seem to be "more product-driven" and look at assessment in less traditional ways based on school-level rather than district-level decisions.

Monitoring and Reporting Student Progress

The district requires that teachers give progress reports every three weeks. Every six weeks, children receive a report card, mailed directly to their homes. Open-house meetings (teacher-parent conferences) are held twice a year in each school. Schools implement the district policy and then, in the words of a district staff member, may "do something extra." The student cumulative folder, maintained for each child, contains SAAS, SAT, ACT, and other standardized test scores and is the key to student progress from year to year. At the end of each year, the teacher must sign off on this folder. According to district staff, these are district-level policies, but most districts in the state use this system. The state sends SAAS scores to the district and the district disseminates them to schools, which in turn send them to parents. The district may also send score data to individuals in the community and to the media.

Professional Development

According to district staff, schools determine the type of professional development provided to them. Every campus looks at the SAAS scores and the different objectives to assess their weak areas, and that assessment drives what is required and provided for staff development.

Parental Involvement

The district supports a staff member who is paid through Title I funds to oversee a districtwide parent initiative. There is a representative for each Title I school, and these representatives in turn work with the parent centers in individual schools to organize volunteers to work in classrooms and assist teachers. As a staff member comments, "I know that our district supports involvement of community and parents."

Resources

The district receives a number of grants, including federal funding for Title I (schoolwide). The Ninth Grade Initiative, a program that encourages 9th graders who are failing in any subject to improve, is another grant the district receives.

Teacher Shortage and Teacher Hiring

Recently, the district has had difficulty filling teacher shortages in some areas such as math and science, special education, and bilingual education.

Recruitment has not been done outside the Rios Calientes area for several years. According to one staff member in Torrijos,

> We pride ourselves on having a good school district, with lots of benefits that attract people. And we've been very successful in attracting teachers . . . both new teachers from the state university as well as those from other districts. I don't think it's quite as good as it was four or five years ago, but we were having people wanting to come to [Torrijos]. I don't know why that has changed. Maybe our salary policy is not as aggressive as it once was when we were paying above what other districts were paying. The year-round school was a draw for some people, too. If a teacher works on the [expanded school year calendar], which is more days than a regular calendar, they can make a very good salary.

Staff comment that the teacher supply is not what it once was and predict that an exodus will occur soon because of retirement. This will exacerbate the shortage in addition to the construction of nine new schools in the next three years in the district, one of the fastest-growing in the state. The district is now paying math teachers a stipend of $1,000 a year as an attraction device.

Partnerships

Torrijos has a Community in Schools program with a number of business sponsors who partner with individual schools. The district also works closely with social service agencies that serve the families of students.

Simon Bolivar Independent School District

Bolivar began in the 1930s as a rural education district with one high school and a few elementary schools; it now has a student population of nearly 50,000. As the second-largest school district in the area, Bolivar is the third-largest employer in Rios Calientes. The district has 61 campuses that stretch from the northeast to the east and southeast areas of the city. The district includes 7 high schools, 11 junior high schools, 34 elementary schools, and 9 alternative schools. In 1998, Bolivar became the first urban school district in the state to be named a "recognized district" for student performance on the SAAS. Nine district schools have been named National Blue Ribbon Schools, while eight others are National Title One Distinguished Campuses. Unlike schools in the other two districts, at least half (30) of Bolivar's schools are rated as recognized. Twelve are exemplary and nine are acceptable. None are low-performing.

A few programs in the district focus on science and mathematics education for both students and teachers. Technology Domes provides state-of-the-art instruction for students and teachers through computers and the Internet. The Net Schools program aims to provide every student with a laptop computer to share with family members. The Teacher Laptop Initiative is supposed to provide every teacher with a new computer.

Demographics

Most of the 46,394 students in 2000–01 were Latino (87.5 percent), with very few white (9.1 percent) and African American students (2.5 percent). About one-quarter (22.1 percent) were LEP, and a large percentage (73.4 percent) of the students were considered economically disadvantaged. The attendance rate was 95.3 percent.

The district practices a policy of open enrollment. Any child who attends a school in Bolivar may transfer to another within the district. District staff report that students from outside the district have been known to transfer to Bolivar schools as well.

Governance Structure

The superintendent, at the highest level, is responsible to the school board. At the next level, a chief academic office (CAO) for the division of academics oversees instructional and academic areas, including bilingual and special education, and supervises all K–12 principals. Under this individual are two executive directors who supervise curriculum specialists assigned by subject area (science, math, and reading) and feeder pattern. The curriculum specialists provide technical assistance and professional development, and they act as model teachers to the individual schools. Also directly under the superintendent, at a parallel level with the chief academic officer, is an associate superintendent who oversees learning standards, assessment, and all special programs. District staff consider their school district "more decentralized than most."

Curriculum

As is true of all districts in the state, the curriculum in Bolivar is based on state standards. The role of the Division of Academics is to ensure that all teachers are trained in these standards and in the expectations for students that underlie them. According to the chief academic officer, "We work within the curriculum to make sure that those standards . . . are what is driving the curriculum." District staff feel that the state standards-driven curriculum correlates highly with the National Academy of Science standards and the Project 2061 Benchmarks.

Textbooks and Supplemental Materials

All districts in the state are obliged to follow the same procedure for textbook adoption that allows each school within a district to vote for a textbook on the state's approved textbook list.[10] According to the CAO, however, "This [requirement] does not preclude schools from teaching and selecting how they're going to teach the curriculum within [the framework provided by] the textbooks and the standards." Principals and teachers may purchase other books or materials as aids to instruction, and schools have a great deal of autonomy as far as supplemental materials are concerned. Those materials must be purchased with school budgets rather than district budgets, although in special cases the district has purchased supplemental materials and equipment used by individual schools.

Instructional Policies

Working within the parameters of the state requirement for seven hours of instruction a day, the district allows schools to apportion instructional time for different subject areas. According to district staff, several years ago the state specified the amount of time that had to be devoted to each subject, and adherence to these requirements was monitored closely. Five or six years ago, the state abandoned these requirements. According to staff, "It was the best thing they could have done because it freed up teachers to spend half a day in language arts or an hour and a half in math, whatever it takes to teach those subjects." Informants at the district level add that the elimination of these requirements also encourages block scheduling.

District staff state that the individual campuses do not do any kind of ability grouping. In fact, in the words of one staff member, "We tell our principals to stay away from that."

Student Assessment

In addition to the administration of the SAAS, which is given according to state regulations, the district provides guidance in appropriate assessments for different skills as well as grading standards. At the school level, there is variability in the frequency of testing, with some campuses administering weekly tests.

Monitoring and Reporting Student Progress

The district monitors student performance in order to identify schools with a high failure rate on the SAAS for assistance. These schools are then asked to develop an improvement plan in conjunction with the district and report on monthly progress. Individual student monitoring is done at the school level. Bolivar requires progress reports to parents every three weeks and report cards every six weeks, but schools are free to report progress more frequently if they wish.

Graduation Requirements

Of the three districts in the study, Bolivar was the first to institute a policy requiring all students to take four years of math and four years of science. This policy was passed by the school board in 1992–93. That same year, all remedial math courses in the high schools were eliminated. The following year, the state abolished all remedial math courses and required that all students complete three years of math and three years of science. Soon, the other two districts (Chavez and Torrijos) also passed four-year requirements in math and science for their students.

Recently, Bolivar adopted a policy (currently being considered by the other two districts) that requires all students to graduate with a "recommended" program.[11] (At the time of the site visit, the state legislature was attempting to pass legislation requiring that all students graduate from a "recommended" program.) Those students who do not graduate at the "recommended" level will be required to attend a prescribed number of hours of community college before entering a four-year college.

Professional Development

At the district level, there is a policy providing six days of professional development to teachers, although it is up to the school to decide the type of professional development that will be offered. Professional development must be tied to each school's Campus Action Plan. The division of academics offers professional development through district curriculum specialists in science, social studies, language arts, reading, and math.

Parental Involvement

The district's biggest parental involvement activity occurs during the summer school program. Parents who agree to send their children to summer school must also agree to attend a two-hour parental involvement workshop once a week. Parent meetings are also scheduled by the Campus Educational Improvement Council (comprising parents, teachers, and community members) three times a year. The district also requires two face-to-face parent-teacher conferences per school year. Schools eligible for Title I schoolwide funding have a parent coordinator who oversees activities to involve parents. The district also has a strong volunteer program and a staff member who holds monthly meetings with the school parent coordinators.

Resources

The district receives Title I monies (schoolwide) as well as funding from Title II, Title VI, and Title IX. There are also state compensatory funds for at-risk students, special education funding, bilingual education funding, and Eisenhower funds.

Teacher Shortage and Teacher Hiring

At the time of the site visit, district staff reported that the district was not experiencing a teacher shortage, although they felt that one was imminent, especially in high school math and science. They attributed this impending shortage to the fact that the local state university (the source of most of their teachers) was not graduating enough teachers in these subjects to meet the needs of the local school districts.

In the words of the chief academic officer, the district plays "a big role" in the hiring of teachers. All applicants are first screened through the district human resources office to ensure that they have required certification and have done student teaching (the office also conducts criminal checks and follows up on references). Principals inform the human resources office of their needs, and this office refers the appropriate teachers to the campuses for interviews. The individual campuses make the final decisions regarding whom to hire.

Principal Recruitment and Hiring

Principals are recruited by the district in what district staff describe as "an internal process." The district has an assistant principals academy that brings all assistant principals together once a month for a half-day meeting that, in the words of the chief academic officer, "starts to prepare them to be good principals." The district hires its principals from this pool of assistant principals. At the academy meetings, the assistant principals learn about the aspects of running a school. The CAO explains that, in general, assistant principals might not always get the opportunity to learn all aspects of school management because they may be assigned to specific areas in their schools. The purpose of the academy is to ensure that assistant principals become "well-rounded and that they know about every aspect of running a school."

Partnerships

Bolivar has a Partners in Education program that identifies business partners and connects them with schools. The district also works closely with agencies that provide social services to the families in the area.

Comparing Policies and Practices across the Three Rios Calientes Districts

Table 5.2 compares the three Rios Calientes districts by their major educational policies and practices to determine the similarities and differences among the districts.

The three Rios Calientes districts are very similar in demographic composition and the major educational policies and practices that guide their operations. One reason for their similarity is the fact that they are located in a state where main education policies are determined and mandated by the state. Another explanation is that all three districts characterize themselves as "decentralized," although Torrijos and Bolivar are more emphatic in proclaiming this than is Chavez. Education policies, therefore, flow from the state to the schools, with very little interference from the district.

Table 5.2. Characteristics, Policies, and Practices of the Three Rios Calientes–Area Districts

	Chavez	Torrijos	Bolivar
Demographics	<u>62,451 students</u> 77% Latino 17% white 5% African American 32% LEP 67% FRPL Average attendance rate: 95%	<u>26,711 students</u> 91% Latino 7% white 1% African American 29% LEP 68% FRPL Average attendance rate: 95%	<u>46,394 students</u> 88% Latino 9% white 3% African American 22% LEP 73% FRPL Average attendance rate: 95%
Governance	Superintendent responsible to school board. Five associate superintendents. Somewhat decentralized.	Superintendent responsible to school board. Five associate superintendents. Very decentralized.	Superintendent responsible to school board. Chief academic officer and associate superintendent. Very decentralized.
Curriculum	State-mandated	Same	Same
Textbooks	State-mandated	Same	Same
Instructional policies	State determines number of hours of instructional time, subject areas, and content. School decides hours spent on each subject.	Same	Same
Ability grouping and inclusion	No state policy. District policy forbids grouping and requires mainstreaming of special education students.	No district or state policy. Left to schools.	No state policy. District discourages ability grouping.

Table 5.2. *(Continued)*

	Chavez	Torrijos	Bolivar
Student assessment	State-mandated	Same	Same
Monitoring and reporting student progress	State requires minimum of 12-week intervals. District requires program reports to parents every 3 weeks and report cards every 6 weeks.	Same	Same
Graduation requirements	Four years of math and four years of science. Above state requirements of three years of each subject.	Same as Chavez	Same as Chavez and Torrijos, but requires all students to graduate from "recommended" program.
Professional development	Some state requirements, but district focuses on curriculum and instruction. School-level funds available.	School-based	District provides six days professional development for teachers through curriculum specialists.
Parent involvement	Federal compensatory programs have parent involvement requirements and funding. District requires parental representatives on campus and district planning bodies.	District-level Title I parent coordinator oversees districtwide parent initiative to organize volunteers to work in classrooms.	Same as Torrijos

(continued)

Table 5.2. *(Continued)*

	Chavez	Torrijos	Bolivar
Resources	Federal: Title I, Title VI State: bilingual entitlement funds, special education, Eisenhower, Innovative Schools, local education organizations, and E-rate	Same	Same
Teacher hiring	Recruit most teachers from two area university programs and a few from nearby military base. Applicants screened by district; final selection at school level.	Recruit within area. Applicants screened by district; final selection at school level.	Recruit within area. Applicants screened by district; final selection at school level.
Principal hiring	Recruit within district employees, usually assistant principals. Hiring at district level. Input from school community.	Same as Chavez	District has a principals' academy for assistant principals and recruits from that pool.
Partnerships	Left to schools	Communities in Schools Program that links business sponsors with individual schools. District works closely with social service organizations.	Partnerships in Education program that links businesses with schools. Social services links.

Sources: Interviews with district personnel in each district and review of district web sites.

LEP = limited English proficient; FRPL = free and reduced-price lunches

6

What Makes Some Rios Calientes Schools Highly Effective?

This chapter examines the characteristics that differentiate highly effective schools (as a group) from typical schools (as a group) in Rios Calientes. Data from both the case studies and the teacher and principal surveys were used in this analysis.

The biggest differences between highly effective Rios Calientes schools and their typical counterparts lie in the effectiveness of the principals and the quality of the teaching force. Principals of effective schools are acknowledged instructional and transformational leaders; they are also advocates for children and effectively involve parents in school activities. The teaching force in highly effective schools is high quality. In addition to possessing the requisite certifications and experience, teachers are culturally adept in working with a diverse student body as well as satisfied with, and committed to, their schools. In the typical Rios Calientes schools, none of the principals is an instructional or transformational leader. Although some typical schools have high-quality teachers[1] who are culturally adept and committed to their students, none have teachers who are highly qualified, culturally adept, committed, *and* satisfied.

Another important difference between the two groups of schools in Rios Calientes concerns how closely the schools adhere *in practice* to the standard that "all children can learn." Highly effective schools are more likely to be flexible in how they use ability grouping, to provide support for teachers working with diverse learners, to have a principal who holds teachers responsible for the success of all students, to have teachers with high expectations for all students, and to have students with high aspirations and knowledge of career options.

Parents of students in highly effective schools are more likely to feel welcome in their children's schools, participate in school activities, volunteer in their children's schools, have contact with their children's teachers, and feel satisfied with the education the schools provide. Effective schools seem to place a higher priority on parental involvement, conducting successful outreach to parents, structuring more attractive parent activities, informing parents of their children's progress, and making a greater effort to ensure that parents have positive encounters with the schools.

Effective schools also seem to make better use of the flexibility and autonomy that is allowed them by the state and the district. This creativity is expressed in schools' efforts to improve instruction, school-level accountability and evaluation systems, professional development for teachers, discipline and order in the school, and extracurricular offerings for students.

The rest of this chapter uses case study material and data from principal and teacher surveys to illustrate how each characteristic mentioned above is evident in highly effective schools and missing in typical schools.

Principal Leadership

Leadership from the top—that is, from the principal—emerged as one of the two most important characteristics of highly effective schools. This leadership manifests as *instructional leadership*—that is, principals' proactive guidance, influence, and involvement in crafting instructional policy and practice; *transformational leadership*, principals' facilitation of reform; and creative problem-solving to improve school climate and environment.

Instructional Leadership

Instructional leadership is one of the two distinguishing characteristics that set principals in highly effective schools apart from principals in typical schools. Although the principals in both types of Rios Calientes[2] schools have similarly varied educational backgrounds and experience, the principals in highly effective schools consciously set out to provide instructional leadership. More important, their teachers acknowledge them as sources of educational expertise who greatly influence teaching. Principals of highly effective schools are extremely involved in coordinating, monitoring, and evaluating curriculum, instruction, and assessment. Often, these principals share leadership with others in the school.

Principals in highly effective schools are respected and recognized as instructional leaders by their toughest critics—their teachers. Teachers' comments about a principal are some of the best indicators about how effective an instructional leader he or she is. Excerpts from the case studies of highly effective schools exemplify how principal leadership in instruction occurs in successful school settings.

About a year ago, Ms. Munoz replaced a very popular, well-regarded principal at Fuentes Elementary School, who left to take a high-level administrative position with the district. With a background in mathematics and a master's degree in education with a specialization in curriculum and instruction, Ms. Munoz exudes competence, energy, and optimism. This young Latina describes herself as "very involved" in determining the curriculum and supervising teachers. She personally conducts 45-minute evaluations of each teacher and supplements those evaluations with informal walk-ins.

Ms. Munoz encourages others in the school to assume leadership roles. Teachers, in particular, have been leaders in staff development. Teachers acknowledge that Ms. Munoz is an instructional leader who is adept and knowledgeable about curriculum matters. They feel she has "a lot of influence" on the way they teach.

An elementary school teacher for eight years, Ms. Echevarria, a young Latina, has a master's degree in education with a specialization in early childhood education and pre-K–12 mathematics. She has been a curriculum specialist for the district and a math/science mentor. She is dynamic, energetic, and focused. As principal of Frida Kahlo Elementary School, she is involved in determining the curriculum and very involved in supervising teachers. She personally conducts all teacher observations because, as she explains, "I want to get to know the teachers." She also does occasional walk-throughs and is developing her own checklist for informal observations. She has encouraged leadership in staff through a leadership committee, comprising teachers from each grade level, who communicate and disseminate information to their grade-level colleagues. Teachers agree that teachers are also leaders in the school.

Frida Kahlo teachers are emphatic in describing Ms. Echevarria as an instructional leader. They feel she has a considerable amount of influence on the way they teach. Further, one teacher comments, "She's the type of person who lets you take risks."

Principals in typical schools, on the other hand, seem less actively involved in curriculum and instruction—and it shows. Their teachers are brutally honest in their opinions regarding these principals' instructional leadership abilities.

Mr. Gomez, a middle-aged Latino who has been principal at Rufino Tamayo Elementary School for four years, holds a master's degree in education with specializations in art, elementary education, and educational administration. He describes his role as "guiding instruction, to make sure that the instruction is going on and that teachers are teaching what is mandated by the state." He shares the supervising of teachers with his assistant principal. The assistant principal comments that the district now stresses

> a lot of going into the classrooms and getting more involved with the programs and the curriculum. It's not like it used to be where you're just an administrator sitting in an office. Now it's more that you're an instructional leader because they want you to know what's going on in the classroom.

Teachers at Tamayo definitely do not feel Mr. Gomez is an instructional leader. According to one teacher,

> I can't count how many times the principal has said, "If you need it, ask me." However, I do not feel that he is knowledgeable about curriculum. He could not come into my room and teach my guided reading group. He couldn't tell me whether I was doing a good job or not.

Another teacher mentions that when teachers are asked on their evaluations to rate the effectiveness of their teaching, these teachers know the principal has no idea what that means. None of the teachers in the focus groups feel the principal has any influence on the way they teach.

Castellanos Elementary School principal Mr. Cortez is a young Latino with a master's degree in linguistics and no previous experience in elementary education. Although he describes his role as principal as that of "instructional leader," teachers in his school think otherwise. One teacher describes him as a "figurehead." Another comments that he is "not deeply involved—doesn't have the content knowledge." Teachers agree, nevertheless, that they are the leaders in this school, sharing ideas with and soliciting criticism from one another.

Ms. Gruber, a middle-aged white woman, has taught elementary school for 14 years and has been principal of Paz Elementary School for five. She sees herself as "very involved" in determining the time spent on academic tasks and supervising teachers and says that her goal in supervising instruction is to model, monitor, facilitate, observe, and provide information and ideas. She describes her main role as principal as trying "to support all I can. I think that's one of my main jobs," adding that she tries to provide as much staff development as possible for teachers. The teachers feel two or three teachers at every grade level are instructional leaders "who give us help when there are questions to be answered and discussed," according to one teacher.

Although teachers feel Ms. Gruber is a leader in the school, when asked specifically if they feel she is an instructional leader, they respond less confidently. One teacher comments, "I think it depends a lot on the individual teacher and on the class she might have." Another adds, "I would say that in content she has a great deal of influence but in style I think that's left pretty much to us." (Content, however, is regulated by the state.)

On a survey of all teachers in each school, results were entirely consistent with teachers' comments about principal leadership in the focus groups. The percentage of teachers in highly effective schools who rate their principals a having a "strong positive impact" on their teaching ranges from 75 to 93 percent, for an average of 84 percent. Forty to 71 percent of teachers in typical schools feel their principals have a strong positive impact on their teachers, for an average of 51 percent.[3]

Transformational Leadership

Principals in highly effective schools also show transformational leadership; that is, they provide intellectual direction and innovation within the school while motivating and supporting their teachers. This dimension of principal leadership is important to school reform; it implies that the principal leads reform efforts by introducing innovation, shaping school culture, and motivating school staff to both implement the innovation and embrace the culture of reform. In these examples, highly effective school principals proactively shape instructional policy and use the flexibility allowed individual schools by the district to spearhead innovative approaches to instructional reform. They also create a child-centered learning environment in their schools while inspiring school staff to adopt compatible ideals and aspirations.

At highly effective Carlos Fuentes, Ms. Munoz has been very involved in changing the instructional process at her school, including encouraging teachers to do more interdisciplinary teaching. She maintains that within the boundaries of the rather stringent state requirements, there is still a lot of curriculum flexibility at the campus level. In her words, although adhering to the requirements is "nonnegotiable, how we get there is left up to each individual campus." She feels that if schools are knowledgeable about the state standards, they can use whatever means at their disposal to design and implement a curriculum that meets those standards.

As principal of a school noted for its academic excellence, Ms. Munoz continues to foster a culture of healthy competition and striving for excellence. One parent says students at Fuentes

> all want to read at higher and higher levels because their friends are reading higher. It's kind of a healthy competition. . . . I can see that kids have a thing about reading in this school. It's like they want to compete against each other; they want to read, they want to read more books.

Ms. Echevarria at highly effective Kahlo Elementary School encourages her teachers to adopt a thematic approach to instruction by integrating subjects around broad themes or concepts, and she encourages teachers to use block scheduling in order to facilitate this approach. Ms. Echevarria has also begun a new program for gifted and talented students that pulls them out of their regular classrooms for special activities planned around major themes and concepts. She has had a T-shirt printed that reads, "Learning for all, whatever it takes," and sees this as her school's motto. She says, "What I've told teachers is that there are no excuses. All children can learn and we just need to meet them halfway."

At Cruz Elementary School, Ms. Fellowes feels that although the school's curriculum is determined by the state, Cruz's strength lies in how it structures instructional strategies to meet student needs. She encourages teachers to identify and implement strategies that will be effective with their target populations. The school has departmentalized grades 4 and 5 in mathematics and science, with both a math and a science specialist on staff; Ms. Fellowes feels this strategy is a strength. She has also seen to it that the primary grades (pre-K through 3rd grade) are very involved in math and science. Many teachers use an integrated approach to teaching science and math. The principal explains that, "This is something that a lot of the teachers here have been trained in and that's the thematic use of units and concepts and they do pretty well with it."

Ms. Fellowes sees herself as a facilitator in working with teachers and with parents and fostering community involvement. She adds, "More than anything else, I am an advocate for the child. That's what it all comes down to." Teachers echo the principal's view of her role, with all agreeing that she is a facilitator. Says one teacher, "She is very good at letting things develop that are positive. If there is anything innovative at all, she encourages it."

When Ms. Baeza arrived at Rivera Elementary School, she discovered that the former principal had been at odds with parents and that parent involvement had been neglected. She also found that, in her words, "the school seemed to be catering a lot to the teachers and [not] so much to the students." In keeping with her two mottoes—"Children come first" and "No excuses!"—she set about remedying the situation. She has opened up the school to parents by increasing activities and encouraging them to visit the school. Consequently, parent involvement in school-sponsored activities increased from almost 0 to 70 percent.

Ms. Baeza has changed the focus of the school to serving students. She expects teachers to facilitate student learning so they are able to adapt their instructional techniques to meet the needs of the individual child. This approach is something new for teachers at Rivera, who in previous years had dealt with learning problems through after-school tutoring. The principal has insisted that whatever special attention a student needs should be given during the school day. She reasons that both children and teachers are tired at the end of the day. Further, because more than 50 percent of the students at Rivera are bused, it is difficult for most of them to stay after school for tutoring. Teachers seem to have internalized Ms. Baeza's messages and to be aware of the importance of high expectations and a belief that all children can learn.

The importance of principals' ability and willingness to act as instructional leaders and change agents in their schools has increased exponentially over the past few years with the growing emphasis on school reform and accountability. All principals in the highly effective schools demonstrate their leadership by introducing progressive instructional strategies, demanding the best performance from their teachers, and supporting these teachers' work through high-quality professional development and other resources. Aside from personal qualities, three major factors seem to contribute to principals' effectiveness as instructional and transformational leaders: educational background and experience, ability to elicit teacher respect and support, and a willingness and commitment to improve education in their schools.

All principals in the highly effective schools have—to varying degrees—a combination of several years of experience as classroom teachers and substantive knowledge of curricular and instructional issues. Although on paper they may not differ greatly in teaching experience and academic background from their counterparts in the typical schools,[4] the much greater respect that they elicit from their teachers is a very good indicator of their superior knowledge of curriculum and instruction and their ability to facilitate school reform.

It is somewhat more difficult to document the third factor contributing to effectiveness in principal leadership: the willingness to act as instructional and transformational leaders. All the highly effective principals describe how they have responded to the identification of instructional weaknesses (reflected in test scores) with changes in instructional strategies: the use of vertical alignment of the curriculum at Barragan; block scheduling and an interdisciplinary approach at Fuentes; and the thematic focus at Kahlo, for example. These principals do not make excuses or blame others (such as the district) for declines in test scores; their attitude seems to be, "Okay, we have identified the problem. Now what are we going to do about it?" Even with the above-average performance of their students, they are still concerned with raising achievement levels. More than one of these principals has confided that even though her school is scoring above average on the state standardized tests, she feels that her students could do more. Ms. Garcia, the principal of Barragan Elementary School, explains why the school has raised its academic standards in the past few years: "Well, we knew that if we wanted our kids to live up to our expectations, we had to raise the bar."

On the other hand, principals at typical schools complain of lack of district support or they focus their efforts on minimum compliance with state requirements. At Paz Elementary School, for example, Ms. Gruber complains that because the district refuses to pay for professional development from a specific provider (that she favors), the school has been unable to use the instructional strategies that she feels are most effective in teaching math. She refuses to purchase these services with the school's funds.

Principals of highly effective schools seem to adapt their leadership strategies to conform to the prevailing "character" of the teaching force. For example, with the teachers at highly effective Barragan Elementary—

a strong, vocal, and self-empowered group with several years of experience at the school—Ms. Garcia expresses her leadership strategy as follows: "You can lead them from the rear, but you cannot lead them from the front because they'll throw rotten tomatoes at you!" Yet she is viewed by her faculty as both a curriculum leader and a supportive principal who empowers teachers.

Other Leadership Challenges: How Principals Cope

Principals of highly effective schools demonstrate other types of leadership ability in dealing with noninstructional issues and problems that they encounter.

For example, Ms. Echevarria has attempted to create a more open and friendly climate at Kahlo Elementary School—and it shows. The walls of the corridors are adorned with student art in a display arranged by parent volunteers. The bulletin boards show lists of honor-roll students and student birthdays. The needs of both students and parents are met with kindness by the front-office staff. Ms. Echevarria comments that the school had been very focused on test results, which "can become very solemn, so I've encouraged them to decorate more." Some students at Kahlo say they would rather be in school than on spring break. And when asked whether parents felt comfortable at Kahlo, one parent responds for all by saying, "Yes. Absolutely."

Ms. Munoz at Carlos Fuentes Elementary School, in addition to complying with the state and district requirements that govern monitoring and reporting student progress, requests that teachers include supplementary information in the three-week progress reports to parents about classroom behavior, absences, and tardiness. Her philosophy is that a parent should never be surprised at the progress or lack of progress that his or her child is making in all areas. She personally reviews the nearly 700 progress reports and signs off on each of them. If something jumps out at her, she calls the teacher and asks for an explanation; as she explains, "this will help me when I conference with the parents later."

In contrast, principals in typical schools do not demonstrate the same decisive, proactive approach to problem-solving as do their counterparts in highly effective schools. The problems, therefore, persist and affect the school climate.

Tamayo Elementary School experienced the most disciplinary problems in the Rios Calientes sample. The principal acknowledges that discipline "required some attention." Teachers attribute much of the problem to the fact that "Central Office acts without talking with teachers and does whatever the parents want, which sends a bad message to parents." The assistant principal may have provided a clue to the source of the problem when he stated that the principal would be leaving for another principalship at the end of the school year and that he "spends 90 percent of his time where they are constructing [his new] school. So, basically, I'm acting as principal here and doing whatever needs to be done."

Ms. Gruber, principal of Paz Elementary School, has a persistent problem with her teachers. When she tried to implement an "open door" policy for parents before school began, the teachers opposed it. So, she gave in to teachers' wishes, even though she liked the idea of welcoming parents and students before school started. When she first arrived as a principal to the school, she says she found "a lot of ignorance and prejudice in a lot of these teachers." Five years later during the site visit, she reports that the problem still exists.

The Teaching Force

Teacher quality, defined as well-prepared, committed, satisfied teachers, is the second most important characteristic of highly effective Rios Calientes schools. In the context of this school district, teacher quality is considered high when *all* the following conditions are present: (1) a high number of teachers have the required certification; (2) a critical mass of teachers has more than three years of teaching experience; (3) a large proportion of teachers is committed to their students and their schools; (4) a significant portion of teachers is satisfied with their schools; and (5) a high percentage of teachers can relate culturally to Latino students, who make up the vast majority of the enrollment in the district. Although the schools in both groups meet the first two conditions, only the highly effective schools meet all five.

The factors that differentiate a high-quality teaching force from a typical one in districts such as those in Rios Calientes are difficult to define. In terms of such standard quality indicators as educational background, certification status, and experience, the teachers in both sets of schools are quite similar. This may be because almost all teachers are recruited from the same pool of teacher education graduates from local institutions. Both groups also have high levels of teacher certification and teaching experience, although teachers in the highly effective schools have been in those schools for less time than their typical-school counterparts: 7.9 years versus 9.9 years.[5] Also, teachers in two of the three typical schools score high on one measure of commitment to their students. Here are some examples from case studies and surveys that describe how conditions 3 through 5 are present or absent in highly effective and typical schools in Rios Calientes.

Commitment

Teacher commitment is expressed in terms of teachers' high expectations for their students and their willingness to "go the extra mile" to ensure that all students are successful learners. As mentioned above, teachers at two typical schools demonstrate that they are willing to go the extra mile for their students, as do teachers in all highly effective schools.

Believing "All Children Can Learn"

Although "all children can learn" is a mantra researchers heard from all teachers they spoke with, differences emerge in actual teacher practices that indicate how seriously teachers take this slogan. One indicator is teacher belief in, and use of, ability grouping as an instructional strategy. Teachers in highly effective schools are almost half as likely as their typical-school counterparts (29 percent versus 51 percent) to report that homogeneous grouping in classrooms is important to their view of education, and they are much less likely to regularly implement this practice in their classrooms. Another indicator is teachers' acknowledgment that student learning is *their* responsibility.

At highly effective Barragan Elementary School, one teacher's statement reflects the attitude of most teachers in the school: "It is our job as teachers to find the means and the methods to make sure kids are learning." These sentiments are supported by the principal, who states that "every teacher here is willing to look and . . . exhaust every avenue, every intervention that's available and possible before deciding that a child needs a special education package."

At Fuentes Elementary School, teachers describe how they implement their approach to student learning. In the words of one teacher, "I think we have a philosophy that all children can learn. You just adapt the instruction to meet different needs, whether they're GT or learning disabled—every year each class is different and you just adapt accordingly." Another teacher adds, "A lot of us teach to the higher expectations and, if they're not getting it, then we move it down a notch so that we can catch them, and then we move it back up." A third teacher states, "I've had students who transfer from other schools say that our expectations are very high."

Teacher comments from typical schools are more tentative. Teachers at Paz Elementary School seem to agree with one teacher who comments, "All children have the ability to learn, but of course we have to look at their mental ability." Tamayo Elementary School teachers, when asked about their expectations for students attending college, explain that a lot of their students are on welfare and their mothers do not work, so the students do not necessarily see the need to go to college in order to get a job.

Going "the Extra Mile"

There are several examples of teachers in highly effective schools who contribute their time and resources to improving the educational environment and instruction in their schools. A notable practice in the Rios Calientes districts is teachers making their own materials to supplement math and science instruction. In most cases, teachers do this on their own time. A much higher percentage of teachers in highly effective schools report making their own materials than do teachers in typical schools (82 percent versus 70 percent in math and 67 percent versus 49 percent in science). Following are other instances of going "the extra mile"—or not.

The principal at Barragan Elementary School says this about her teachers' commitment to the school: "If teachers are not willing to give it their all, they will not succeed in Barragan." She adds

> I can tell you that the majority of our teachers are not 7:45 to 3:15 people. . . . They're not going to go home and collapse. If they do go home, it's to pick up their kids and bring them back to dinner [that evening the school is sponsoring an enchilada dinner for parents]. . . . I am not going to have to ask them to do it. It's going to come from within.

At Fuentes Elementary School, teachers have contributed their own time to forming student organizations, and most of them are willing to accommodate parents by arriving at school earlier or remaining later than required by the schedule.

In contrast, Ms. Gruber at typical Paz Elementary School comments that although teachers were offering tutoring to students when she first arrived, they would cancel it if they had something else to do. She found it necessary to insist that teachers show up at their scheduled tutoring sessions when other competing demands arose, even though teachers think that this is unfair. Also, she mentions that teachers do not want parents and students to come into the school building before classes begin because they want quiet in which to work.

It is interesting to note that higher percentages of teachers at highly effective schools are likely to cite the following four factors as motivating them to accept positions at their schools: the school's good reputation; the principal; professional development opportunities; and the school's educational philosophy. This suggests that these teachers are more likely to have accepted jobs at schools that they feel are performing well and that embody their own views of education, hence their greater commitment to the school.

Satisfaction

Teacher satisfaction among the teachers in Rios Calientes encompasses their respect of their principals as leaders, their view of the adequacy of resources that they have to work with, and their feelings of empowerment.

Respect for Principals

Teachers are not shy about expressing their approval or disapproval of their principals' leadership abilities. The previous section on principal leadership contained several quotes from teachers from highly effective schools praising their principals' leadership in instructional matters as well as quotes from teachers in typical schools who are highly critical of their principals as instructional leaders. In all cases, teachers at highly effective schools express respect for their principals as both instructional and institutional leaders. This is definitely not true for typical schools, where teachers have harsh criticism for two principals' lack of knowledge regarding instruction and curriculum. The third principal is given mixed reviews on instructional leadership. Survey data from all teachers in the schools support these divergent views.

Satisfaction with Support

Teachers in focus groups discuss their satisfaction with access to support, mostly professional development opportunities. Teachers in highly effective schools are pleased with both the access to, and the quality of, the professional development they have received.

At Cruz Elementary, teachers comment that their school provides more resources for professional development than the district does. As one teacher explains, the principal "actually finds more money on the campus level than the administrators [at the district level]." Another teacher comments that the principal "is willing to send you to in-services or training . . . whatever you need." Most professional development in this school is provided at the campus level, reflecting the preferences of both the principal and teachers.

Teachers at Kahlo Elementary School seem to feel that there are plenty of opportunities and resources for professional development. They also feel that all the professional development they have received so far has been useful. As one teacher puts it, "I take everything that my principal puts in my box for professional development as a 'Go' because if it wasn't important enough, she wouldn't have put it in my box." Teachers also agree unanimously that opportunities for professional development are distributed equitably.

In general, teachers in typical schools have issues with both access to, and the quality of, their professional development. In two schools, teachers complain of inequitable distribution of professional development opportunities among teachers.

Teachers at Castellanos Elementary School complain that the principal "hand picked" teachers to go to professional development workshops. They comment that teachers in the school's dual-language program are given priority and that a lot of the resources are used for that program. As one teacher expresses, "If you want to go, you are told a lot of the time that there is not money for that. So you end up spending your own money." Teachers in this school also give mixed reviews to the quality of professional development they have received.

Teachers at Tamayo Elementary School, while admitting that there are a lot of different professional development resources, believe that access to these opportunities is not equitable. They comment that the principal picks the same people over and over to attend these activities. They also feel that the professional development that they have received is a mixed bag in terms of usefulness.

Teacher Empowerment

Surveyed teachers in highly effective schools report having more autonomy and control over various aspects of the school, including curriculum/ texts, assessments, daily schedules, and professional development.[6] This finding is supported by data from the principal survey, where more principals of effective schools report greater influence of teachers in school policy areas.

At Rivera Elementary School, teachers stress that decisions are made through group consensus. They feel that teachers serve a strong leadership role at Rivera. The principal agrees that teachers in the school have considerable influence over school policies. She comments, "I'm hoping that they feel that they have had a strong voice."

At Barragan Elementary School, Ms. Garcia encourages teachers to take on leadership roles. "I would not be surprised," she says, "if you took a survey of all the administrators in the district, how many come from Barragan." Teachers say the principal "empowers us in just about everything." Teachers also feel that since they have had four different principals in seven years they have developed a sense of cohesiveness and independence. As one teacher explains, "We're a strong faculty and I think that the faculty here is going to do what they think is best for their students whether they agree with the administrators or not."

Although the principal at Tamayo Elementary, a typical school, feels that teachers "had quite a bit of influence as far as instruction and things of that nature," the teachers themselves seem to disagree. Almost half responded on the teacher survey that they have no control over the curriculum or texts. Teachers also attribute problems with student behavior outside the classroom to lack of support from the central office.

Cultural Sensitivity

A very large proportion of the students in the Rios Calientes schools is Latino. Many students also have low-income, LEP, and immigrant status. For teachers to be effective instructors of students with these characteristics, it is important that the teachers understand the children's cultural backgrounds and experiences.

All but one school in the Rios Calientes sample has a teaching force that is more than 60 percent Latino. Except for that one school, the percentage of teachers who report speaking fluent Spanish ranges from

49 to 74 percent. There is some indication that having a bilingual, largely Latino teaching force enhances students' learning experiences. Fluency in Spanish also increases communication between teachers and newly arrived immigrant parents. Although most schools have parent centers and a parent coordinator, having teachers who can communicate directly with non-English-speaking parents contributes to a warm and welcoming environment in the schools.[7]

Asked how they tailor instructional strategies to the cultural and linguistic needs of their students, most teachers at highly effective Cruz Elementary School generally agree that they do so but could not explain how. (At Cruz, 68 percent of the teachers are Latino and 52 percent speak fluent Spanish.) One teacher states that since she has always lived on the border and taught in border schools, "it's just part of my culture as well." But another teacher, who is a recent arrival from Michigan, reveals, "You guys do a lot of adapting for different languages and all those things that doesn't take place elsewhere." A third teacher chimes in: "It just becomes second nature." When students do not understand a certain word, teachers might use a visual aid to get the point across. Other teachers might provide the Spanish translation. And learning is not a one-way street. Says one teacher, "We also learn about culture from the kids."

The above example contrasts with the situation in one typical school where teachers do not seem to recognize the need for adjusting instruction to students' linguistic and cultural needs. At Paz Elementary School, where 31 percent of teachers are Latino and 28 percent speak fluent Spanish, teachers respond defensively when asked about tailoring instructional strategies to meet linguistic and cultural needs of students. One teacher seems to reflect the general attitude of teachers in this school when she states

> I have never felt that to be an issue in my classroom. It just has never been a negative issue. The majority of the children I think feel very secure in their identities and it's just that we have a number of programs about being a human being and treating all people well.

The principal sheds some light on the teachers' attitudes when she describes the ignorance and prejudice she found upon arriving at the school five years ago. An anecdote shared by the principal illustrates the point. Teachers were attributing Latino students' lower achievement scores to Latino parents' "poor" parenting skills and suggested that the school hold parenting workshops targeting Latino parents. According to the principal, "my Hispanic teachers were very upset with us. They said, 'That is not fair to Hispanic students, because we're not like that.' " She also describes what she sees as "ignorance and prejudice" on the part of teachers regarding African American and "mixed race" students in the school.

High Expectations

High expectations held by principals and teachers emerged as an additional characteristic that differentiates highly effective from typical schools. At highly effective schools, high expectations for all students are an integral part of the school environment. Principals set the tone through their leadership, and teachers reflect this philosophy in their instructional behaviors. To assess whether a school maintains a climate of high expectations, researchers focused on how each school approaches the issue of ability grouping; the support and guidance provided to teachers in dealing with diverse learners in the classroom; and other evidence, including how the principal encourages high expectations among his or her staff, teacher attitudes toward the possibility of higher education for their students, and students' exposure to the possibility of college and career options.

Approach to Ability Grouping

Highly effective schools seem to differ from typical schools in their use of ability grouping. Although both types of schools acknowledge using some within-class grouping, primarily in reading, all highly effective schools emphasize the temporary nature of this approach; two of the typical schools do not. A much higher percentage of teachers in effective schools responds that they do not group students by academic ability (57 percent versus 31 percent). Teachers in highly effective schools are also more likely to base ability grouping decisions on daily observation and teacher test scores (which require more frequent monitoring) than on standardized test scores (which are reported once a year). A much lower percentage of teachers in highly effective schools (29 percent versus 51 percent) responds that homogeneous grouping is important to their view of education; they report being less likely to regularly implement homogeneous grouping in their schools.

Fuentes Elementary School, a highly effective school, uses what the principal calls "skills grouping" (mostly in reading and mathematics), where students who are having problems with certain skills are pulled aside for special instruction. According to Ms. Munoz, this approach differs fundamentally from ability grouping or tracking:

> It's not like identifying a student as a poor reader and keeping him in the low reading group. It's a matter of looking at the skills the child needs and then saying, "Okay, these children need this skill and when they learn it, they'll leave the group." They won't always be in the same group, and the groups will always change.

Fuentes parents confirm this assertion with anecdotes about their children who are put in a special group because they are not reading at grade level and then move out of that group when they catch up with the rest of the class.

Kahlo Elementary School does not officially group students according to ability within classes, although Ms. Echevarria observes that students are grouped informally by ability—particularly reading ability. She maintains, however,

> it's not like the years when we went to school and they had the bluebirds and the buzzards and the buzzards were always the buzzards. The groups here change. So in essence, I guess, there ARE groupings, but they are flexible groupings that could be based on ability or interest or experience of different things. Kids do work together in ever-changing groups.

Staff at the typical Tamayo Elementary School, however, feel differently about ability grouping. The assistant principal at Tamayo acknowledges that whereas "in the old days we used to group students [by class] according to ability, nowadays we don't do that any more. We put them . . . as the low, the middle, and the high in the same classroom." He explains, however, that reading classes are the exception. According to the assistant principal, the decision on how to group students is classroom-based and left to the teacher. In general, teachers speak positively about ability grouping. One teacher says, "We use a lot of cooperative learning and I have found that if you group them by ability they challenge each other and work harder." Another adds, "When you are teaching skills it really has to be by ability grouping."

Working with Diverse Learners

Schools that are serious about making the "all kids can learn" mantra a reality must support and guide their teachers in instructing a classroom of diverse learners. Survey data from teachers show that teachers at effective schools receive more of this type of assistance than their counterparts in typical schools, although teachers in two of the three typical schools acknowledge receiving support in teaching diverse learners. Teachers in highly effective schools are more likely to have studied methods of working with students of different races and ethnicities and students with disabilities; not surprisingly, they are also more likely to report feeling prepared to overcome stereotypes about Hispanics and math and science learning.[8] These teachers also speak more eloquently about adapting instruction to reach students at different levels as well as students of different cultural backgrounds.

The math coordinator at Cruz Elementary explains the school's policy toward diverse learners this way:

> We're very much aware on this campus as far as how our children are learning and we adapt our techniques in that respect. If the bulk of the class is learning like this, then we can teach the bulk of the class this way, but for those students whose needs are not met, let's do something different for them and the rest of the class can certainly benefit from that other way of teaching, too. I would say that's true of maybe 85 percent of our teachers here. They would go out of their way to make certain that everybody's needs are being met as far as different learning types and diverse populations.

Cruz Elementary teachers comment that because of the school's location in a border community they are just used to diversity. Says one teacher, "The materials are here because they are used to working with a diverse population." Teachers also have recourse to a learning resource center with staff who go into classrooms to work with students experiencing difficulty in working at the classroom level.

When asked how Kahlo Elementary School deals with diverse needs of students in the classroom, both the principal and teachers respond that the district and the school provide a great deal of support to help teachers meet these challenges. Kahlo teachers talk mainly about the needs of LEP students and point out that teachers do not modify their language but find other ways of communicating with students. For example, teachers bring in background knowledge to make the vocabulary meaningful. One teacher says that if a student really cannot understand a word in English, she will just tell the student what it means in Spanish. (Seventy-four percent of teachers at Kahlo are fluent Spanish speakers.) One teacher's comment—"We accommodate the students' needs"—sums up the attitude of these teachers.

The Kahlo principal explains that she expects teachers to modify their teaching in the classroom to adapt to individual children's learning needs: "We've given them a list of different types of modifications they can use and have talked about it at staff development sessions and meetings." The assistant principal adds that this is "just good teaching."

By contrast, one typical school's teachers do not see the need for tailoring their instructional approaches to different types of learners, while another's teachers feel that they do not receive the necessary support to teach diverse learners.

Most teachers at Paz Elementary School feel that tailoring instruction to the needs of diverse learners is not required. According to one teacher, "I don't think we really have had to address this." One bilingual teacher, nevertheless, describes how she uses "Hispanic activities" to "bring in the culture" in her classes, and another mentions how students express their culture through music. The principal acknowledges that racism and prejudice on the part of the mostly Anglo teaching force toward the mostly minority students in the school is a problem.

Teachers at Castellanos Elementary School make some effort to tailor instructional approaches to the cultural and linguistic needs of their students. One teacher says, "I use a lot of movement and I try to connect it with prior knowledge." But another adds, "It's very difficult. I scrounge. I make them copies from Spanish books." A third teacher comments that there are not a lot of support opportunities to help teachers deal with diversity in the classroom. The math coordinator reports that the school has held some workshops on diversity, but "that's normally left to our bilingual teachers or the dual-language program teachers."

Other Evidence of High Expectations

Principals of highly effective schools are more emphatic than their typical-school counterparts in insisting that school staff adhere to the belief that "all children can learn" and that teachers demonstrate this adherence through their approach to teaching. This attitude is exemplified by Ms. Baeza at Rivera, who feels that "every child can be successful, no matter at what level or what he comes with. . . . We're in the 'no excuse' business." She expects teachers to facilitate students' learning and be able to adapt their instructional techniques to meet the needs of the individual child. Teachers at highly effective schools, from their comments in the focus groups, seem to take this principle seriously.

Typical-school principals may not be as forceful in requiring that their teachers hold high expectations for all students, because teachers' remarks indicate they are not as fully committed to this ideal. Nowhere is the difference in attitude clearer than in teachers' expectations that students will attend college. At all typical schools, teachers express grave doubts about the possibility that students might attend college, given their socioeconomic backgrounds. Surprisingly, students at two of the three typical schools, together with their parents, enthusiastically endorse the idea of going to college.

When teachers at Castellanos Elementary School are asked whether they expect their students to go to college, they are quiet for a good while. No one responds right away. Then, one teacher says, "Realistically, no." Another observes, "I talk to them as if 100 percent are going to college, but I think realistically that's not going to happen." All the students in the focus groups, however, have plans for the future. One boy says that he wants to be "a naturalist, like the Crocodile Hunter." A few say that they want to be veterinarians, lawyers, doctors, police officers, and teachers. All feel that it is important to go to college and say they will do so. They agree that college is important for getting a good job, and several tell stories about family members who did not go to college and how that has limited their lives. Parents, too, are optimistic that their children will go to college.

Teachers at Paz Elementary School express hope that their students will go to college, but, as one teacher puts it, "It's hard to tell." Teachers speak about motivating students to attend college, and a teacher mentions putting a graduation certificate up on the wall "so students could see it." Students at Paz are very hesitant to answer this question, and no one has anything to say immediately. One girl observes that she is not even sure that she wants to go to college. Another student wants to be an "emergency doctor." A third student wants to be a professional football player but wishes to have a "real career" to fall back on in case he gets injured. (His second choice is to get a master's degree in math or science and be an astronaut.) A fourth student says that he wants to pass high school and then study Egypt.

When asked about their expectations that their students will attend college, teachers at Tamayo Elementary School explain that a lot of their students are on welfare and their mothers do not work, so children do not necessarily see the need to go to college in order to get a job. One teacher says students going to college is "our hope, but not according to the statistics." Another responds, "Most [students]? No."

Tamayo students, on the other hand, seem to realize that attending college will help them obtain jobs with higher salaries, and they are all emphatic about the importance of going to college to make money. Says one, "You're not going to get anywhere if you don't go to college." Another student observes, "There are only a few jobs where you don't need a college degree—janitor or McDonald's." These students express the wish to support their parents when they are older, however, and felt that this might make going to college more difficult. They are all concerned about how much college costs. One student mentions saving all his birthday money for college. Asked whether students feel prepared to go to college, one responds, "I think I will be very scared, but prepared." Another observes wisely, "We will lose some friends."

At all effective schools, however, most teachers are upbeat about their students' college-going prospects. Students themselves heartily proclaim their intentions to attend college. Many are well-informed about the importance of college and seem knowledgeable about career options. Parents, too, seem to support their children's college-going plans.

Teachers at Barragan Elementary School all feel that most of their students will attend college. Parents agree enthusiastically. Some joke about their children's aspirations and the fact that the kids may already have picked out a college. Says one parent, "They've got long-term goals that they've thought about for a long time." All students in the focus groups agree that college is inevitable and necessary for getting a good job. Many have ideas of which schools they want to attend. They also mention several professions, including policemen, veterinarians, and marine biologists, that they want to pursue.

At Rivera Elementary School, most teachers, while acknowledging the odds against their students going to college, are very positive. In the words of one teacher, "We hope. [College-going] is something we address all the time. In the classroom I will say, 'When you go to college' and 'We need to start planning for how to get to college.' " Students are optimistic and ambitious about their futures. They respond enthusiastically to questions about their career plans, with some mentioning ambitions to enter such fields as law, engineering, and medicine. All maintain that it is very important to go to college. Most cite reasons related to making a good salary, and several mention that their mothers, because they did not have college degrees, would not be able to support the family if something happened to their fathers. Parents generally agree that their children will be attending college after graduation.

Parent Involvement

How deeply parents are involved in their children's schools is another important factor that differentiates typical schools from highly effective ones. This involvement can be measured by parents participating in school-sponsored activities and volunteering in the school. Effective-school principals estimate that 74 percent of parents regularly participate in school activities; only 33 percent of typical-school principals report this level of parent involvement. Four of the five effective schools report having parent-teacher associations, while only one of the three typical schools does. And at effective schools, 26 percent of parents volunteer for school service, compared with 17 percent of parents at typical schools.

Teacher survey data also support the conclusion that parental involvement is greater at highly effective schools. Teacher responses to the survey show a higher percentage of teachers at effective schools reporting high rates of parents volunteering, attending teacher conferences, and attending class functions. Parents whose children attend highly effective schools are satisfied with how the schools extend access to parents, offer meaningful activities, and provide good educations for their children.

The School as a Welcoming Place

Highly effective schools seem to do a better job of creating a welcoming environment for parents than do their typical counterparts. They do this by establishing lines of communication between school staff and parents, whether through frequent correspondence or meetings on the school premises; encouraging parents to talk frequently with teachers, the principal, or other school staff; and ensuring that the front-office staff treat parents who visit the school in a warm and welcoming manner. The provision of translation services or a parent liaison bilingual in English and Spanish also helps parents who are monolingual Spanish speakers access the school. At effective schools, parents in our focus groups frequently comment on how welcome they feel in their children's schools.

"The teachers [at Barragan] have always welcomed parents, as has the administration."
"It's just an easy feeling to know that not only are you welcome [at Barragan], but you have something to offer."

Parents joke that they have "trained" the principals at Barragan over the years to have attitudes of openness and accessibility. In the words of one parent, "We say this in fun, but it's because we're very involved and we try to keep up to date on what's going on in education and in the community. . . . It's important that our kids do well in school."

Cruz Elementary School parents also observe how welcoming the school is to parents. As one says,

> What's impressive, too, is that our principal is welcoming and she remembers your name. The teachers and the personnel, they know who you are and they know your kids and we're all such proud parents that it makes you feel like you're part of the school.

"Yeah," responds another parent, "when the 5th grade teacher knows your 1st grade child, you're like . . . is that good or is that bad?"

Several Fuentes Elementary School parents comment on the welcoming atmosphere of the school. Says one, "The teachers have an open-door policy, and I don't think I've ever been afraid to ask a teacher a question." Adds another, "As a new parent, I found that all the teachers are so friendly and that's what's made me want to volunteer. It just makes you more involved."

In contrast, some staff at Tamayo, a typical school, seem clueless about the reasons behind their school's failure to involve parents. While the parent coordinator and teachers attribute low attendance at school activities to parents' feelings of inferiority or safety concerns, parents say that the school, especially the front office, does not make them feel welcome. One teacher, discussing how difficult it is to get parents involved in the school, comments, "I think that parents are afraid to come to this school." Another observes, "They are embarrassed." A third teacher adds, "It's not a safe place for them." But parents, while agreeing that most Tamayo teachers are helpful and willing to make time after school to talk with them, say they do not feel welcome in the school. Says one parent, "It's just the front office that's unfriendly, but the teachers are fine." Another parent disagrees: "Well, sometimes it's . . . good and sometimes it's not. It depends on which teacher you encounter."

Parent Involvement in School Activities

Highly effective schools have a much higher rate of parent involvement in school activities, including volunteering, than do typical schools. This seems a function of whether schools are successfully offering activities that appeal to parents, whether parents feel a part of the school community, and whether the school infrastructure facilitates parental involvement. As Title I schools, both types of schools receive funding for parent liaisons. Highly effective schools, however, are more likely to have committed parent liaisons and to offer useful, appealing courses for parents.

Barragan Elementary School boasts the involvement of about 70 percent of parents. About half the parents have volunteered for school service. Teachers say that the presence of a parent on schoolwide committees ensures that parents have a voice. There are book fairs and book nights when parents come in to read. They sit on interview committees when the school hires administrators. One teacher describes the school's strategy for involving parents: "We just have to invite them and feed them, let them know they are appreciated, empower them, give them recognition, make them feel needed." Another teacher concurs, "These efforts have been pretty successful. Parents are at the school all the time. . . . They want to be here. They want to help."

Ms. Baeza at Rivera succeeded a principal who was described by a staff member as "at odds with parents." The new principal invested considerable effort before the school year began in reaching out to parents, polling them about the types of activities that they wanted at the school and ensuring that they had a voice in school decisions. Parents have suggested several activities, among them a Halloween party at the school, a cookout, an Easter outdoor activity, a Christmas program, and a talent show. Many of these activities also bring in community members and are very well attended. The parent involvement at Rivera is now at 70 percent. Programs offered at the school for parents include ESL classes, computer skills, and a women's support group. Free babysitting is available during some parent meetings. The parent coordinator also sends parents notices once a month with activities to do with their children at home.

At typical school Paz Elementary, however, the parent coordinator does not seem to realize that the lack of parent involvement on the part of at least the monolingual Spanish-speaking parents might be due to the school's failure to communicate in Spanish. The parent coordinator says that she tries to find out via surveys to parents what they might be interested in, but although "I might not hear it directly from the parents, I will hear it from Spanish-speaking office workers" (apparently, the parent coordinator does not speak Spanish). The school, which has a very low rate of parent participation, does not offer translation services for non-English-speaking parents either, although like most schools in Rios Calientes, Paz has a large enrollment of students with monolingual Spanish-speaking parents.

This same school offers a contrasting picture of how teachers view parents' contribution through volunteering in the classroom. Teachers at Paz mention that because so many parents work, sometimes grandparents of students become involved. Of the parents who volunteer in class, one teacher comments,

> Some of them just come in to watch and see what's going on. I've shown some parents how to work with their children and that seems to go over well. Some of them are uneducated and are grateful to have this kind of help.

Parent Satisfaction with Children's Education

Highly effective schools have parents who are very satisfied with the education provided to their children. These schools often structure activities that pair parents and children in learning and that involve parents in their children's education by informing them of their children's progress. The Rios Calientes districts require that all schools provide regular feedback to parents on student progress by mail and that schools schedule mandatory parent-teacher conferences twice a year. Therefore, all schools, regardless of effectiveness, provide these opportunities at a minimum for parents to become involved in their children's education. Highly effective schools, however, seem to go above and beyond this basic requirement.

Kahlo Elementary has scheduled times when parents can call teachers, and several parents do call. One teacher explains, "If a parent needs to talk, we don't turn them away [even if it's outside the specified hours]." Another teacher says that she gives her home number to parents if necessary. In addition to the required progress reports, some teachers send home weekly notes that the parent has to sign. Three-quarters or more of the teachers at Kahlo report that in order to involve parents in their children's education teachers have contacted parents, held open houses, provided child care, sent written communications, and discussed their students informally.

Kahlo offers a dual-language family reading program, where parents pick up a backpack with a study guide and cassette tapes and return the completed guide when they have gone through the exercises. The parent coordinator gives parents lessons on how to read to their children so they can complete these exercises together. Parents are satisfied with the information they receive on their children's progress. According to one mother, "We always know that we can always ask the teacher how our child is doing." Parents seem to feel strongly that their children are progressing at Kahlo and learning in school.

Similarly, parents at Cruz say they have almost daily contact with their child's teacher, mostly around how their children are doing in school. Says one parent, "It's so nice to have that daily input from your kid's teacher." Parents also describe how, in addition to the required progress reports and report cards, they receive weekly reports on their child's progress as well as other information from teachers. As one parent says, "My son's teacher sends all the paperwork he's done stapled in a folder. She signs off on it and dates it and I'm supposed to sign it so she can see that I've reviewed all the papers."

Parents are enthusiastic about the job that Cruz has done in educating their children. Says one, "Oh, I love this school." Another adds, "I'm so pleased with the teachers." A third parent, who had been a teacher, concludes, "I've worked in a lot of other elementary schools, which has helped me compare where my child is . . . and I'm very impressed and happy with the school." Parents think that Cruz is above-average in terms of how far along students are, particularly in math and science.

Parents feel that Fuentes Elementary School is doing a splendid job of educating their youngsters. They describe the environment as one that encourages students to learn more and more. Even students are enthusiastic about being in school, and all are eager to share the reasons they liked school, including the "nice and friendly teachers." Parents confirm that the teachers and the school make a special effort to keep parents involved in their children's education. Comparing Fuentes to schools that their other children have attended, parents' compliments about the school are glowing. In the words of one parent, "I can't remember working as hard with my other three kids. I am more involved with my child in this school." Says another, "You can't even compare that other school [that my other children attended] with this."

Parents of students at typical schools are much less satisfied with the level of communication provided to them by the schools. Sadly, as can be seen from this vignette, parents seem resigned to the mediocre education that their children receive.

Asked whether they are satisfied with the information they receive from the school on their children's progress, parents at Tamayo express dissatisfaction. One parent observes, "Sometimes we do [get information] and sometimes we don't." Another complains, "They say it's up to us to come and ask, but as far as them communicating with us, that doesn't happen."

Parents agree that the school seems to wait three weeks before letting them know about problems. In general, parents feel that their children could do better than Tamayo. They feel, nevertheless, that the school is basically the same as other schools in the district. As one parent comments, "It depends on the teacher you get, but what they learn is pretty much the same."

The Role of the Principal

Principals of highly effective schools seem to place a higher priority on involving parents than do their typical-school counterparts. This emphasis is evident from the efforts made by the principals and staff of effective schools to conduct outreach, offer attractive parent activities, and ensure that parents have positive experiences with the school. For example, principals of two highly effective schools have replaced a home liaison or a parent coordinator who was not working effectively with parents. In one case, the principal herself has assumed responsibility for outreach to parents.

When Ms. Munoz noticed a few months after arriving at Fuentes that the parent volunteer group membership was declining, she assumed responsibility for outreach. The school now has a very high participation rate for parents who are active in school-based activities—75 percent. On the topic of parent attendance at parent-teacher meetings, one parent comments:

> It's not a question of, "If you want to come. . . ." You're told: "This is the time you can come. If it's an inconvenient time, I'll work with you and I'll make a different time." So as a parent I didn't even question it. I just thought, "This is my job and I'm doing it."

The parent coordinator at Rivera has been the unofficial coordinator for one year but has been volunteering at the school for six years. She is in charge of 25 parent volunteers who assist the teachers, usually reading for kindergarteners and 1st graders, decorating the walls with student work, and other tasks to help teachers. According to the principal, the current budget clerk was the parent-home liaison, but she did not work out because she was unwilling to visit students' homes. The principal explains why she replaced the former liaison:

> When a child is sick I would like her to go. Well, she would like the parent to come. Sometimes that's good, but sometimes it isn't. I myself have gone to children's homes. . . . Whatever it takes. No excuses, no excuses!

At two of the three typical schools, on the other hand, outreach to parents does not seem a priority to the principals, who relegate the task to the parent coordinator. In these two schools, the parent coordinators are not effective at outreach; thus, parent involvement is low or nonexistent.

At Paz Elementary School, the parent coordinator is a former teacher who sees her role as working with the children, "going into the classrooms and providing lessons for the whole class." She runs a parent volunteer program that involves 10 parents. In describing the school's efforts to reach out to parents, whose participation is very low (10 percent), she explains that there is nothing on campus currently, but that she plans to get something in place for next year. She complains that previous activities planned for parents were poorly attended and that although the school has altered times and locations to try to attract more parents, "it's usually the same parents attending." (The parent coordinator does not speak Spanish and the school does not offer translation services for non-English-speaking parents.)

Flexibility and Autonomy

This indicator of effectiveness explores how schools in Rios Calientes work within the rigid confines of state and, to a lesser extent, district requirements to improve the instruction provided to students. Because state requirements in these districts so strongly dictate the way various areas within a school are implemented, few options are left to individual schools.[9] Looking at how the two groups of schools use their limited flexibility and autonomy to improve outcomes reveals much about the principals' leadership capabilities as well as the quality and commitment of the teaching force. All the highly effective schools in the study use opportunities for flexibility and autonomy creatively and effectively to improve instruction. The main areas where this flexibility is put to good use are curriculum and instruction (which includes the use of instructional time), the accountability/evaluation system, professional development offerings, disciplinary practices, and student extracurricular activities.

Curriculum and Instruction

When principals and teachers are asked whether they feel their school has sufficient autonomy and flexibility to work effectively within state and district requirements, all—except staff from one school—say yes. Almost all comment that although the state requires that the curriculum be aligned with state standards and that official textbooks be state- or district-mandated, schools are allowed wide latitude in supplementing instructional materials. Effective schools, however, make greater use of additional commercially produced instructional kits or teacher-made materials. Teachers in highly effective schools report using supplementary materials at the rate of 92 percent in math and 82 percent in science, compared with teachers at typical schools, whose reported rates of use are 85 percent in math and 68 percent in science.

Effective schools tend to perceive mandated curriculum and textbooks as representing the minimum levels of instruction, and they seek to exceed these levels in their offerings to students. Highly effective schools are also more likely to use flexible instructional time to implement such innovative instructional approaches as block scheduling for interdisciplinary teaching and thematic units to integrate several subject areas.

For example, while teachers at Cruz Elementary School feel they have little control over textbooks required by the district, in the words of one teacher, "Whatever we want to supplement, I think we are free." Another teacher adds, "We pretty much make up our own [supplementary] materials or do what we have to." Similarly, Fuentes Elementary School has chosen to limit class size in the 5th and 6th grades to 22 students per class. Teachers are encouraged to take advantage of block scheduling to do more interdisciplinary teaching. The principal explains:

> What we're moving to is using science as a hub and then you begin to pull in your literature studies, your mathematical concepts, and your social studies. It just makes for a more connected, relevant, meaningful area of study for students.

As a contrasting example, the principal at Paz Elementary School acknowledges the need for additional instructional materials. But she blames the lack of these materials in her school on the district's failure to provide her with sufficient support and funding.

Accountability/Evaluation System

The state mandates that schools report student performance to parents every 12 weeks, while all three districts require more frequent reports (teacher reports every three weeks and report cards every six weeks). Four of the five highly effective schools describe additional monitoring and reporting practices, while none of the typical schools go beyond district requirements. According to the principal survey, four effective schools use district-generated school-level reports on standardized test scores to monitor student progress, whereas no typical school reports doing this. Some effective schools also communicate constantly with parents about their children's progress—face to face, on the phone, and through notes.

The learning resource center at Cruz Elementary School conducts numerous assessments to identify gaps in student learning and, subsequently, areas where professional development might be provided. Teachers are required to document student progress continuously, and the principal requires teachers to communicate with parents at regular intervals. According to the principal, "Communication with parents has to be a constant and not just a progress report every third week of the grading period."

To facilitate this communication, every child has a self-organizer, in which students write their daily assignments. Parents must sign the book and return it daily. Teachers use this book as a form of communication with parents. A parent says that through this regular communication, "the teachers make the parents accountable."

Fuentes Elementary School uses similar systems to evaluate student progress. The principal requests that teachers include information on classroom behavior, absences, and tardiness in the progress reports that go to parents every three weeks. She reviews and signs off on every progress report and, if she spots potential problems, she calls the teacher in for an explanation. The school monitors the progress of classes monthly and reviews the school's overall progress every semester. Also, before SAAS scores are distributed by grade to teachers, the principal identifies achievement gaps between groups of students; planning and resource decisions are made based on these gaps.

Although none of the typical schools collect student progress information over and above that required by the district, Tamayo Elementary School has elicited parent criticism for its failure to proactively communicate about student performance. Parents complain that they do not receive sufficient and timely information from the school if there are problems with their children's academic progress. One parent complains, "The school really should communicate a little more with us . . . we don't really know how they're doing in the classroom until the third week."

Professional Development

Teachers at typical schools report participating in more professional development than do those in highly effective schools. Quantity, however, does not equate with quality. While the state requires that staff development be predominantly campus-based and aligned with campus performance objectives, highly effective schools seem to make a greater effort to tailor professional development offerings to the specific needs of the school. This is reflected in the fact that these schools are more likely to provide buildingwide workshops on cultural communication. Effective schools' principals and teachers report more campus-based professional development tailored to perceived needs identified by gaps in student achievement. In many effective schools, teachers who attend out-of-school professional development activities are required to share what they have learned with peers. Many teachers in these schools comment that teachers themselves are professional development resources for their fellow teachers.

Although Cruz Elementary School has set aside funds to send teachers to training, Ms. Fellowes mentions a different, "very successful" practice. For the past two years, the school has customized training to meet the needs of the staff and the students. After looking at disaggregated standardized test score data, for example, the school as a whole identifies areas where there are "patterns of low scores across grade levels or within grade levels" for targeting by professional development. "We go out and hunt for someone who has strengths in these areas, set up training sessions, and address [the problems]." Most professional development occurs on campus because, according to the principal, teachers prefer to stay at the school: "They are at home; they're able to work with their colleagues at the same time."

Ms. Echevarria at Kahlo has initiated the practice of having more campus-based staff development so the school can use travel funds for other purposes. Because of her extensive background in staff development at the district level, she is eminently qualified to provide some training herself, which she does. She explains the school's strategy:

> I didn't so much send people out, but I tried to bring things in. Many times, when you send people to conferences they pick up ideas, but they don't get in-depth instruction. It's more superficial. So we did away with a lot of that and brought things to campus.

In addition, teachers who receive training off campus are expected to provide training for other teachers in the school.

Tamayo Elementary School, on the other hand, offers very few on-campus professional development opportunities. Teachers complain that the professional development they have received is not always useful. One teacher comments, "Sometimes they have been useful and sometimes not. Sometimes you are absent too many days from the classroom. You can fall behind—this is hard on teachers and students."

Discipline and Order

As required by the state, all schools have disciplinary policies that are widely disseminated to students, parents, teachers, and staff. Although no schools in the Rios Calientes sample (except one typical school) seem to have serious problems with discipline, indicators show that the discipline at highly effective schools is better than that at typical schools, as reported by the principal survey. Effective schools also report fewer incidents of vandalism (1.75 versus 6.00) and theft (0.50 versus 1.33) on school property. The teacher survey supports this finding, with more effective-school teachers reporting a higher percentage of students exhibiting desirable student behavior in classrooms.

The majority of principals at highly effective schools credit their teachers with encouraging good discipline, stating that teachers assume the responsibility of dealing with behavior problems in the classroom before they escalate. Teachers feel they are able to exert their authority effectively because they have parental trust and support.

Discipline problems are rare at Fuentes Elementary School. Ms. Munoz attributes this to the fact that teachers take responsibility for and handle a lot of the minor disciplinary lapses in their own classrooms. She also feels that the school's family-oriented, nurturing environment helps. The teachers, many of whom have been at the school for several years, know the families of their students, so an atmosphere of trust has built up that deters students from committing serious disciplinary infractions because parents are supportive of teachers. In the words of the principal,

> You can walk into any of the classrooms, from kindergarten to 6th grade, and [you will find that] the teachers, who have been here for several years, know the community. A lot of the children who are in these teachers' classrooms, they've had brothers and sisters or even mothers and fathers come here. So the teachers are really familiar with the community. . . . And because of this, the community has trust and faith that teachers are going to do right by their kids.

Discipline problems at Kahlo Elementary School, when they do come up, are not serious, and most problems are resolved in the classroom. Teachers claim that students know the rules and act accordingly. Ms. Echevarria credits the new assistant principal and his student counseling, character education classes, consistent teacher enforcement of the rules, and a great deal of parent support for the order and discipline that reigns in this school. She comments, "Very rarely do we have a parent who opposes any of the things that we're doing, and I think that the key to that is the way we communicate with the parents." She adds that the assistant principal consults with parents to gain their consent before determining disciplinary action.

Typical schools, in accounting for the greater incidence of student disciplinary problems on their campuses, blame external forces such as the influence of television, lack of parental support, and the proximity of another school for these problems.

The assistant principal at Tamayo Elementary School, for example, where discipline "required some attention," attributes the six incidents of vandalism and two of theft on school property to the fact that "Today children have television and a lot of things have changed. Now they're not afraid [to come to the principal's office]. So you have to find different ways of dealing with student behavior." One teacher describes the "bad kids" as students who "are very defiant . . . They could care less if you punish them." Another supports this view: "Kids here don't fear discipline."

Teachers give other reasons for the behavior problems in the school. One observes, "Some parents act badly . . . and their kids see that as acceptable since their parents are doing it." Another says the central administration's lack of support for teachers' disciplinary actions "sends a bad message to the parents."

Ms. Gruber at Paz Elementary School describes discipline as a "minimal problem." She attributes the 10 incidents of vandalism and two of theft on school property to the fact that students from a neighboring school share a campus with Paz. A few teachers, however, complain that they have had a difficult year discipline-wise with students in their classes.

Student Participation in Extracurricular Activities

In general, effective schools report greater student participation in extracurricular activities than do typical schools. Several effective schools provide activities for students that involve parents and the entire community. It is typical for these schools to offer intramural and extramural sports, student government, art/music/dance/drama, and after-school math and science programs.

Student participation in extracurricular activities is high at Barragan Elementary School. Ms. Garcia attributes this to the fact that parents are so involved in school activities. Several teachers sponsor student activities, including a teacher who gives arts and crafts classes after school for any student who wishes to attend. According to the principal, teacher sponsorship of activities is spontaneous. She comments,

> Nobody has asked them to do it. Not one has come to me and asked, "How much am I going to get paid?" It's just that they have a great deal of ownership. They love this campus.

A high percentage of students at Cruz Elementary School also participate in some type of extracurricular activity, of which the school boasts a great variety. Students are satisfied with the range of activities offered and say that they could not participate in any more. Cruz also offers student support services such as tutoring on a regular basis outside school hours.

Typical schools report lower student participation in extracurricular activities, even though students express the desire for more activities. Indeed, these schools tend to offer fewer activities. For example, a low percentage of students participates in extracurricular activities at Paz Elementary School, although students say they would like to be involved in more after-school programs, particularly football and swimming. Castellanos Elementary School also has a very low rate of student participation in extracurricular activities, although students comment that they would like to participate in more activities. All student activities are run on a volunteer basis by the teachers, rather than supported with school funds. According to the principal, if the school had more funds, it might be able to do more.

In Summary

Rios Calientes's state employs a top-down educational system. As a result, it is difficult to identify large differences in individual schools' policies and practices that contribute to effective learning since so many of these are mandated by the state. Several state requirements ensure that all schools implement policies and practices known to benefit learning (i.e., small class sizes, standards-based math and science curriculum, a good accountability/evaluation system, and so on) at a minimum level.

What then separates highly effective from typical schools becomes how far highly effective schools go beyond the state minimum and how they use whatever flexibility and autonomy is allowed by the state to improve their instruction and the educational environment in their schools. The characteristics that differentiate these highly effective schools from typical schools can be attributed to the willingness of key staff in the schools to do more than is required of them to ensure a high-quality education for all students. Like Avis, they try harder.

PART III
What the
Study Concluded

7

Lessons Learned and What They May Mean for Educational Reform

This effective schools study compares two very different sites, Cumberland City and Rios Calientes, to draw some general conclusions about factors that contribute to school effectiveness. It raises some provocative questions that merit further examination and exploration. It also presents implications for policymakers, educators, and researchers and suggests policy changes that could increase the number of highly effective schools.

Looking across Districts: Are Findings Generalizable?

Several factors characterize effective schools in both districts. How these factors are present in each district, however, differs, for several possible reasons. Differences between districts in state or district policy and characteristics of the area or city in which each district is located might help explain how effectiveness attributes manifest in each district.

Some Things *Do* Make a Difference

This study focuses on individual schools. Therefore, it is important to make distinctions between *external factors,* which are outside the school and school control and serve as context, and *internal factors,* which are within the school and at least to some degree within school control. In some cases, external factors can be useful to understanding why shared indicators of effectiveness manifest differently in each district.

The Cumberland City and the Rios Calientes–area districts are very different—geographically, ethnically, and demographically. Different, too, are the contexts under which they were operating at the time of the study, including different state mandates and the presence or absence of teacher and administrator unions. Nevertheless, the study has identified five characteristics that differentiated highly effective and typical schools in both districts.

Principal Leadership

In both the Rios Calientes–area districts and in Cumberland City, all the highly effective school principals are instructional leaders, while none of the typical-school principals or the principal of the formerly effective school are.

Principals in highly effective schools in Cumberland City, however, are not as strong transformational leaders as Rios Calientes highly effective principals are. While motivating teachers is a part of their jobs, Cumberland City principals' efforts focus more on improving individual teacher performance than on whole-school reform. Three of the four highly effective schools have schoolwide educational philosophies, all of which were in place before the principals came to their schools. Tellingly, none of the schools chose to participate in a district pilot effort that gave principals and staff the power to hire teachers. In Rios Calientes, all five principals at highly effective schools lead their schools' reform efforts. They spearhead innovative instructional strategies to address perceived weaknesses and motivate the school community to support reform efforts.

Principal leadership has been cited repeatedly in countless school effectiveness studies as an important factor in effective schools (Waters, Marzano, and McNulty 2003). Marks and Printy (2003) identify two conceptions of leadership—transformational and instructional.[1] They distinguish between instructional leadership, in which the principal assumes the central and exclusive role in setting instructional policy, and an integrated form of leadership, where principals share this role with teachers and others in the school. Principals who are transformational leaders and who collaborate with teachers in an instructional leadership role practice an integrated form of leadership. In a small study of 24 restructured schools, Marks and Printy find that such principals have a substantial influence on school and student performance. In a meta-analysis of 70 studies on leadership since the 1970s, researchers at the Mid-Continent Regional Educational Lab find a substantial relationship between leadership and student achievement (Waters et al. 2003).

High Teacher Quality

In both the Rios Calientes–area districts and in Cumberland City, highly effective schools have a higher-quality teaching force than do typical schools. What differentiates teacher quality, however, differs by district. Teachers in highly effective schools in Cumberland City surpass typical-school teachers on such traditional measures of teacher quality as graduate credits, completion of college-level mathematics and science courses, teacher certification, experience teaching, and experience teaching at their current school. In the Rios Calientes–area districts, teachers in both types of schools are comparable in these quality indicators. They differ, however, in their satisfaction with work and their commitment to teaching, with teachers in highly effective schools showing greater satisfaction and commitment. In both Cumberland City and the Rios Calientes area, highly effective school teachers appear more committed to their schools and more willing to "go the extra mile."

Internal factors that help ensure that satisfied, committed teachers are hired by effective schools differ for each study site. In Rios Calientes, where principals have the final word in teacher hires, effective principals are able to hire teachers who meet their criteria and who would fit in well with the school community. Cumberland City principals, who cannot make any hiring decisions about teachers, face a more difficult task: effective principals have to work around union and district regulations to have at least some influence on teacher selection.

External factors may have contributed to the differences between the two districts on indicators of high quality. The teachers hired by the Rios Calientes–area districts come from a very homogeneous pool of teacher candidates trained by a few area universities and colleges. This may account for their similarity in preparation and experience. Cumberland City, on the other hand, recruits from a much wider range of sources and, therefore, a much more diverse pool. Also, availability of qualified teachers willing to work in the district seems more of a problem for

Cumberland City than for Rios Calientes, forcing Cumberland City schools to hire teachers who do not meet traditional qualifications.

Although much of the research in the past 40 years has supported the contention that high-quality teachers increase student achievement, some researchers have gone even further in suggesting that teachers are the most important factor influencing student outcomes.[2] In their review of the literature on teacher quality, Goldhaber and Anthony (2003) define the characteristics that go into teacher quality as those that appear to produce growth in student achievement. Although research findings on the importance of traditional measures of teacher quality—graduate degrees, licensure, years of experience—have been mixed, Goldhaber and Anthony agree that the evidence tilts toward confirming the benefits of teacher experience up to the first five years. Teachers with fewer than three years of experience have been found less effective than more senior teachers, but the benefits of experience seem to level off by about five years (Darling-Hammond 2000). Ferguson (1991), in combining measures of teachers' qualifications such as scores on licensing examinations, master's degrees, and experience, finds that these qualifications account for more variation in student reading and mathematics achievement than student socioeconomic status does.

High Parent Involvement and Satisfaction

Parents in the Rios Calientes–area districts are much more likely to participate in volunteering and school activities in highly effective schools than in typical schools. In Cumberland City, the differences are not so much in the degree of parent participation but in parent attitudes and the existence of parent-friendly policies. For example, the four highly effective schools have open-door policies that welcome parents to the school at any time. In the three typical schools and the formerly effective school, however, parents are required to make appointments before visiting the school.

External factors may account for the low parent involvement in Cumberland City typical and highly effective schools. These reasons included welfare-to-work requirements that prevent parents from volunteering and attending school activities and fear for personal safety in attending nighttime events. The Rios Calientes–area districts do not seem to have external reasons depressing parent involvement. Internally, highly effective schools in both districts make efforts—through parent-friendly policies and practices—to reach out to parents and welcome them to the school. Typical schools in both districts, on the other hand, make fewer and less effective efforts at parental outreach, with the expected results.

The rationale for involving parents in their children's schools is based on the assumption that parents' involvement helps children's learning. In investigating the influence of parents' involvement in student educational outcomes, Hoover-Dempsey and Sandler (1995) first examine the reasons parents become involved in their children's education. They find that this involvement occurs because parents construe involvement as part of their parental role; they have a sense of personal efficacy regarding helping their children do well in school; and they perceive opportunities, invitations, or demands from their children or the school to become involved. Hoover-Dempsey and Sandler conclude that parents help their children succeed in school by three main mechanisms: modeling of school-related behaviors and attitudes, reinforcement of specific aspects of school-related learning, and direct instruction. Jeynes's 2003 meta-analysis of 21 studies investigates the impact of parent involvement on minority children's academic achievement. He finds that while parental involvement affects all academic variables (grade point average, standardized tests, and other measures) by at least two-tenths of a standard deviation, the effect size is double for African American and Latino children. The conclusion of this meta-analysis is that parental involvement benefits African American and Latino children more than it does Asian American children.

Good Student Discipline and School Climate

The severity of student discipline problems differs greatly between Cumberland City and the Rios Calientes area. In Cumberland City, student bad behavior centers around physical violence—hitting and fighting—while in the Rios Calientes area, student bad behavior is more related to students talking instead of paying attention and not using good manners. In both areas, nevertheless, teachers in highly effective schools apply discipline more consistently and are more likely to take responsibility for disciplining their own and other teachers' students.

An external factor that might explain the difference between districts is the culture of poverty in Cumberland City that is much less pronounced in Rios Calientes. As discussed previously, students in Cumberland City schools bring more serious problems to school than their counterparts in Rios Calientes. Many are undisciplined and respond with physical violence to attempts to discipline them. Teachers complain that students' violent actions mirror the way their parents behave; teachers often feel that parents do not support them in attempts to improve their children's behavior. For lower-income residents, Cumberland City is a place of economic decline and loss of hope, whereas Rios Calientes is growing demographically and economically.

Most research on safe and orderly schools centers on student behavior and the effectiveness of efforts to improve behavior (National Institute of Justice 2004). Researchers have paid less attention to the relationship between safe and orderly schools and student achievement. In a notable exception, Lee, Chen, and Smerdon (1996), who studied 8th graders in almost 400 schools, find that students in orderly, safe schools have higher math, reading, and science achievement. Students are also more engaged in these schools. A second study finds school environment makes the greatest difference between highly effective and typical schools (Mid-Continent Research for Education and Learning 2005).

High Expectations for Students

In both Cumberland City and the Rios Calientes area, teachers in highly effective schools have higher expectations for their students than do teachers in typical schools; highly effective school teachers are also more likely to take responsibility for their students' learning. In addition, teachers in Cumberland City highly effective schools report teaching math at higher levels of learning than do teachers in typical schools. This is not the case in Rios Calientes, where what is taught is more strictly prescribed by state requirements for curriculum and instruction. In Rios Calientes, teacher expectations are measured by teachers' attitudes and approaches toward ability grouping; teachers in highly effective schools are much less likely to group students by academic ability and less likely to consider homogeneous grouping important to their views of education. These teachers are also much more likely to expect their students to go on to college.

Research on teachers' perceptions or estimates of a student's full potential to succeed, especially when the teacher and the student are of different races, is germane to the concerns of this study. An additional consideration is whether biases in teachers' perceptions of future performance affect test scores. Baron, Tom, and Cooper maintain that "the race or class of a particular student may cue the teacher to apply the generalized expectations, therefore making it difficult for the teacher to develop *specific* expectations tailored to individual students. In this manner the race or class distinction among students is perpetuated" (1985, 251). Ferguson (2003), in discussing teacher bias in estimating latent potential, cites research by Jussim, Eccles, and Madon (1996) as the only work that has tested for racial differences in impacts of teachers perceptions on future test scores. According to Ferguson, these researchers, who collected teachers' perceptions of 1,664 6th graders' current performance, talent, and effort in math, find that

> for both grades and scores . . . the estimated impact of teacher perceptions was almost three times as great for African Americans as for whites. Effects were also larger for girls and for children from low-income families. Further, the effect was cumulative across disadvantages or stigmas: black children from low-income backgrounds experienced the effects of both race and income. (2003, 472)

While Ferguson interprets this finding to mean that teachers are less flexible in their expectations for the performance of African Americans, females, and students from low-income households, other researchers speculate that some groups of students may be more vulnerable in responding to teacher expectations (Weinstein 1985).

The research literature supports that the five factors found by this study to characterize highly effective schools *do* make a difference. Because of context and external factors, however, these factors played out differently in Cumberland City and the Rios Calientes–area districts.

Do Cumberland City and Rios Calientes Differ in Meaningful Ways?

Although Cumberland City and Rios Calientes effective schools share several characteristics of effectiveness that differentiate them from their typical counterparts, external factors affect how these differences play out in each district. Among the most striking differences between the two districts are differences in student performance levels, the role of state and district policies in the schools, and the demographic and economic outlook of the regions.

Differences in Achievement

Within the Rios Calientes–area district, the gap in student achievement between highly effective and typical schools is much narrower than the gap in Cumberland City. In Cumberland City, 42 percent of students in highly effective schools score proficient or above on the SAT9 math test, compared with 11 percent of students in typical schools, a difference of 31 percentage points. In the Rios Calientes–area districts, the difference is 17 percentage points; 61 percent of students in highly effective schools score proficient or above in math on the SAAS, compared with 44 percent of students in typical schools.

While Cumberland City and Rios Calientes use different tests, as reported in chapter 2, the tests seem to cover similar areas. In Rios Calientes, "proficient" means 85 percent or better, while in Cumberland City, "proficient" represents solid academic performance, indicating that students are prepared for the next grade. Assuming that these definitions are even somewhat equivalent, it seems clear that 4th graders in Rios Calientes are achieving at higher levels than are 4th graders in Cumberland City, whether they are in typical or highly effective schools (figures 7.1 and 7.2).

This narrower gap in student achievement between typical and highly effective schools in Rios Calientes compared with Cumberland City (and

Figure 7.1. Fourth Grade Students Scoring Proficient or Above in Math

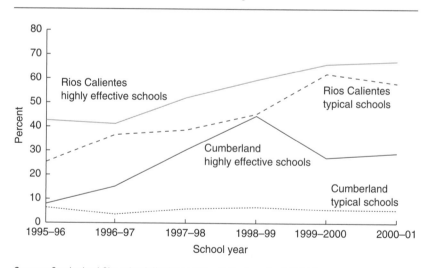

Sources: Cumberland City school district and Rios Calientes school districts.

Note: "Cumberland highly effective schools" includes Andrew Jackson (the formerly effective school), since it was originally selected as a highly effective school.

Figure 7.2. Fourth Grade Students Scoring Proficient or Above in Reading

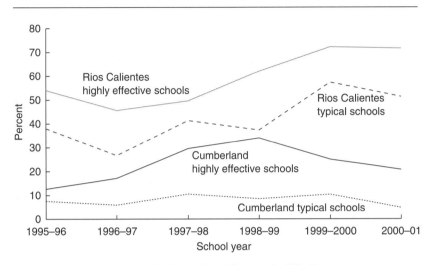

Sources: Cumberland City school district and Rios Calientes school districts.

Note: "Cumberland highly effective schools" includes Andrew Jackson (the formerly effective school), since it was originally selected as a highly effective school.

the overall higher performance of Rios Calientes–area students) may be related to differences in state policies and the alignment of state and district policies. Simply put, students in the Rios Calientes districts—in both effective and typical schools—may be achieving at a higher level than their counterparts in Cumberland City because of factors at the state and district level that benefit Rios Calientes schools and give them an advantage over Cumberland City schools.

State and District Policy Differences

State A (where Rios Calientes is located) mandates most education policies from the state level through the districts to the schools in a top-down approach. State B (where Cumberland City is located), on the other hand, is more decentralized. State A, unlike State B, mandates class size, textbook selection, and use of student data from standardized test scores to align instruction. Both states have statewide K–12 academic standards and high-stakes tests based on those standards.

Alignment of state and district policies. State A has one set of academic standards and one set of tests to measure achievement of those standards. At the time of this study, however, public schools in Cumberland City had two different sets of standards—one district and one state—each with a series of tests used to measure how well the standards were being met. These two sets of standards were not aligned, and the Cumberland City district eventually had to revise its standards to bring them closer to the state standards.

Class size. In general, the maximum class size mandated by the states is much higher in Cumberland City schools (K–2: 30 students; higher grades: 33 students) than in the Rios Calientes–area schools (K–4: 22 students).

State accountability in education. The educational accountability efforts of State A have been considered stronger than those of State B, according to a research study that rated the State A accountability at 5 on a scale of 0 (low) to 5 (high), while rating State B's efforts at 1 (Carnoy and Loeb 2002).

Teacher hiring. In Cumberland City, the hiring of teachers is a district function. In the Rios Calientes area, districts screen teachers, but the decision to hire is up to the individual schools. Teachers in Rios Calientes are recruited from a local, homogeneous pool of teacher candidates who have been trained at a few local area universities and colleges. Teachers in Cumberland City are hired from a much wider, diverse pool that more closely reflects the typical national teaching pool.

Textbooks. State A provides districts with a list of approved textbooks. State B does not have such a list.

NSF-funded math and science improvement efforts. The Rios Calientes–area math and science improvement effort is located within a local university and serves various area districts. In Cumberland City, the math and science improvement effort is integrated within the school district and works only within the district. In the Rios Calientes area, the math and science improvement effort supplements existing district math and science reform efforts. In Cumberland City, it *is* the district math and science reform effort.

Differences in Region, Area, or City

Size. Cumberland City has a much larger and more ethnically diverse population than the Rios Calientes area. Cumberland City's population is declining, while the population of the Rios Calientes area is increasing.

Economic outlook. The relative geographic isolation of Rios Calientes can mean that Rios Calientes employers often need to look locally to fill their employment needs. This need, coupled with the loss of low-skilled jobs to Montecito across the Mexican border, may have stimulated the local production of higher-skilled workers and put pressure on schools to provide students with sufficient skills and knowledge to qualify for high-skilled jobs or admission to local colleges. Cumberland City, in contrast, as part of the northeast corridor, can draw higher-skilled workers from various areas and institutions. Rios Calientes employers usually recruit local residents; Cumberland City employers usually do not. In addition, Cumberland City is home to several elite colleges and universities and draws its higher education student body from throughout the world, unlike Rios Calientes, where college students are overwhelmingly from Rios Calientes and Montecito.

Demographic match and mismatch. The vast majority of the residents of the Rios Calientes area are Latino, as are most teachers and students. In Cumberland City, about the same percentage of residents are African American and white; teachers are predominately white, and students in the school district are predominately African American.

External factors, such as state or district policies and area demographic and economic conditions, play an important role in how attributes of effectiveness manifest in these effective schools. Still, across districts, the study found five common benchmarks of effectiveness that differentiate highly effective schools from typical schools: principal leadership, high teacher quality, high parent involvement and satisfaction, good student discipline, and higher expectations for students. The commonality of these effectiveness characteristics across districts with such different external factors is a good indicator of their generalizability.

Speculations: Food for Thought

This section explores the possible effects of such areas as diverse as cultural congruence and district disruption on student achievement. It also challenges some common assumptions, such as that low income level is the best indicator of poverty and that schools serving low-income minority students will not be as good as schools serving higher-income students.

Students in Predominately Low-Income Schools Can Achieve at Levels Comparable to Students in Schools with Few Low-Income Students

Highly effective schools for low-income students exist throughout the United States, although not in high numbers. In these schools, low-income students seem to achieve at the same level as students in wealthier schools. The findings in Cumberland City are a case in point. As shown in table 7.1, 4th grade students in the five highly effective elementary schools, which have mostly low-income students, are compared with 4th graders in the 25 elementary schools in the district where 20 percent or fewer of the students are low income. The differences are not just in terms of income. Ninety-three percent of the students in the highly effective schools are minorities, compared with 46 percent of students in schools with smaller shares of low-income students.

Based on the 1999 SAT9 scores, students in the highly effective schools are not only performing at higher levels than the district as a whole, they

Table 7.1. Performance Levels of Cumberland City 4th Graders on the 1999 SAT9 Math, Science, and Reading Assessments by School Income Level (percent)

	Math basic or above	Math proficient or above	Science basic or above	Science proficient or above	Reading basic or above
4th graders in the 5 highly effective, predominately low-income schools	77	42	76	31	72
4th graders in the 25 schools where 20 percent or fewer students are low income	78	38	78	31	84
All district 4th graders	52	17	56	14	60

Source: Cumberland City school district.

are also performing at levels comparable to schools where 20 percent or fewer students are low income.

Taking Individual Responsibility Is Key to School Effectiveness

An earlier study looking at similarities across effective schools found that taking responsibility was "an important improvement strategy" and that the schools in the study worked to create an environment in which all educators shared a sense of responsibility for school improvement and the attainment of the school's goals. In their effective schools, "school leaders created a collective sense of responsibility for school improvement" and the schools "fostered in students a sense of responsibility for appropriate behavior" (Charles A. Dana Center 1999, ix).

In the UI effective schools study, differences are found between highly effective and typical schools in teachers and other staff taking responsibility in various areas, including student behavior and student learning. For example, in the highly effective James Monroe and John Tyler schools, teachers' attitudes are that "each staff member is not just responsible for the children in their class, they are responsible for every child in the school," according to one teacher. In the highly effective schools, there is common discipline and responsibility for the behavior of other teachers' students. At the other extreme, in typical schools George Washington and Martin Van Buren, the principals express concern that teachers do not even take responsibility for discipline with the students in their own classes.

In typical school James Madison, while the principal feels it is "our responsibility to find out how [students] can learn and meet their needs," she also feels it is unfair that "teachers and administrators are held accountable for standardized test scores because they can't control what students are doing at home." Compare this with highly effective Thomas Jefferson, where both teachers and the principal feel that student success is their responsibility.

Differences are also seen in teachers' taking responsibility for decision-making. Teachers in typical school George Washington do not see themselves as part of the decisionmaking process. Their principal agrees, saying that most teachers "don't want to participate [in policy issues] because they don't want that burden." At highly effective school James

Monroe, teachers volunteer for a cadre that meets before and after school to create policies and go over guidelines.

In Rios Calientes, findings are similar to those for Cumberland City. Highly effective–school teachers are much more likely to accept responsibility for their students' learning, and their principals are much more likely to expect teachers to do so. In the words of Ms. Echevarria at Kahlo, "What I've told the teachers is that there are no excuses. All children can learn and we just need to meet them halfway." Another principal of a highly effective school states firmly, "We're in the 'no excuses' business," and she says she expects teachers to do whatever it takes to meet the instructional needs of their students.

Unanimously, teachers in the Rios Calientes highly effective schools confirm both that their principals expect them to take responsibility for their students' learning and that it is a position that they themselves hold. As one teacher at Rivera says, "I think that . . . you have this child and no matter what baggage they are coming in with, he has the ability to learn and it's just our job to find a way to reach him and help him to learn." Principals of highly effective schools provide the leadership and set the tone and expectations for the school and teachers to take responsibility for student learning. Teachers, for their part (at least those who remained in the schools), embrace and implement this approach.

Such is not the case in the typical Rios Calientes schools. The principal at Castellanos, for example, complains that it is difficult to get teachers to take ownership for their problems in the classroom; instead, they expect him to provide the solutions. At another typical school (Paz), the principal explains that many Anglo teachers feel that the disparities in achievement levels between Anglo and Latino students are mainly the result of Latino parents' poor parenting practices. Teachers at a third typical school suggest that because many students are on welfare with mothers who do not work, students do not see the necessity of going to college in order to get a good job (and by implication, that students do not feel that they need to do well in school).

Cultural Congruence between Teachers and Students in Rios Calientes May Play a Role in Raising Student Achievement Levels

Assuming that SAT9 and SAAS classifications of "proficient" are approximately the same, Rios Calientes students perform at a higher academic level than Cumberland City students. As discussed in earlier chapters, several differences between the two districts—including differences in class size, state mandates, and parent involvement—may contribute to this disparity in achievement levels. An additional factor, however, may be the greater cultural congruence among teachers, students, and the community in the Rios Calientes area.

The cultural matches and mismatches between students and teachers in Cumberland City and the Rios Calientes area can be measured in terms of race/ethnicity and language. In the Rios Calientes area, 83 percent of the public-school students, 56 percent of the teachers, and 78 percent of the general population is Latino. In the Rios Calientes schools in the study, Latino student enrollment ranges from 72 to 97 percent, averaging 89 percent; LEP students make up from 23 to 53 percent of the enrollment, averaging 39 percent. The shares of Latino teachers in the eight Rios Calientes schools range from 35 to 86 percent, averaging 68 percent, with an average of 62 percent of teachers speaking fluent Spanish.

In Cumberland City, the pattern is quite different. Sixty-five percent of public school students are African American, as are 43 percent of the general population and 36 percent of the public-school teachers. The proportions are reversed for whites. Sixteen percent of students are white, as is 45 percent of the general population and 62 percent of the public-school teachers. In the sampled Cumberland City schools, African American student enrollment ranges from 20 to 99 percent for a per school average of 57 percent, while the Latino student enrollment ranges from 0 to 79 percent for a per school average of 35 percent. Across the eight schools, almost 60 percent of the teachers are white, 25 percent are African American, and 12 percent are Latino. The percentage of African American teachers in individual schools ranges from 12 to 35 percent, while the share of Latino teachers ranges from 0 to 20 percent. Only about 15 percent of teachers speak Spanish.

Cultural matches and mismatches may have implications for teaching and learning. Research studies have shown that having a teacher of the same race or ethnicity can increase the achievement of minority students as measured by standardized test scores. Although most of these studies have involved African American students (Dee 2001; Hanushek 1992; Murnane 1975), one focuses on Latino students (Clewell, Puma, and McKay 2005). According to that study, having a teacher of the same ethnicity results in higher test score gains in reading and mathematics for Latino 4th grade students. Clearly, the Rios Calientes teachers—

even many Anglo teachers—are familiar with the culture of their Latino students, with most sharing their culture. As one Anglo teacher explains, since she has always lived on the border and taught in border schools, "it's just part of my culture as well." A second Anglo teacher adds: "It just becomes second nature. I don't know that we necessarily adapt so much as we are just used to the [diverse] groups by being here for a few years." In the focus groups, the Rios Calientes Latino teachers say they are unaware of doing anything differently in their classes to accommodate cultural diversity, but an Anglo teacher who has recently arrived in the district comments, "You guys do a lot of adapting for different languages and all those things that doesn't take place elsewhere."

In general, Rios Calientes teachers feel more prepared than Cumberland City teachers do to teach recent immigrants (1.8 versus 2.5 on a scale of 1 [prepared] to 4 [unprepared]). They also feel somewhat more prepared to overcome societal stereotypes about Latino students and math and science (1.3 versus 1.6) and equally prepared to overcome societal stereotypes about African American students and math and science (1.5 versus 1.6), although Rios Calientes teachers are less likely than Cumberland City teachers to have studied methods of work with students from different racial or ethnic groups in the previous 12 months (19 percent versus 31 percent).

Where Differences between Teachers Are Minimal, the Principal Appears to Tip the Scale

In Rios Calientes, teachers are "good" by the traditional measures in both the typical and highly effective schools—the major difference lies in the principals. Although in most Rios Calientes typical schools, teachers seem to have qualifications similar to those of their highly effective–school counterparts, it does not seem to be enough. Principals in highly effective schools provide five things that make a difference: instructional leadership (encouraging innovative instructional approaches, for example), a supportive environment for teachers (providing appropriate professional development and other resources), giving teachers autonomy and fomenting creativity, making parent involvement a schoolwide priority, and setting the tone of high expectations for students for the entire school. In Rios Calientes, 85 percent of teachers in highly effective schools say that their principals have had a "strong positive impact on their instruction," compared with 50 percent of teachers from typical schools who make a similar claim.

Among the Possible Factors Contributing to the Minimal Differences among Rios Calientes–Area Teachers Are the Selection Processes and a Restricted, Relatively Homogeneous Pool

Unlike in Cumberland City, differences between highly effective– and typical-school teachers in the Rios Calientes area are often small and are not always in the direction that might be expected, given the findings on teacher quality. (For example, Rios Calientes teachers in *typical* schools are more likely to have recently taken a math content course and to have spent more time on math instruction than are teachers in *highly effective* schools.) Why might the quality gap be narrower between Rios Calientes and Cumberland City teachers in highly effective versus typical schools? One factor may be employment options. Unlike Cumberland City, which is surrounded by suburbs and other cities, the relative geographic isolation of Rios Calientes means that teachers are limited in their choices of districts in which to work. If Rios Calientes residents want to teach, they teach in the Rios Calientes districts. If Cumberland City–area residents want to teach, they have myriad choices.

Teacher selection may be another factor contributing to fewer differences between Rios Calientes–area typical-school and highly effective–school teachers. In the Rios Calientes area, once the district approves teacher candidates, principals select the teachers themselves. It can be assumed that the principals select the most qualified teachers available whom they feel best fit the school. In Cumberland City, principals do not have a role in teacher selection. Teachers are assigned to schools, and the principals have little or no control over whom they get. Most of the highly effective–school principals and other staff members, however, work to circumvent the official teacher assignment process in order to hire or keep the teachers they want, presumably the more qualified ones. This could help account for the greater differences between highly effective– and typical-school teachers in Cumberland City.

Rios Calientes teachers also seem to come from a more homogeneous pool than do Cumberland City teachers. For example, 90 percent of the Rios Calientes teachers have received their bachelor's degrees from a state university—most often, according to interviews, from the local university, State University at Rios Calientes. For 75 percent of the Rios Calientes teachers, the bachelor's degree is their highest academic degree. Almost 50 percent of Cumberland City teachers have graduated from a state university, about 40 percent from private colleges and universities, and the rest from state colleges. Over 60 percent of the Cumberland City teachers in highly effective schools and about 40 percent of the teachers in typical schools have advanced degrees.

District Upheaval May Have a Greater Impact on Highly Effective Schools Serving Low-Income Students Than on Other Schools

After the 1998–99 school year, there were a number of changes in the Cumberland City school district, including multiple changes of superintendents, a threatened state takeover, privatization of some district schools, threatened strikes, and the threatened removal of teacher certifications. As the following figures indicate, these changes appear to have had a greater impact on student achievement in the highly effective schools than in their typical neighbors.

Between 1998–99 and 1999–2000, the average share of students scoring proficient or higher on the 4th grade SAT9 math test declined at all five original highly effective schools from 45 to 27 percent, staying at about that level (29 percent) in 2000–01. Individual school declines ranged from 11 percentage points to, in the case of formerly effective school Andrew Jackson, 40 points. Typical-school percentages declined by only 1 percentage point between 1998–99 and 1999–2000 (from 7 to 6 percent; see figure 7.3). In 2000–01, they decreased another percentage point. Only one typical school declined in 2000, although all three had declined by 2001.

Results were somewhat similar in reading, where the average share of students scoring proficient or above declined from 34 to 25 percent between 1998–99 and 1999–2000, decreasing another 4 points to 21 percent in 2000–01. Four of the five original highly effective schools saw declines in both 2000 and 2001. Typical-school scores moved from 9 percent to 10 percent in 1999–2000 and then to 5 percent in 2000–01 (figure 7.4). As in math, only one typical school declined in 2000, although all three had declined by 2001.

The average science score for highly effective schools declined from 35 percent in 1998–99 to 25 percent in 1999–2000 and again to 22 percent in 2000–01. Between 1998–99 and 1999–2000, three of the original five effective schools experienced declines. Typical schools continued their pattern of small up-and-down changes, going from 3 percent in 1998–99 to 7 percent in 1999–2000 and back to 4 percent in 2000–01 (figure 7.5).

Figure 7.3. Cumberland City 4th Graders Scoring Proficient or Above on the SAT9-Math

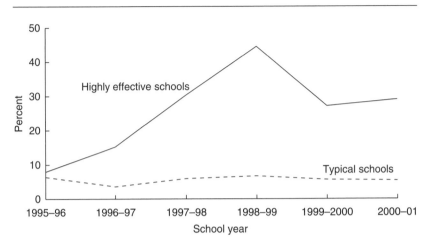

Source: Cumberland City school district.

Note: "Highly effective schools" includes Andrew Jackson (the formerly effective school), since it was originally selected as a highly effective school.

Figure 7.4. Cumberland City 4th Graders Scoring Proficient or Above on the SAT9-Reading

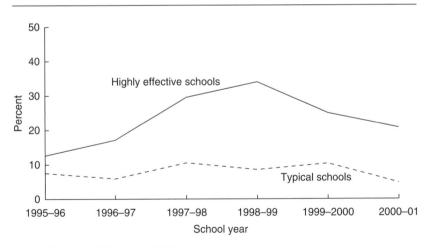

Source: Cumberland City school district.

Note: "Highly effective schools" includes Andrew Jackson (the formerly effective school), since it was originally selected as a highly effective school.

Figure 7.5. Cumberland City 4th Graders Scoring Proficient or Above on the SAT9-Science

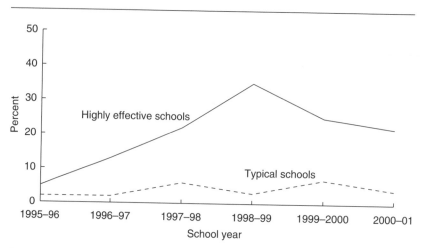

Source: Cumberland City school district.

Note: "Highly effective schools" includes Andrew Jackson (the formerly effective school), since it was originally selected as a highly effective school.

In table 7.2, 1999 scores and 2001 scores of students in the selected high-poverty, highly effective schools are compared with all district 4th graders and with 4th graders in district schools where 20 percent or fewer students are low income.[3] The data reveal a disturbing fact: at proficiency levels in all three subjects, the students in the highly effective low-income schools show by far the greatest decline in achievement from 1999 to 2001. This suggests that highly effective predominately low-income schools are the most vulnerable to detrimental change and upheaval at the district level. Since 93 percent of students in highly effective schools are minority students, compared with 46 percent of students in schools with fewer low-income students, this vulnerability may have negative effects on racial achievement gaps as well.

Income Level May Not Predict a Culture of Poverty

The schools in this study all serve low-income students. All eight Cumberland City schools and four Rios Calientes–area schools have at least 85 percent of their students eligible for free or reduced-price lunches.

Table 7.2. Performance Levels of Cumberland City 4th Graders on the SAT9 Math, Science, and Reading Assessments by Income Level, 1999 and 2001 (percent)

	Math Basic or Above		Math Proficient or Above		Science Basic or Above		Science Proficient or Above		Reading Basic or Above	
	1999	2001	1999	2001	1999	2001	1999	2001	1999	2001
All district 4th graders	52	56	17	19	56	62	14	14	60	62
4th graders in the 5 highly effective, predominately low-income schools	77	69	42	29	76	71	31	21	72	62
4th graders in the 25 schools where 20 percent or fewer students are low income	78	75	38	34	78	78	31	27	84	89
4th graders in the 78 schools where more than 49 percent of students are low income	43	50	11	13	48	53	9	9	50	53

Source: Cumberland City school district.

The shares of low-income students at the other four Rios Calientes–area schools are 80 percent, 70 percent, 60 percent, and 47 percent.

Although highly effective schools generally have fewer discipline issues than do typical schools, the differences between the discipline problems in Cumberland City and in Rios Calientes are dramatic. In Cumberland City, the major discipline concerns are fighting and hitting. Students hitting teachers happens often enough that one teacher in a highly effective school comments, "When a child curses or hits me, it ruins my outlook." In Rios Calientes, discipline issues center on students talking and not remembering or using their manners.

Students in Rios Calientes focus groups, when complaining about their classmates' behavior, cite such minor infractions as chatting in class and passing notes. Bad behavior for substitute teachers is mentioned often. Says one student, "When we have substitutes, kids just go crazy and start saying bad words." Although students in one typical school characterize their classmates' behavior as "terrible," they go on to describe it as passing notes and whispering in class.

In Cumberland City, student descriptions of bad behavior in even the highly effective schools are quite different. Students in highly effective schools speak about "troublemakers" and "evil kids, bad kids," saying that some "kids act like animals, not like teachers expect, they jump around, curse, catch attitudes, sometimes curse at the teacher and fight." Students in the typical schools speak about how some students in their classes act "bad," explaining "they fight, they talk, they run around, they hit each other."

In Cumberland City, teachers and principals see a strong disconnect between the values and culture of the school and that of the surrounding areas. For example, one highly effective school principal explains, "Fighting is what is taught at home. [It is] okay to hit someone at home, not here." At that same school, the school home coordinator is only allowed to make home visits if accompanied by a police officer. She sees the biggest barriers to student learning as "drugs, alcohol, mental illness, some kids get themselves up and into school. They have all the social issues in the world and we have to help them." The picture is similar in the other Cumberland City schools, where there are worries about gangs outside the school, drugs, gunshots, and how students are being cared for. One typical-school principal's response to what the expression "all children can learn" means to him is "I don't want to hear any excuses, [students] didn't eat, mother's an alcoholic, father's on crack, all children can learn." He goes on to say that while "these folks don't get out of [the surrounding neighborhood] they see how cops, how the government deals with people they don't like . . . through violence, through force." Perhaps the most poignant description comes from a highly effective–school teacher:

> You watch kids deteriorate as years go on, behaviors and attitudes change. It is a survival skill. If they are too nice, they will get beaten. . . . They don't know what the word "friend" means, don't know how to be kind, no sense of loss, don't know how to miss someone.

This is not the situation in the Rios Calientes area. While drugs are a problem in high school, no informants in the elementary and middle schools mention drugs as a problem. One of the more serious concerns raised is that many children in one school are on welfare and their mothers do not work so the children do not necessarily see the need to go to college in order to get a job. It is obvious that teachers, students, and parents belong to the same community and share values. In some schools, teachers know the parents of students well because they have taught their students' siblings or, in some cases, the parents themselves. As Ms. Munoz at highly effective school Fuentes explains:

> You can walk into any of the classrooms, from kindergarten to 6th grade and [you will find that] the teachers, who have been here for several years, know the community. A lot of the children who are in these teachers' class-rooms, they've had their brothers and sisters or even mothers and fathers come here. So the teachers are really familiar with the community. . . . And because of this, the community has trust and faith that teachers are going to do right by their kids.

What factors can explain the differences? The Rios Calientes area is relatively geographically isolated with a common culture, a large share of immigrants, an economy whose workforce depends on workers who come out of the area public schools, a smaller population, a lower cost of living . . . Whatever is behind those differences, looking at income level alone can clearly lead to inaccurate, incomplete assumptions about children and their environments.

Implications

The research findings of the UI effective schools study contain several implications for researchers, policymakers, and educators. This section lays out these implications separately.

Implications for Researchers

The finding that several characteristics shared by effective schools in Cumberland City and Rios Calientes manifest differently in each area leads to the conclusion that external factors, such as state or district policies and area demographic and economic conditions, play an important role in how attributes of effectiveness play out in these effective schools. What are the implications of these findings for effective schools research?

External Factors Affect How Research Is Conducted and Interpreted

Although generic terms such as "quality of the teaching force" and "high expectations" may be used to describe the characteristics of effective schools, how these factors are expressed in diverse settings is as important as the identification of the factors themselves. In districts such as Rios Calientes, traditional indicators of teacher quality are widely represented in both effective and typical schools because of external factors, such as homogeneity of the teaching pool and availability of qualified teachers. In these districts, nontraditional indicators of teacher quality, such as teacher satisfaction and commitment, may emerge to differentiate effective from typical schools. But in Cumberland City, which experienced a shortage of qualified teachers (and thus had to recruit from a broader, more diverse pool), traditional quality indicators matter and suffice to differentiate effective from typical schools.

Because of the Influence of External Factors, Outlier Studies Should Be Conducted within the Same District

If conducting outlier studies within districts is not possible, districts should be matched for similarities in policies, practices, and education reform status. For example, the three Rios Calientes–area districts are comparable in policies, practices, and education reform status because they all operate within the context of a top-down, state-driven education reform mandate that regulates most aspects of K–12 education. The startling differences in context between the Cumberland City and Rios Calientes districts and the observed effect of external factors on attributes of effectiveness clearly illustrate the danger of comparing effective and typical schools across districts.

Many external factors affect the quality of a school and the education it provides. Yet the finding that schools in each district in the UI effective schools study report several common benchmarks of effectiveness that differentiate them from other schools is encouraging to the generalizability of effectiveness characteristics. Support for these findings has also been found in the research literature on student achievement and in the effective schools research canon.

Implications for Policymakers and Educators

The second set of implications applies to policy at the state and district level as well as to policy governing schools that serve low-income minority students.

State and District Educational Standards and Assessments of Those Standards Should Be the Same or Closely Aligned

The Rios Calientes–area districts and the School District of Cumberland City provide contrasting cases of high-minority, low-income school districts with both high- and average-performing schools. In the case of the Rios Calientes districts, differences between typical and highly effective schools in school quality and achievement scores are much smaller than differences in Cumberland City. At least some of the contrast between the two districts may be because of State A's stricter alignment between state and district policies. At the time of this study, all State A districts used the same assessment based on the same standards. In State B, the state had one set of standards and assessments and the district had another. To be effective, districts and the state should not be working at cross purposes but should be following either the same standards and assessments or different standards and assessments that supplement and support each other. It goes without saying that the standards in all cases should be of the highest quality.

Principal Leadership Is Key

With the school reform movement and the increased focus on educational standards, the need for principals who are instructional and transformational leaders has intensified. A critical mass of "good" teachers is not enough to ensure that schools serving low-income students succeed.

Although the presence of high-quality teachers is a necessary component for success, it is insufficient, as the Rios Calientes districts demonstrate.

This finding argues for careful attention to the selection of principals who are knowledgeable concerning school reform, curriculum, and instruction, and who are effective motivational leaders. Once hired, and with the involvement of their faculty, these principals should be granted autonomy in hiring and dismissing teachers, developing a professional development plan for the school, making curricular and instructional choices, and so on. Principals should be held accountable for the results of these actions. An effective principal in a low-income, minority-serving school should be an instructional and transformational leader who has a clear vision for his or her school and who strongly influences the direction the school chooses.

Parent Involvement Is Crucial

Involving parents in school activities has often been seen as a challenge by low-income schools. Many parents of students in these schools have demanding work schedules and may be intimidated by the school and its personnel. School policies need to go beyond merely welcoming parents to the school and should make it clear that parents have a right to visit the school when they choose and to be kept informed of their children's progress. Such policies may or may not lead to an increase in parental involvement, but they can affect parental attitudes toward the school as well as reflect the attitude of the school toward parents.

In Cumberland City, where levels of parent involvement are low, parents at highly effective schools feel that they have access to the schools, whereas parents at typical schools feel that they do not belong in their children's schools. This difference is reflected in parent attitudes toward the schools. In the Rios Calientes districts, where highly effective schools enjoy much higher levels of parental participation in school activities than typical schools, effective schools cultivate a welcoming environment, update parents frequently on their children's progress, and structure meaningful activities for parents. It also does not hurt school-parent relations that the majority of teachers and the parent coordinator in these high-Latino-enrollment schools speak fluent Spanish and that the school provides Spanish translations of materials and meetings.

Because many low-income schools receive Title I funds, they have access to monies for supporting parent involvement strategies. More emphasis should be placed on disseminating, at the state or district level, effective parental involvement strategies and increasing the schools' accountability for parental involvement and satisfaction.

Well-Prepared, Committed, and Satisfied Teachers Are Vital

This dictum is clearest in Cumberland City, where there is a marked contrast between the typical and effective schools in teacher quality and experience. In the Rios Calientes districts, teacher quality and experience are uniformly high.

Low-income schools that serve minority students have a greater need for high-quality, experienced teachers. States and districts should make it a priority to provide incentives in order to attract and retain well-qualified teachers in low-income schools. The final decision to hire a teacher should be left to the school. This will increase the chances that teachers who are a good "fit" will be hired. In addition to being more effective teachers, such hires will be more likely to be committed to the school and to enjoy working in the school setting.

Cultural Congruence Matters

Teachers who are knowledgeable about and comfortable with the culture of their students are an important part of an effective low-income school. It is especially important in schools where a nonmainstream culture is predominant that teachers be familiar with the culture and home environments of their students. To the degree possible, teachers of similar cultures should be hired in these schools. Professional development can also help other teachers understand and work with students of other cultures; teachers should learn to adapt instructional strategies to the cultural and linguistic needs of their students. It is extremely important, moreover, that all teachers in these schools be familiar with the culture of poverty.

High Expectations and Responsibility Are Important Hallmarks of Effectiveness

One factor that differentiates typical from highly effective schools at both sites is a culture of high expectations for all students and the corresponding assumption of responsibility on the part of teachers and principals for fulfilling those expectations. States and districts should hold schools accountable for the achievement of high standards (once they are given adequate resources to achieve them), and principals should expect high expectations and responsible attitudes from their teachers and include these in their teacher evaluations.

A Safe and Orderly Environment Provides a Setting for High-Quality Learning

Not only should districts and schools have clear codes of discipline that spell out expectations for student behavior and the consequences for infractions, but this code should be written down and widely disseminated to parents, teachers, and students. Disciplinary policies should also be upheld and consistently enforced. It is important that teachers assume responsibility for student behavior in their classrooms as well as for the behavior of all students within the school when they are outside the classroom. Principals should support teachers' fair and consistent application of disciplinary measures. Parental knowledge, buy-in, and support of the discipline code is important as well.

Special Care Should Be Taken to Protect Highly Effective Schools for Low-Income Minority Students during Changes and Economic Misfortunes

Highly effective schools for low-income minority students may be more vulnerable to district upheaval and loss of resources. "Outliers"—low-income schools where students are performing well—may be subject to greater risk than either middle-class schools or low-income, low-achieving schools when there is district upheaval or when education funds are cut. The state or district should identify these schools and, when adverse situations arise, ensure that they are protected due to their greater vulnerability.

Conclusion

The UI effective schools study's findings regarding the important role of principals and teachers in increasing school effectiveness are striking. Principals can become real instructional leaders, regularly observing and working with teachers to improve instruction, being aware of curriculum strengths and weaknesses, and using that knowledge in decision-making. They can promote innovative, effective curricular and instructional strategies and motivate the school community to embrace education reform. They, with teachers and others, can come up with a clear discipline plan that is shared with school personnel, parents, and students and ensure that it is fairly enforced. They can work to make their schools more welcoming to parents.

Teachers can take responsibility for all the students in the school, seeing any misbehaving or out-of-place student as their responsibility. They can work with the principal to establish a consistent instructional philosophy for the school and they, too, can work to make the school a more welcoming place for parents. They can make a commitment to their students' learning that will ensure that the instructional process is meaningful no matter what cultural or linguistic diversity their students bring to the process. They can invest the phrase "all children can learn" with purpose and truth.

These steps will not change the world, but they can start changing a school.

APPENDIX A
Sample Cumberland City Case Studies

John Adams Elementary
A Highly Effective School

As the two researchers follow a small learning community coordinator down the hall for their initial tour of the school, there is sound of an adult yelling. Everyone immediately stops while she opens the door, looks in, and then closes the door. "I thought it was a teacher," she explained, "and we don't allow teachers to yell at students. But this was a DSS [Department of Social Services] worker, and we have no control over them."

John Adams School is a K–6 elementary school in North Cumberland City with a 2000–01 student enrollment of 705.[1] Since 1996–97, John Adams School's enrollment has ranged from 705 to 803. The community around John Adams School is predominately Latino; two-thirds of the residents are Latino and about a third are African American. The demographics of John Adams School reflect those of the surrounding community. Over the past six years, most John Adams School students (75 percent) have been Latino, while the remainder have been African American. The students are overwhelmingly from low-income families. Over 90 percent of John Adams School's students qualify for free or reduced-price lunches (96 percent in 1996; 91 percent in 2001), and about 56 percent qualify as low income under Cumberland City's stringent definition.[2] Each year, slightly less than half the students either enroll after school starts or leave before school ends. Still, almost 90 percent of John Adams School teachers expect 80 percent or more of their students to remain with them throughout the school year.

John Adams School is a "Success for All"[3] school and was among the earliest implementers of the bilingual version, "Exito Para Todos." The school day runs from 8:30 am to 2:45 pm. There are 46 teachers in John Adams School, including eight SLC coordinators. Along with the classroom teachers, there are 12 specialist teachers, a nurse, a counselor, and interns. Since the school has a large Title I population, there are a number of extra teachers on staff, including a "teacher in charge" who covers classes so other teachers do not lose their preparation periods. Almost 88 percent of the teachers are women. Forty-four percent are white, 35 percent are African American, and about 20 percent are Latino. The student-to-teacher ratio is 16:1.

School Programs

John Adams School houses the North Star After-School Program, a Congreso de Latinos Unidos (Congreso) after-school program that provides an array of activities including academics, recreation, arts, drama, dance, and cultural enrichment. A Saturday program serving 60–70 students provides extra support for students in need as well as programs for gifted students. In addition, while John Adams School is a nine-month school, it has an intensive pre-K–8th grade full-day summer program. Students can attend a full-day Congreso camp, a full-day John Adams School summer program, or a summer program that is half John Adams School, half Congreso. The principal estimates that 31–50 percent of students participate in extracurricular activities.

John Adams School has several out-of-school partners including a college-based medical program, DARE, Evil Eye (a medical program), and Asthma Busters. Other partners include Dunkin Donuts, Fannie Mae, a local college, and the local police. John Adams School also has a club for junior fire fighters and an FBI club, and the school is starting a collaboration with a local Boys and Girls Club to provide more activities. Along with two other highly effective schools (but no typical schools), John Adams School has its own web site that provides information on the school including virtual visits to computer, art, science, and physical education classrooms.

The school has a Home and School Program, a school council, a community assistance program, and Wednesday parent meetings. The Home and School Program does fundraising to provide teachers with supplies for classes, for school projects, and to give children money for trips. The school council does everything from making and selling T-shirts to working on the school budgets. They do, in the words of one parent, "whatever needs to be done." In the community assistance program, parents help the nurse and help teachers in the classroom. At the Wednesday parent meetings "parents as parents help other parents and the community."

Student Achievement

SAT9 data in math, science, and reading were collected for 4th grade John Adams School students from the 1995–96 school year through the 2000–01 school year. As figure A.1 indicates, there was a strong pattern of increase in the percent of 4th grade students scoring at or above proficient from 1996 through 1999, but math and reading scores decreased in 2000 and reading again in 2001. It should be noted that 2000 and 2001 were times of great turmoil for the entire district.

Figure A.2 shows the percentage of students scoring basic or above on the SAT9. The share increases consistently for math, science, and reading over the six-year period, except for a slight decrease in reading in 1998. For the same cohorts of students who took the SSA as 5th graders,

Figure A.1. Percent of John Adams 4th Graders Scoring Proficient or Above, 1996–2001

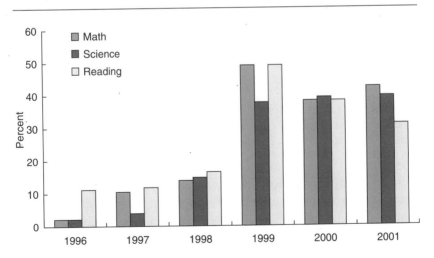

Figure A.2. Percent of John Adams 4th Graders Scoring Basic or Above, 1996–2001

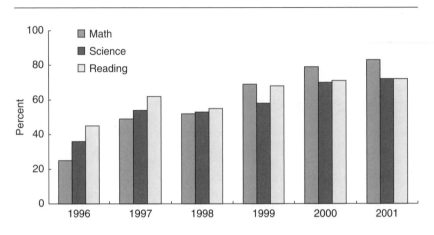

the percentage scoring at high-middle or above in mathematics increased from 20 percent in 1997 to 56 percent in 2000.[4]

The principal estimates that about 10 percent of the 1999–2000 students were not promoted to the next grade. However, almost three-quarters of the teachers report that all their 1999–2000 students have been promoted. Other teachers report from 1 to 22 percent of their students were not promoted. John Adams School follows state and district criteria for promotion where students have to score at least below basic III on the SAT9.[5]

School Leadership

> I took over a school that was running well. I need to build on that. . . . I am a team member as well as a leader. I run it as a family and as a business. You have to build on both aspects.—Principal George Lindsey

The principal, George Lindsey, is a white man with a background in elementary teaching and curriculum who is fluent in Spanish. He has both a master's of arts in teaching and a master's in education. Having arrived as principal for the 1999–2000 school year, he is relatively new to the school. He characterizes his leadership style as soliciting advice from staff but having sole responsibility for final decisions. He sees his overall role as an instructional leader who serves as a team member in creating a shared value system. Defining himself as "a facilitator [and] as a catalyst for change," the principal rates himself as very involved in all aspects of instruction. Part of his role, he feels, is "to support the curriculum standards that the school and district set up and to streamline those to meet the needs of the school." The school's program, Success for All, was instituted under another principal. Teachers feel, however, that this principal's influence on instruction may increase as they start a new reading series, *Balanced Literacy*, a districtwide curriculum.

The interviewed teachers see the principal as someone who is "usually accommodating" and tries to be "very supportive." "If you need something for your class he finds a way to do it," says one teacher. An SLC coordinator sees him as "an educational leader and the person who facilitates the improvement of the physical environment." This SLC coordinator comments that the principal is "really good at fixing the facility . . . He cleaned up things that have been around forever [like] the nasty dumpster kids had to pass on their way to lunch." This SLC coordinator also sees the principal as the educational leader who "sets the feeling for the school, pushes the academics."

Mr. Lindsey's leadership skills are seen as different from the previous principal, and some people are having a hard time getting used to him, feeling the "other principal did more of our jobs. [Mr. Lindsey] expects more [from staff]." Others, including another SLC coordinator, agree about the increased expectations and are "happy with him." The custodian feels Mr. Lindsey "runs a tight ship." He says that the former principal "set the standard and [Mr. Lindsey] picked it up and advanced it."

Mr. Lindsey is a very visible principal who tries to get in every classroom every day and is able to do so four to five times a week. Unlike the other schools where students did not mention the principal, John Adams School students have opinions about Mr. Lindsey. Two students do not like him because "he screams at you when you are bad" and students have to go him when they "get in trouble," while a third student likes him.

Forty-five percent of the teachers surveyed say the principal was very important to their decision to come to the school. However, all but one teacher were referring to an earlier principal, not Mr. Lindsey.

The principal says he does not have any other staff involved in leadership positions in the school, but he does see the SLC coordinators, who meet once a week, as a leadership team, "a tremendous support," and "an extension of the principal." The teachers see the SLC coordinators and some of the teachers as school leaders. "All children know when [they] see certain staff members in the building that they have to get it together." One SLC coordinator says her role is

> to help the teacher so they are left alone to teach. My job is to release outside pressures for the teacher—to take care of discipline, to be a case manager. It is a grandma kind of job, to support teachers, to teach and give back. I can do lessons if they need it, helping them do their job better.

Teacher Quality

All the John Adams School teachers are certified, and only one has an emergency certification. Two-thirds of them have at least master's degrees, and about 20 percent speak Spanish fluently. Teachers have taken an average of 3 undergraduate math courses and 1.3 undergraduate science courses.

John Adams School teachers are very experienced. Their teaching experience ranges from 3 to 40 years, for an average of 17 years. Only one teacher has been teaching for three years or less. Teachers have also been at John Adams School for a long time. On average teachers have been at the school for 12 years; only one teacher is new to John Adams School, having been there for two years or less. Teacher attendance is very high, with 75 percent having at least 95 percent attendance. This high teacher attendance, combined with student attendance, led to the school receiving a $98,000 bonus.

Teachers are very involved in professional development. During the 1999–2000 school year, all John Adams School teachers spent at least 10 hours on mathematics-related professional development and at least 10 hours on science-related professional development, according to the principal. The teachers themselves report an average of 6.9 different professional development activities during the 1999–2000 school year, with three teachers indicating that they had done none of the possible activities listed. A majority of teachers say they have read district math standards (67 percent) and district science standards (56 percent) and have spoken informally with colleagues about implementing math standards (53 percent). During that same time, 29 percent of teachers had taken a science course or studied science concepts in depth; 12 percent had done so in math.

By extending the instructional day by six minutes, John Adams School banks time to increase the time available for professional development.

Bank time is used for traditional professional development activities. It is also used when a child goes to a new teacher or a new community, so the old and new teachers can get together to talk about the child.

The interviewed teachers do not perceive professional development was done well this year. They do, however, "take small pieces from different professional developments and make it work" individually. Interviewed teachers could only think of one example of excellent professional development, a workshop on computer networking. An SLC coordinator feels that lots of professional development was offered outside the school, but it was hard to get people out on Saturdays. She feels the professional development on literature and *Balanced Literacy* was good but that math and science professional development "didn't happen." The principal, however, is concerned that the teachers are "somewhat professional developmented out."

Teacher autonomy is another component of teacher quality. There are some differences in perceptions of teacher autonomy. The principal sees teachers as having great influence on deciding the content of staff development programs, acquiring educational technology, and setting policy on tracking or otherwise grouping students. He sees them as having moderate influence on curriculum, scheduling, budgeting, and determining professional and teaching assignments. They, and he, have no influence over hiring. Among the teachers surveyed, 50 percent say they have partial control over the curriculum and textbooks they use, 21 percent say they have total control, and 24 percent say they have no control. About 50 percent say they have partial control over the professional development content, while 40 percent say they have no control. One SLC coordinator feels teachers play a large role in decisionmaking regarding curriculum and pedagogy:

> The SLC coordinator brings up a menu of issues and they find consensus. The team [of teachers and SLC coordinators] decides. They meet and discuss curriculum, supplies, and materials.

Instruction

John Adams School teachers spend almost five hours (4.8) a week in mathematics instruction and about an hour and a half (1.6) a week in science instruction. While most teachers use *Math Wings*, the Success for All math curriculum, others use Heath's *Mathematics Connections* and Creative Publications' *Mathland.* Most teachers use *Science Today* as their science curriculum. The school uses the district-mandated *Balanced Literacy* for reading and language arts.

Among the 26 teachers who teach math, half (50 percent) report expecting students to go beyond performing procedures and be able to perform analysis and reasoning in most of the math areas they cover. Of the 19 teachers who teach science, around half (47 percent) expect students to go beyond performing procedures and be able to perform analysis and reasoning in most of the science areas they cover.

Teachers rated the importance to their view of education of 13 different pedagogies ranging from inquiry-based learning to basic skills development. While they feel all 13 are at least somewhat important to their views of education, they feel that basic skills development is the most important, with all the teachers surveyed giving it the highest rating. This basic skills focus was also seen in teacher ratings of the practices they are able to implement in their classrooms, with 78 percent saying they implement basic skills development regularly. In addition, 66 percent implement drill-and-practice for skill development, 38 percent implement inquiry-based learning, and 41 percent are able to implement strong content learning in individual disciplines regularly.

Almost 90 percent of teachers do some homogeneous grouping of students within classes for instruction, most often for reading (82 percent), because, as the principal explains, "it is the Success for All model and it is working for them." Focus group teachers speak about explicitly choosing homogeneous or heterogeneous student grouping often based on efficiency. As an SLC coordinator explains,

> I try to be efficient about ways to run the business of education. Sometimes it is more efficient when there is homogeneous grouping; other times heterogeneous grouping. The decision requires discussion, thought, and then consensus.

Teachers speak of doing "homogenous grouping when it is conducive to what is going on." In reading, for example, they see homogeneous grouping as "more efficient in part because there are more people involved in teaching reading." In math, they use heterogeneous grouping "because the math program is so structured." They feel, "It is neat when you can see improvement in lower-level kids when the higher-level kids [are] helping them."

Students were asked what their teachers do that helps them to learn and what their teachers do that does not help students learn. "Explaining things" is the best thing most interviewed students feel teachers do to help them learn. Other things students mention are "when people don't do the work, he helps them" and the teacher "almost tells us the answer but doesn't. It helps us a lot." Also if a student does something bad, the teacher "makes us stay in and learn—if [we] do it again he will call [our] parents."

Getting mad is the major thing students feel that teachers do that does not help them learn. Speaking of one teacher in particular, students said, "He yells and gets red." Also, "He gets really mad and says do it yourself; it's like he turned into the devil," and, "When he writes the homework on the board, he erases it fast—he does it because he thinks people are not paying attention."

All nine interviewed students think most of the kids in class are learning pretty much what the teacher wants them to learn. Math is most often mentioned as what the students are learning, with students saying they are learning decimals, fractions, times tables, division, and counting by tens. Students are also learning spelling, how to say big words, that English has a lot of words, and how to read in two languages. Other things they are learning include "how to do things on your own without help," "how to share," and "how to help people when they are down."

In another measure of student engagement, during the 1999–2000 school year, 46 percent of the students attended school at least 95 percent of the time, as did 44 percent during the 1995–96 school year.

Expectations for Students

The principal, six teachers, and one SLC coordinator were asked what the phrase "all children can learn" means to them. The principal believes that "all means all, that every child can and will learn given the proper supports." Individual teacher responses center around student strengths and potential "even if they come at different levels." The SLC coordinator feels that "to say they can't learn, it is a sin. We need to make the school a safe haven—they can eat and they can be safe and they can learn." One teacher explains that this belief that all children can learn is

> part of a philosophy. You are taking kids from where they are at, taking them from a low level and modifying instruction. This may not happen overnight or over a couple of weeks, but you do see growth and learning. You understand that it can happen.

High expectations show up in another area as well. Most teachers at John Adams School, an SLC coordinator reports, mark low. Students get As on tests but Cs and Ds on report cards because the students are not performing at grade level.

All interviewed students but one think that going to college is important because they feel without college they will not get a good job. Students have not really thought about whether they will be prepared to go to college, but the two parents interviewed feel that their children are being prepared to go to college. The SLC coordinator reports that students ask about college and if they can go there. The school is also part of such programs as the College Medical Program, which offers students college-level career information and opportunities. At this point, student career plans reflect those of most elementary school students: doctor, lawyer, computer person, singer, teacher, nurse, basketball player, and FBI agent (this student is a member of the FBI club).

In another indication of expectations, focus group students say they want to learn more history, more about computers and technology, more science including more experiments, more basketball and gymnastics, and how to make "stuff" like paper.

School Climate

> Teachers help us a lot; every day I want to wake and go to school.—Student

The nine 3rd, 4th, and 5th grade students interviewed, including one special education student and one special-needs student, all really like John Adams School, except the lunchroom, which is generally hated. Almost all of what students like about the school is academic: computers, math, science, and reading. Even when students say gym is what they like about John Adams School, they are quick to point out that gym is "different from recess. In gym you do exercises and different activities than recess." An SLC coordinator supports this, saying the students "appreciate the fact that they are learning." The school climate also seems to reflect this comment from another SLC coordinator:

> The school needs efficiency. It's not different from any other industry. The way to achieve success is for everyone to be responsible and to raise the bar for effectiveness.

Student Behavior

Unlike other schools, John Adams School does not have a special accommodation room for disruptive students. Rather, an accommodation policy includes having a private conference with the student. If the conference does not work, the next step of the policy is to contact the parent. Subsequent steps include a plan with the SLC coordinator, a plan with the counselor, and, finally, the district's individual plan for special-needs students. Under this principal, teachers say, "the behavioral standards have become more structured; kids are being held more accountable." The principal feels that to have good discipline,

> we have to have support for the kids. Children act up because they have a need. I have had [teachers] who felt children should be transferred and isolated because of disciplinary incidents. But I don't believe that. I believe in progressive discipline, not to transfer a child after the first incident.

An SLC coordinator agrees: "One big thing we do—we are able to listen to somebody when children need to be listened to."

The interviewed teachers feel that "teachers are all different in terms of style and how they respond" to student behavior but that, in the words of one teacher, "all teachers hold their students accountable. There are consequences for the student from the teacher for their behavior." A second teacher agrees: "Our mission should be to teach. If a student is damaging the opportunities for others to be successful, there need to be consequences." There is a focus on getting students to take ownership of their behavior, using time outs and behavior modification and a focus on positive reinforcement. Some teachers use "incentives to try promote the behavior of students doing the right thing, to promote and reward the good citizen." An SLC coordinator comments, "Kids don't see anything positive about themselves. I let them see their own positive." There is a need, she feels for more services for the younger students. There "needs to be some way to get them out of the classroom for a couple of days and teach them about life lessons, manners, how to act."

On a day-to-day basis, the "SLC [coordinator] takes care of behavior problems and if the SLC [coordinator] is not available, then it is back to the classroom teacher." As an SLC coordinator explains, "If the kid is banging his head against the wall when the teacher is trying to teach fractions, then I take the kid." In addition, the teachers see teachers as highly qualified professionals who are responsible for teaching and discipline. "Very effective planning and very appropriate lessons" contribute, they feel, to good discipline and cements the teacher as the one in charge of the classroom. Saying "I'm the grown-up and you're the kid" is a release for the children because "they don't have to be in charge."

The principal rates discipline as a problem as 2 on a scale of 1 (not a problem) to 4 (a significant problem). During the 1999–2000 school year,

there were no thefts and five incidents of vandalism. There are no suspensions unless the child does something "really, really bad." The principal doesn't "want kids to stay home, so I don't like suspensions. I even
want them to come here when they are sick."

About 90 percent of the teachers surveyed feel that most of their students are familiar with classroom routines, make transitions between
activities smoothly, and are not disruptive. Almost 80 percent feel that
most of their students try hard, work seriously, and are engaged in pursuing the substantive content of their lessons, and that they do not waste time
when making transitions in and out of the classroom.

All the focus group students are very positive about the school and
about what they are learning. Their feelings about other students' behavior are mixed. Two students feel the other students are nice and "act like a
bunch of angels," and a third student says that students generally obey the
teacher. As the following quotes indicate, the remaining students disagree:

> Kids act like animals, not like teachers expect, they jump around, curse,
> catch attitudes, sometimes curse at the teacher and fight, don't do work
> when supposed to and never listen.
> A lot of bad kids (all the boys—[there is] only one good boy and a girl in
> the class) talk nasty, act horrible.
> Some act bad, some good, some people always be fighting, some boys get
> suspended.
> My class so bad. They jump up, hit each other and make fun of people
> who aren't bad, fight, start trouble, most of time get suspended.

The custodian says that although there are fights, "I never really see
anything more than a [fist]fight. Maybe one weapon the whole [four
years] I've been here." The two parents interviewed feel that John Adams
School is doing a good job on discipline and that their children are learning that fighting is wrong.

Teacher Community

Teachers are important to each other at John Adams School. No teacher
asked for a transfer out of John Adams School this year, and a third of
the teachers say that the other teachers are a very important component
of their decision to teach at John Adams School. Most teachers give and
receive advice from other teachers and share resources regularly. Teachers, SLC coordinators, and the custodian all spoke about staff commitment to the school and to each other.

The custodian, for example, thinks John Adams School "is probably the best school. . . . Other schools aren't as friendly, not such a friendly atmosphere. There's a camaraderie, togetherness, everybody gets along." Sample teacher comments include the following:

> We work together, share with each other, help each other.
> The key piece is the support that we get from each other. Ours is a team that cares.

One way that this caring is evidenced is in teacher behavior. For example, teachers volunteered for recess duty under a special project, although that stopped once the project was over. Currently, one staff member does lunchroom and recess duties voluntarily, even though it is against the contract. The researchers found the staff very alert, friendly, and helpful, not just to the researchers but also to every adult and child who came into the school while the researchers were present.

The principal feels that John Adams School provides "a nurturing environment for teachers." There is breakfast for Teacher Day and lunch at the end of testing, as well as senior teachers who mentor other teachers. The principal gives teachers "much praise" and provides them with opportunities to staff any extra programs that the school gets. Not surprisingly, even though by contract Mr. Lindsey cannot recruit teachers, he has no problem filling positions. One way he does this is through internships. Currently there are several interns at the school whom the principal wants to stay on after they receive their certifications.

Parent and Community Involvement

> If you want community involvement, then they should be able to come whenever they want and [there should be] people there who speak the language.—Principal George Lindsey

There is a great deal of parent and community involvement in John Adams School. During the 1999–2000 school year, 80 percent of parents participated regularly in school activities and 50 percent volunteered for school service, according to the principal. Interviewed teachers also speak about the high level of parent involvement, explaining that "the parents are supportive. If they can, they will come, if they can't, they will do something." The teachers and principal feel the school has "a pretty strong Home and School Program and a community assistance program."

The principal has an open-door policy for parents. "Parents," he says, "have an open-ended invitation to come to visits any time they want. . . . We don't put a show on. Parents are welcome to visit any class at any time." Teachers agree, saying, "Parents have an opportunity to see what it is like in the classrooms." The principal credits the high involvement of parents to the "nonthreatening environment . . . [Parent involvement] is high because people feel comfortable. From principal to building engineer, parents can talk to anyone." There are no appointments for parents. "They come in and I talk to them." Interviewed teachers agree, feeling the principal "talks with parents and is supportive."

Why John Adams School Is a Highly Effective School

At John Adams School, it appears that the principal, teachers, and students are working together and taking responsibility for their actions. The principal, the teachers, and the students have high expectations in academic and behavior areas, and these expectations are being met. Among the components of John Adams School that influence its position as a highly effective school are these six:

A Strong Principal. Although relatively new to the school, the principal is a strong leader, seen by himself and others as an instructional leader and manager who is supportive and highly visible in the school and in the classrooms. Following another strong principal, this principal did not attempt to change what was already working and but rather is using momentum and standards set by the previous principal to establish his own vision. The principal sees himself as a team member and feels he needs to run the school as a "family and a business"; other staff members recognize this need for efficiency. He believes in holding everyone, including himself, accountable for their actions and behaviors, and students and teachers are aware of that. The principal not only focuses on the academics but also looks to improving the school climate and environment for teachers, students, and parents. This effort includes improving the physical environment, working to create a "nurturing" environment for teachers, and applying discipline techniques that focus on support for students' needs.

Great Teachers. Of all the Cumberland City schools participating in the study, John Adams teachers are the most experienced, have the lowest turnover rate, have the best attendance, and have taken the most math and science college courses. They are involved in a great deal of professional development; indeed, administrators feel the teachers may be "professional developmented out." Even though interviewed teachers do not think the professional development was done that well recently, they still take bits and pieces of it and make it work in their classrooms. Teachers take responsibility for their own development and for the students. "You're the grown-up; they are the kids, it is your responsibility." There is also some indication that teachers and administrators feel responsible for every student, regardless of the class and teacher to whom the student is assigned.

High Expectations for Students. Teachers and the principal see teachers and staff as primarily responsible for student success. While there is a strong basic-skills focus, perhaps the strongest of the schools in the study, about half the teachers expect students in math and science to be learning at higher levels beyond "performing procedures." There is a great deal of homogeneous grouping, and there is a degree of intentionality about the grouping—an analysis of where it is and is not appropriate for a class.

Few Discipline Issues. Student behavior and discipline do not seem to be problems. Various enforced and effective disciplinary policies are in place to deal with student behavior. Out-of-school suspension is not favored; students are expected to be at school, "even when they are sick." Teachers are very explicit about holding students accountable for their behavior and use incentives and positive reinforcement for good behavior. "Very effective planning and very appropriate lessons" are seen as important tools to prevent discipline problems.

Teacher Community. Staff commitment and involvement in the school and with each other is strong, as is the nurturing environment for teachers. The teachers support each other and the school, with personal and professional support.

Strong Parent Involvement. The school has a great deal of parent involvement and an open-door policy for parents. There seems to be an integration with community programs as well.

Martin Van Buren Elementary
A Typical School

The Martin Van Buren School is actually two schools. Grades 1 through 4 are housed in the main building in a busy neighborhood, while the kindergarten students are in an annex a few miles away. Walking into the office of the main school, one is confronted by a buzz of activity. It is crowded with staff, desks, and computers. Both Spanish and English are being spoken. The researcher is shown to one of two vice principals who coordinates the interviews and gives a tour of the school, all the while fielding questions from students and teachers who come up to him in the hall.

Martin Van Buren School is a large K–4 elementary school in north-central Cumberland City with a 2000–01 enrollment of just over 1,400 students. The school's enrollment has been consistently increasing from its 1995–96 enrollment of 1,235 students. The surrounding community is racially mixed with about 60 percent of the residents Latino, 20 percent African American, and 16 percent white. Students in the school are over two-thirds Latino, one-quarter African American, and 3 percent white. The major change in Martin Van Buren School's demographics over the past five years has been a decrease in the percentage of white students (from 16 percent to 3 percent) and a resulting increase in African American students.[6]

Over 90 percent of the students qualify for free or reduced-price lunches with 54 percent qualifying as low income under Cumberland City's stringent definition.[7] Each year, about half the students either enroll after school starts or leave before school ends. Over three-quarters of the teachers, however, expect at least 80 percent of their students to remain with them throughout the year.

Martin Van Buren School's school day runs from 8:45 am to 3:00 pm. The school has 69 teachers, including four SLC coordinators, special education teachers, and content specialists. There are also two counselors. The majority of the teachers are women (87 percent); 54 percent are white, 26 percent are Latino, and 12 percent are African American.

Martin Van Buren's four SLCs serve in some ways as schools-within-the-school. Students remain in the same SLC for the entire time they are at Martin Van Buren School. It is hoped that students and teachers within these smaller environments will get to know each other better. Martin Van Buren School also has Adaptive Learning Environment Model (ALEM) classrooms where special education students are mainstreamed into traditional classrooms and special education and mainstream teachers team-teach.

School Programs

The principal estimates that 11–20 percent of the students participate in extracurricular activities. Martin Van Buren School has various after-school activities including drama, cheerleading, writing, public speaking, and math and science programs such as the Animal Discovery Club, the George Washington Carver Science Fair, Extended Day Clubs, and clubs for the "academically at-risk" and the "mentally gifted." According to the principal, the most popular activities are cheerleading, the mentally gifted club, and safety monitors, and students "work hard for those spots." The six interviewed students participate in numerous after-school activities including safety monitors, the mentally gifted club, Boy Scouts, Sister to Sister, Girl Scouts, the homework club, and the math club.

Martin Van Buren School has several community collaborations including one with the B and A Enrichment Services, which has placed three social workers in the school, and the North East Treatment Center, which works with children and families that need more intensive psychiatric services. Martin Van Buren School is part of the Partners Program, a local university initiative that matches urban and suburban schools that then pursue yearlong academic and social activities. It also works with the Police Athletic League Center, which provides Martin Van Buren School students with athletic opportunities, homework clubs, computer outreach programs and self-esteem workshops. The school also participates in Library Power, an initiative to focus on the library as a place to raise student achievement by refurbishing the library, updating and increasing book and software collections, and providing professional development opportunities for staff.

Parent outreach programs include such monthly seminars as *Helping Your Child with Math* and *Understanding Learning Disabilities,* Family Nights, parent-teacher conferences, teacher home visits, and a parent resource room, where parents may bring younger children and borrow reading materials. There is also a Home and School Association and GED and English as a second language (ESL) programs for parents. Martin Van Buren School also participates in the Safe Corners programs where parents on the corners watch out for students; the interviewed parent says it helps "parents know each other and look out for each others' kids."

Student Achievement

SAT9 data in math, science, and reading were collected from 4th grade Martin Van Buren School students from the 1995–96 school year through the 2000–01 school year. With the exception of the 2000 scores, only 6–8 percent of Martin Van Buren School students scored proficient or above in math, science, and reading (figure A.3). It should be noted that 2000 and 2001 were times of great turmoil for the entire district.

As figure A.4 indicates, the percentage of 4th grade students scoring basic or above on the SAT9 during 1996 through 2001 generally fluctuated with slight increases in 2000 but never rising over 50 percent in science, math, or reading. Martin Van Buren School is a K–4 school and thus has no 5th grade SSA scores to report.

The principal estimates that 18 percent of 1999–2000 students were not promoted to the next grade, while slightly less than half the teachers report that all their students were promoted in 1999–2000. Martin Van Buren School follows the state and district criteria for promotion where students have to score at least below basic III on the SAT9.[8] In addition, the students must get a passing grade in English language arts and mathematics.

School Leadership

Tamara Jones was appointed principal in late 2001, after filling the role as acting principal for a year and a half. She had previously taught elementary school. Her specializations include mental and physical disabilities

Figure A.3. Percent of Martin Van Buren 4th Graders Scoring Proficient or Above, 1996–2001

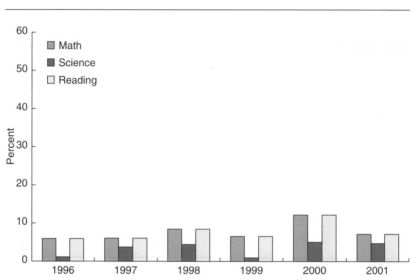

Figure A.4. Percent of Martin Van Buren 4th Graders Scoring Basic or Above, 1996–2001

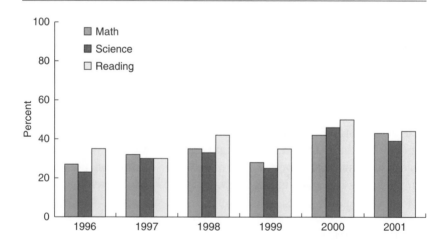

with a focus on hearing impairment. An African American woman, her highest degree is a JD.

Ms. Jones describes the many aspects to her role as educational leader, curriculum planner, stakeholder, and community and children's advocate. She feels that it is her responsibility to "make certain that all students have equal access to educational opportunities and the best instructional practices available." Her style of leadership is, she says, collegial; she solicits advice from staff but has the sole responsibility for decisions. "If I hear a voice, I'll listen to it."

The five interviewed teachers and the four SLC coordinators describe the principal's role as that of a "delegator" or "facilitator," with one commenting that the principal "is very good at delegating; she likes her SLC coordinators to be autonomous, and we make the decisions." The teachers feel that "in urban education, you don't have an instructional leader" so, in reality, the principal deals with "cleanliness, ordering materials, [and] paperwork issues." The SLC coordinators and teachers also feel that the principal's role is limited by the structure of the district: "She's eager to implement new programs and things, but a lot of the decisionmaking has been from the cluster."

The principal reports that she is very involved in supervising the teachers, although being involved also includes delegating those tasks to others. She considers the SLC coordinators the first level of supervision, although they cannot evaluate the teachers because they are in the same union bargaining unit. The assistant principals perform teacher evaluation and supervision for the principal. Martin Van Buren School uses the school district's Teaching and Learning Observation Form, which covers such areas as personality, preparation, technique, and pupil reaction.

Other leadership positions within the school are those of the two assistant principals, the SLC coordinators, and teachers who do in-service professional development. The interviewed teachers and the SLC coordinators say the assistant principals play a big role in discipline and within the operations of the school; the staff add, "The vice principals are very teacher friendly; they are the backbone of the school." The principal comments about their importance as well: "It's like I have four other arms. They assess things and make decisions. They know exactly what to do."

The SLC coordinators each oversee around 13 classrooms and fill various roles. The principal feels they nurture and mentor the teachers and also help "select materials, identify . . . in-service [professional development] and best practices," and share behavioral strategies and techniques. The SLC coordinators describe their roles this way:

> Coordinator of interventions and strategies to help kids learn better, help the teacher acquire those skills.
> We are allowed to make decisions [regarding curriculum selection and implementation], share what we think. We do have a big say.
> We plan a lot of cultural activities.
> We are involved in every aspect of school. We sit with the principal, with the bilingual community, [and] counselor, whatever issues are affecting the school at the time.

Teacher Quality

Less than three-quarters of the Martin Van Buren School teachers are fully certified (73 percent). One teacher is not certified, and another 12 have emergency certifications. One-third have at least master's degrees, and one-quarter speak Spanish fluently. On average, teachers have taken 2.2 undergraduate math and 1.1 undergraduate science courses. While they have been teaching for 11 years on average, individual teaching experience ranges from being in their first to their thirtieth year. One-third of all teachers are new to teaching, having taught for three years or less. Martin Van Buren School teachers have a high rate of turnover; 42 percent of teachers have been at the school for two years or less. On average, Martin Van Buren School teachers have been there for just over five years. Teacher attendance is low. During the 1999–2000 school year, only 53 percent of the teachers had at least 95 percent attendance.

Martin Van Buren School banks time for professional development and uses it for school meetings, special events, and discussing academic and behavior problems.[9] Yet, the principal reports that only 1 percent of teachers spent at least 10 hours during 1999–2000 on math-related professional development and 1 percent of teachers spent at least 10 hours on science-related professional development. Martin Van Buren School teachers report doing an average of 4.9 different professional development activities during the 1999–2000 school year, with six teachers indicating that they had done none of the 27 activities listed. Almost one-quarter of the Martin Van Buren School teachers report studying methods of teaching math or attending formal meetings on math standards, 16 percent report studying methods of teaching science, and 8 percent and 6 percent report studying math or science content, respectively, in the prior year. Ten percent each say they worked on a school curriculum selection committee for math or science.

Interviewed teachers say they have access to a lot of professional development including ALEM training and writing workshops. The principal agrees, describing such professional development opportunities as district workshops/seminars on math and science content and reform, Project Seed training for teachers and parents on introducing pre-algebra concepts, mentoring programs for beginning teachers, and release time and/or financial support to attend other professional development or to take graduate-level courses.

Martin Van Buren School also does in-house professional development where teachers give training in their areas of expertise to each other. "If our administrator sees that a teacher has a good handle on it," an SLC coordinator explains, "[the administrator] will ask that teacher to provide some professional development." Three teachers taught or facilitated in-service math workshops during 1999–2000; two of these same teachers also did a science in-service, as did one other teacher during 1999–2000. Interviewed teachers like the in-service. They feel that an in-house teacher doing the professional development "goes through what we go through [and] has the same type of kids." Learning from "people that are really, really teachers . . . that is practical." In addition, SLC coordinators help with lesson planning, classroom management, teaching ESL, and working with peers, and teachers may also go to another classroom to observe a different style of teaching.

During 2000–01, there was a big professional development focus on *Balanced Literacy,* the district-mandated reading and language arts curriculum. The school, according to an SLC coordinator, concentrates "on different subject areas different years. If a new program comes in, we concentrate on that." Because of the focus on *Balanced Literacy,* SLC coordinators feel that teachers did not receive enough professional development that year to be effective math or science teachers. There was some science professional development in the beginning of the year covering both content and instructional strategies, but math was not covered heavily. SLC coordinators anticipate using a new math curriculum, which comes with professional development from the vendor, for the upcoming year.

Surveyed teachers feel professional development has had a strong positive impact on their instruction, rating it a 3.9 on a scale of 1 to 4 (4 = strong positive impact). Interviewed teachers feel some of the professional development is "useful and beneficial and some a waste."

Another component of teacher quality is teacher autonomy. While the principal feels teachers have little influence on curriculum selection, 60 percent of the teachers feel they have partial control over the curriculum and textbook selection, 13 percent feel they have total control, and only 24 percent say they have no control. Interviewed teachers say they no longer have the freedom to choose the materials they want, unlike under the former principal, who let teachers make more decisions on instructional materials. The SLC coordinators, however, say they "order what the teachers want . . . whatever they want we try to get."

The principal feels teachers have a great influence on the content of professional development offered, but almost half the teachers (44 percent) say they have no control and another 50 percent say they have partial control over what professional development is offered. To select professional development opportunities, the principal says she asks teachers what they would like or what they need, looks at student test scores and grades, and then looks at what professional development is available from the cluster and textbook publishers.

Interviewed teachers say the principal has no influence on the way they teach: "We have freedom to decide what we are going to do in our classrooms, but not [to choose] materials."

The principal feels that teachers have moderate influence on setting policy on tracking or otherwise grouping students and determining the schedule. She feels teachers have little influence on planning budgets, determining specific teaching assignments, or hiring new personnel.

Instruction

Teachers spend on average 4.2 hours a week in mathematics instruction, higher than the school policy of 100 minutes (1.67 hours) a week for kindergarten students and 225 minutes (3.75 hours) for the upper grades. With the exception of the bilingual classes, which use *Matematicas Mi Ventaja,* most teachers use *Math Connections* by Heath. Next year, the principal says, the school is changing to *Everyday Math.*

Teachers spend on average over two hours a week in science instruction (2.3 hours), higher than the academic learning time policy for kindergarten (90 minutes a week) and close to the policy for 1st through 3rd grade (135 minutes, or 2.25 hours, a week) but lower than the policy for 4th grade (180 minutes, or 3 hours, a week). Other than the bilingual classes, which use *Naturaleza Y Sociedad Santillana,* the principal and the teachers say they use *Discovery Works* by Silver Burdette for science.

Of the 41 teachers who teach math, just over one-third expect students to go beyond performing procedures and be able to perform analysis and reasoning in most of the math areas they cover. Of the 38 teachers who teach science, just over one-third also expect students to go beyond performing procedures and be able to perform analysis and reasoning in most of the science areas they cover.

Teachers were asked to rate the importance to their view of education of 13 different pedagogies ranging from inquiry-based learning to basic skills development. While they feel all 13 are at least somewhat important to their view of education, Martin Van Buren School teachers consider multiple learning styles, basic skills development, and student-centered work most important. For the building blocks of elementary education, almost two-thirds of the Martin Van Buren School teachers feel they are able to implement basic skills development regularly in their classrooms, compared with less than half who implement drill-and-practice for skill development and over one-quarter who implement inquiry-based learning regularly.

About 80 percent of the Martin Van Buren School teachers do some homogeneous grouping of students within their classes for instruction by academic ability, most often for reading (71 percent), though some group for math (19 percent). The policy, the principal says, is heterogeneous grouping within class and grade, but there is variation among classes. Interviewed teachers' opinions on grouping vary:

> I think you need to be grouped homogeneously within [the] classroom, but heterogeneously among classrooms. When kids were just at the one level, they made much more growth.
>
> I love heterogeneous grouping in the first grade. It's so important for the weaker children to learn from the stronger children. I found the weaker children grow stronger, while with the homogeneous grouping, the lower level is stigmatizing.

Discussions with SLC coordinators and teachers about ability grouping reveal little continuity or planning in their grouping of students, either because of too few or too many levels in a classroom or because of the number of students who transition in and out during the school year:

> All my second grade reading level transferred. I had really low and no high [and] need the middle to have some balance.
>
> We tend to group by behavior—not all the time, but a lot of the times.
>
> We have so much transition. . . . as kids come in they are plugged in.

I don't think it's good to have a class too mixed, two or three different levels is okay. With one teacher in the room, it's too much with too many different levels.

The interviewed teachers say they reach children of different abilities by teaching them at their instructional level. They "teach concrete experiences, talk about more than [the] abstract [and use] various types of assessments so everybody's needs are being met." They also use hands-on learning. In ALEM classes, where there are two teachers in the room, teachers feel they can be more successful in reaching the greater variety of student levels in one classroom. Teachers also have ESOL support for their bilingual students. Teachers report teaching in English about 80 percent of the time and in Spanish almost 20 percent of the time.

The six interviewed students were asked what their teachers do and do not do to help students learn. The types of things teachers do to help them learn, students say, include helping them individually, having another student who knows the material help them, and making learning fun by doing "stuff with money for learning math." In addition, they feel teachers help them learn by fully explaining the topic, doing it "step by step," and by asking students what they don't get in order to be able to "make it clearer."

Students have definite ideas of what their teachers do that does not help them learn, including teasing them: "If we get a good grade, she'll say we failed again," or letting them draw during health and art: "When we are supposed to be learning, we are drawing pictures and stuff," or by making them sit until "she's done. We sit for like 15 minutes and look at the board." All six students think that most kids in their class are not learning what the teacher wants them to learn, but they do feel that they are learning reading and spelling, math including fractions, science, and social studies.

In another measure of student engagement, during the 1999–2000 school year, only 25 percent of students attended school 95 percent of the time.

Expectations for Students

When asked what the phrase "all children can learn" means to them, the interviewed teachers respond, "All children have potential and can achieve to the best of their ability," while the principal feels the responsibility rests more with the teacher: "We have to find that point where they can learn and grow them from that point." The interviewed teachers feel that success for their students is "if they are self-sufficient . . . self-supporting." Teachers want and expect students to get a job and "get along, think critically, and be good decisionmakers." The interviewed students, half of whom are in the mentally gifted club, see themselves as growing up to become lawyers, artists, boxers, or scientists. They all feel it is important to go to college, because "you have to learn if you want to do something." In general, they feel they are being prepared to go college, although one student admits that she does not have all the education she needs yet but feels she will once she gets out of high school.

School Climate

> It's a nice school because it teaches the kids as much they can.—Student

The six 4th graders interviewed all think of their school as "nice" or "good." Three students like the school because "they teach you new stuff," and two students say their teachers are "great." The principal feels that overall, the school climate is a positive one in which the administration shows that it values the teachers and where the school is as safe as they can make it. However, she adds that when a teacher is mugged outside the building, a teacher dies suddenly, or a teacher's car is keyed, these situations negatively affect the climate of the school.

Student Behavior

Discipline is seen at Martin Van Buren School as somewhat of a problem, with the principal responding that it "required some attention" during the 1999–2000 school year. During that time, there were 45 suspensions, no reported incidences of vandalism, and one theft.

Martin Van Buren School's discipline policy entails handling discipline in five ways: the accommodation room, after-school detention, the Comprehensive Support Process/Functional Behavior Assessment, conflict resolution/peer mediation, and, finally, out-of-school suspension. The accommodation room's purpose, as it is written in the discipline policy, is to give students a temporary place (a maximum of 45 minutes) to "cool off" if they are disrupting the class. Teachers comment that some students do not see going to the accommodation room as a deterrent; rather, they ask for it. After-school detention is for students who have already been to the accommodation room several times.

Both the assistant principals and SLC coordinators deal with discipline problems. The SLC coordinators see their role in dealing with behavior as encouraging teachers and providing them with assistance with disruptive students, helping to write behavior plans, or talking to parents to see "how we can get it turned around." The principal comments, "The best intervention when a child is misbehaving is the intervention administered by the person the child is misbehaving with." She feels that teachers "abdicate" their power when they send the children to the administration for discipline and feels the teachers need to "take ownership of what's going on in the classroom." Teachers feel enforcement of the discipline code "is not consistent . . . it really depends on the teacher," and that the consistency depends "on the mood of the day." However, "if you want to suspend [students], the administration is very responsive."

Interviewed teachers feel that schoolwide, discipline "is the major problem" because "disruptive students . . . take so much time, exhaust the teachers, and rob from the other kids." Teachers feel that because of the behavior problems, they are no longer only a teacher, they are "counselor, parents, judge." Yet interviewed teachers say that within their own classrooms, most students are "agreeable and compliant . . . when they are treated with respect, they are respectful." Interviewed students worry about behavior as well, saying some students in their class act "bad" explaining "they fight, they talk, they run around, they hit each other." The custodian comments that the students with behavior problems are "not the majority" but that "the few they have in here . . . make the whole school look bad."

Teachers say the student behavior problems schoolwide stem from a lack of social skills and lack of respect for authority figures. They feel the "laws of the neighborhood are a lot different than the school. . . . We are fighting a battle; we are teaching them one way, and once they step outside the door, it's totally different." Teachers feel that some students not only do not learn social skills at home, but their parents "will tell them to fight—tell them to hit," so the students learn the "cycle of abuse . . . and that's how they deal with frustration and anger." Other reasons for behavior problems as noted by interviewed teachers include staff turnover every year, attendance and tardiness, unmedicated emotional disturbances, and frustration if their academic level is low in a particular area.

However, about 85 percent of the teachers surveyed feel that most of their students are familiar with classroom routines, make transitions between activities smoothly, and are not disruptive. About three-quarters of teachers feel most of their students try hard, work seriously, and do not waste time when making transitions in and out of the classroom. They also feel that most of their students are engaged in pursuing the substantive content of their lessons.

Teacher Community

One-third of the teachers at Martin Van Buren School say the other teachers were a very important component of their decision to teach at the school. About 60 percent of Martin Van Buren teachers regularly interact with other teachers to give or receive advice and to share resources. When asked what resources and support they have, the interviewed teachers mention they get support from their SLC, though they "really don't talk too much outside the SLC"; they also have "other teachers" for support. In fact, the interviewed teachers, all from the 1st and 2nd grades, regularly eat lunch together in one of their classrooms. The interviewed teachers call the two vice principals the "backbone of the school," feeling they are very teacher friendly. The principal also says the "administration shows that it values the teachers" by providing lunches, gift certificates, and other recognition.

Parent and Community Involvement

The principal reports that 5 percent of parents participated regularly in school activities and 2 percent of parents volunteered for school service during 1999–2000, while the parent coordinator says that for parent-teacher conferences, they can have about 95 percent of the parents. All workshops and notices home are offered in both English and Spanish.

A majority of teachers (83 percent) note that they had contact with at least 75 percent of their parents during the 1999–2000 school year; one-quarter said they had contact with all their parents that year. Over half (55 percent) say that the majority of parents attended parent-teacher conferences during 1999–2000, and 38 percent of teachers say that at least one-quarter of their students' parents contacted them about their child during 1999–2000. In reaching out to their students' parents, Martin Van Buren School teachers report most often discussing students' progress informally with parents (83 percent), contacting parents when their child does something good or noteworthy (77 percent), and sending written communications to parents in multiple languages (70 percent) to get parents and others involved in students' education.

The parent coordinator says she tries "very hard to get the [parents] in." She uses fliers and telephone calls, and speaks to parents when possible. She comments that evening meetings are better for reaching parents because many work or go to school during the day, especially since welfare reform. Martin Van Buren School works with Motivation Education Training Center and Even Start to encourage parent and family participation because, the principal says, many times "we have to teach parents what good parenting skills are and that means involving them in the school. If the parent didn't have a good experience or if they feel it's negative, they don't want to come up here."

Why Martin Van Buren School Is a Typical School

The management of a K–4 elementary school with more than 1,400 students, two buildings, 42 percent of the 69 teachers at the school for less than two years, and one-third of the teachers new to teaching requires a strong leader with a clearly articulated vision and the successful delegation of many responsibilities. It appears that the management of this school organization is a challenge for the current principal.

An Uninvolved Principal. While the principal sees herself as an educational leader and curriculum planner, the interviewed teachers and administrators see her as delegating those tasks and only being involved in "paperwork issues." The assistant principals are important to the running of the school; the teachers call them the "backbone of the school." It appears the principal is removed from the day-to-day instruction, discipline, and activity of the school. One teacher goes so far as to describe the principal as an example of where "teachers who can't teach become administrators." Teachers feel that while this principal has ideas to implement, she does not go out of her way to work around a difficult system to make things happen. In addition, principal and teacher perceptions differ in such areas as teacher autonomy over the content of their professional development, their influence on curriculum, and their involvement with parents.

Less-Qualified Teachers. Teachers are not as strong in Martin Van Buren School as in the highly effective schools, although they have taken as many undergraduate courses in math and science. Over a quarter are not fully certified, and only a third have master's degrees. A third are new to teaching, and over 40 percent are new to the school. Although teachers have access to a lot of professional development, they do relatively little of it. The school's approach to focusing on one area for professional development each year may also do teachers a disservice—the previous year, the SLC coordinator felt the teachers were not effective teachers of math or science because of a focus in literacy that year. There is also little continuity or planning in their instructional grouping of students.

Ineffective Discipline. There is a structured discipline policy, but teachers feel its enforcement is inconsistent. The accommodation room does not seem to be working and may be counterproductive. One teacher says students see going to the accommodation room "as a reward." The principal feels the teachers should be dealing with discipline issues within their classrooms, while interviewed teachers feel it is not classroom discipline but schoolwide discipline that is a major problem. Within the classroom, teachers speak of students being respectful "when they are treated with respect." However, there is no expectation that students will listen to teachers outside their classrooms. Rather, it is felt that students do not respect authority figures, that "you have to have a relationship with them. Some kids will just ignore you." One teacher attributes at least part of the schoolwide discipline problem to the "large changeover of staff every year."

Lower Student Expectations. The principal's response to "all children can learn" emphasizes the teachers' role in making this happen, while the teacher responses do not. Interviewed teachers do not expect their students will go to college; rather, their hopes for students center more around self-sufficiency than academic achievement. Only a third of the surveyed teachers expect their students to go on to learn higher-level skills, beyond performing procedures in math and science. Student attendance is low.

Some Teacher Community. The school is very large and in two sites, making it difficult to administer and to form into a community. As such, the SLCs appear to be the main unit in which teachers and students communicate. The teachers regularly interact and use each other as professional resources, and the SLCs form the basis for this support and interaction, with one teacher commenting, they "really don't talk too much outside the SLC." One-third of the teachers say teachers at the school were an important reason for deciding to teach at Martin Van Buren.

Mixed Parent/Community Involvement. There is some disagreement about the degree of parent involvement. The principal says there is almost no parent involvement, while the teachers say they have a lot of involvement with their parents. The parent coordinator also says there was a lot of involvement in the parent-teacher conferences. Although the parent coordinator says, "we try very hard to get [parents] in," there are differing accounts to how many parents are involved, and it is unclear how much outreach is done for parents. While there appear to be many programs for parents, it is unclear how much effort is placed on getting the parents involved. The parent coordinator will send fliers home in both English and Spanish and may phone the parents or talk to them, but there is no mention of home visits or other strategies to increase parent involvement.

APPENDIX B
Sample Rios Calientes Case Studies

Diego Rivera Elementary
A Highly Effective School

Every child can be successful, no matter at what level or what he comes with. . . . We're in the "no excuses" business.—Ms. Baeza

Diego Rivera Elementary School is in the southern part of Rios Calientes County near the Mexican border in an area characterized by a large, stable, low-income Latino population. The school's accountability rating from 1995–96 to 2000–01 showed steady improvement from acceptable to recognized and exemplary.[1]

In 2000–01, there were 485 K–5 students at Rivera. Most students (94.2 percent) were Latino, with few white (1.9 percent) students. Of the 485 students, 50.1 percent were LEP, 11.5 percent were enrolled in the special education program, and most (92.4 percent) were classified as economically disadvantaged.[2] The school averaged a 22.9 percent mobility rate, a high attendance rate of 96.8 percent, and zero disciplinary placements.

During 2000–01, there were 36 teachers. Of those, most (88.9 percent) were Latino, followed by white teachers (11.1 percent), and most (86.1 percent) were female. The average class size in K–4 was 28 students, and the average for grade 5 was 27 students.

Factors Related to Effectiveness

Several attributes of a positive school climate as well as numerous enabling conditions contribute to Diego Rivera's effectiveness.

School Climate

The school climate is characterized by the principal, Ms. Baeza, as "one of warmth, friendliness, security." The main messages that the principal wishes to convey are "Children come first" and "There are no excuses." Parents and some staff concur that this focus has been made clear during the short time the principal had been in her position. Site visitors observe a clean, bright, well-maintained building bustling with the presence of parents and students.

At the time of the site visit, Rivera was in transition from one principal to another. Ms. Baeza, who had been in her position for about almost a year, mentioned that the main areas of change within the school had been an increase in the number of parent activities offered, an increase in class size in grades K–4 to the maximum allowed by the state, increased monitoring and follow-up of student progress, and increased emphasis on professional development of teachers and staff. This was supported by comments from teachers, staff, and parents. Parents commented that the academic rigor of the school had also increased. In the words of one parent, "It's more advanced this year than what it has been in the past."

The school buses about 50 percent of its students, who come from other neighborhood schools in the district. A large percentage of parents do not speak English, and many families are headed by single parents. The principal noted that several parents had died that year, making the school year difficult for many students.

High Expectations for Students

Ms. Baeza feels that "every child can be successful, no matter at what level or what he comes with. . . . We're in the 'no excuses' business." She expects teachers to become facilitators of their students' learning so they are able to adapt their instructional techniques to meet the needs of the individual child. This approach is somewhat new for teachers at Rivera, who in previous years had dealt with learning problems through after-school tutoring. The principal has insisted that whatever special attention a student needs should be given during the school day. She reasons that both children and teachers are tired at the end of the day. In addition, because more than 50 percent of the students at Rivera are bused, it is difficult for most of them to stay after school for tutoring.

Teachers seem aware of the importance of high expectations and a belief that all children can learn. In the words of one teacher, "I think that with the phrase 'all children can learn' you have this child and no matter what baggage they are coming with, he has the ability to learn and it's just our job to find a way to reach him and help him to learn." Most teachers, though acknowledging the odds of their students going to college, are very positive concerning their students' futures. In the words of one teacher, "We hope. I think [college-going is] something that we address all the time. In the classroom I would say 'When you go to college' and 'We need to start planning for how to get to college.' "

Students are optimistic and ambitious about their futures. They respond enthusiastically to questions about their career plans, with some mentioning ambitions to enter such fields as law, engineering, and medicine. A few students plan to go into professional sports. They seem to have responded to their teachers' encouragement to enroll in college, however, because all maintain that it is very important to go to college. Most cite reasons related to making a good salary, and several mention that their mothers, because they do not have college degrees, would not be able to support the family if something happens to their fathers. Some typical comments from students are "I think it's [a college degree] important so that you don't end up working at McDonald's"; "If you don't go to college, you ruin your life"; "I think it's very important to have a college degree. That's how you get whatever job you want"; and "I think college is important because you become a low-life [without it]—you start doing drugs and other bad stuff." Students all agree that they will be ready for college when the time comes. Parents are in general agreement that their children will go to college and that the school will prepare them well.

Although the principal asserts that the school had no formal policy regarding ability grouping, most teachers agree that in a few subjects, such as reading, ability grouping is appropriate. For other subjects, such as math and science, teachers feel that students learn more by being around other students at different levels of proficiency. As one teacher explains,

> When we are doing a small group instruction for reading, it has to be the children that have the same ability level and that's the only thing I group by ability. For something like science and math I like to have a mixed group so that somebody strong can help someone who doesn't understand as well.

This perception among teachers is supported by survey data that show 58 percent of teachers use ability grouping, 100 percent of whom use it in reading, while only 39 percent and 11 percent of those who group do so in math and science, respectively. Ability groups, when they are used, are determined more by daily observation than by test scores, parent request, or teacher-made tests. Over half the teachers (55 percent) feel that heterogeneous grouping is important to their view of education, with 41 percent feeling that they are able to implement this view in their classrooms regularly.

Principal and teachers are asked how they handled the teaching of diverse groups of students. Ms. Baeza reiterates her expectations for the teachers to provide "whatever the child needs, whether it's reading or math or one-to-one conferencing with a student over a composition." Teachers mostly respond in terms of how they use more or less Spanish with students depending on the grade level, with a large proportion of the class taught in Spanish at the kindergarten level and then decreasing as the grade levels increased. Teachers agree that they have access to a lot of resources for dealing with diversity and that they are able to use these resources when they need them. Says one teacher, "When we are confronted with an issue like diversity, our district is always very good. They provide a wealth of resources for us."

Order and Discipline

Ms. Baeza states that discipline is not a serious problem for Rivera. She feels that there are fewer problems because the school does not have 6th graders. She also comments that as of the current year, children have more of a place and a voice at the school and that this may have improved their behavior. Two incidents of vandalism and none of theft occurred on school property during the previous academic year (1999–2000).

Behavior problems are generally handled in the classroom by the teachers. Teachers agree that students are generally very well behaved and attribute this to the school's Life Skills and Character Education classes as well as the small size of the school. One teacher attributes the good behavior to "good communication with the parents" and explains that teachers have telephones in their classrooms to facilitate that communication. "When there is a problem we can call [parents] right then and there." Students themselves seem to have a different view of their behavior. They maintain that fellow students are disruptive, but say that most of the bad behavior is in the form of chatter in the classroom.

Organized Curriculum

While agreeing that the state standards "run everything in the state," the principal maintains that standards are research-based and aligned with both national standards and state frameworks. The school uses the district-adopted textbooks (Harcourt Brace) for mathematics and science, but the principal feels that using supplemental materials as aids to the district-adopted textbooks gives schools sufficient flexibility and autonomy regarding the curriculum. She comments that for science, Rivera uses *Windows of Science* as a supplement, together with hands-on teacher-made materials that teachers prepare over the summer. The Urban Systemic Program (USP)—a National Science Foundation–funded initiative of which the school is a part—has provided mentors in the past to work with teachers in the school. The teachers also work with Mexican American engineering students and scientists, who come to the school periodically to help with instruction and labs. The principal observes, "It's important that our children feel that science is also very important." In mathematics, the school is using hands-on materials and manipulatives from a private professional development provider as well as other supplemental materials.

Overall, a large majority of teachers (77 percent) acknowledge using supplementary teacher-made math materials. A majority of those who do (79 percent) use self-made supplementary materials for math instruction, and 46 percent use materials made by other teachers. Supplementary materials are less likely to be used for science, with a little over half of teachers (55 percent) saying that they use these materials. About half (48 percent) say that they use self-made materials in teaching science, and about 20 percent acknowledge using materials made by other teachers.

Enabling Conditions

Several enabling conditions are evident at Rivera. To start, a good principal leads a team of capable teachers. A highly structured accountability and evaluation system is another positive sign. In addition, the school makes good use of the flexibility and autonomy granted by the district, and teachers use their instruction time well. Finally, the school offers many activities for both students and parents, making the school a welcoming place for the whole community.

Effective Leadership

This is Ms. Baeza's first year as principal at Rivera. The previous principal was her classmate and friend in high school and undergraduate school and goes to Rivera twice a week to help Ms. Baeza. She states that she feels comfortable calling on him for assistance and feedback when she needs it. Ms. Baeza is a mature Latina with a master's degree in education with specializations in special education, bilingual education, elementary education, supervision, and administration. She is maternal and nurturing and seems passionately committed to the students' education and general well-being. She feels that she is "very involved" in determining the curriculum, determining the time spent on academic tasks, establishing policies on class size and grouping, and supervising teachers. She sees her overall role as principal in supervising instruction as being "an instructional leader who supports, facilitates, monitors, demonstrates the school mission statement." She feels that her leadership style is collegial, leading by consensus.

Ms. Baeza's leadership style seems very different from that of the previous principal. It was her perception that the school "seemed to be catering a lot to the teachers and [not] so much to the students." Ms. Baeza has changed the focus to serving students and, as part of that, has opened up the school to parents by increasing activities for parents and encouraging them to visit the school. For example, school staff report that the school had not had a PTA under the previous principal because "the previous principal and the parents were at odds." Ms. Baeza wants to start the PTA again. She has also been trying to work with teachers to develop thematic units that integrate reading, language arts, math, science, and social studies.

According to the principal, she tries to obtain input from teachers, students, and parents that assists her in incorporating their wishes into her school plan. She shares leadership responsibilities with an assistant principal, a literacy leader, and a Title I support teacher. Teachers at Rivera state that since the principal is a new administrator they are not yet sure about her leadership abilities. They comment, nevertheless, that they expect their principal to be involved in all aspects of the school.

They also stress that decisions are made through group consensus. In the words of one teacher, "There is a group that gets together and decides" (the group is made up of teachers, parents, and community members elected by their peers). Teachers feel that in addition to the principal, teachers serve a strong leadership role at Rivera. Although the focus group teachers say they are not yet able to assess the principal's abilities as an instructional leader, 75 percent of the teachers at Rivera respond in the survey that the principal exerts a "strong positive impact" on their instruction. This is one of the five most important influences (out of 16 possible influences) on instruction at the school.

Rivera's principal communicates academic goals to teachers, staff, parents, and students by giving speeches and presentations; posting goals in prominent places in the school building; listing them in the staff handbook; including them in written communications that go out to parents, teachers, and staff; and distributing them to the Campus Educational Improvement Council. The principal feels that the academic goals exert a strong influence on all aspects of decisionmaking, from establishing the curriculum to parental involvement.

Capable Teaching Force

Rivera has 31 classroom teachers who teach math and/or science. Twenty-eight (or 90 percent) are female, and three (10 percent) are male. In racial/ethnic distribution 78 percent are Latino, 3 percent are African American, 10 percent are white, and 10 percent classify themselves as "other," while one chose not to respond. The average teacher is 41 years old, with a significant proportion of teachers in the 46- to 50-year-old range. The large majority has children (71 percent), and only one lives outside the Rios Calientes area. Eighty-one percent grew up in the Rios Calientes area, and 65 percent speak fluent Spanish. A large majority holds a bachelor's degree in elementary education (84 percent), while one has a bachelor's degree in science. Five have bachelor's degrees in fields outside education, including history, management, political science, psychology, and sociology. Five (16 percent) have master's degrees; of these, three have master's degrees in elementary education, one in bilingual management, and one in technology. Twenty-one teachers, or 68 percent, have had more than five years of teaching experience, and none are uncertified or emergency certified. Seventy-seven percent have been teaching at Rivera for three years or longer. The average amount of teaching experience is 11.6 years, and the average Rivera teacher has been at the school for 8.6 years.

The most important factors in teachers' decisions to teach at Rivera are that they are selected for the position (48 percent); professional development (52 percent); and the school's educational philosophy (46 percent). Only one teacher has a child who has attended or is attending Rivera. The principal says that in hiring teachers she looks for

> a teacher who's proactive; a teacher who's energetic and is a hands-on person. One that has a gleam in his or her eye, who loves learning, and who knows that learning also occurs outside the classroom. . . . One who is willing to dare to go where others have not gone.

Being committed to the ideal that "all children can learn" is an important determinant of who gets hired at Rivera.

All the teachers at Rivera received at least 10 hours of professional development in math curriculum, the teaching of mathematics, or some related topic during the previous year. The same applies for science. The principal explains that as part of the greater campus action plan, the school provides 1.5 hours of professional development a month. It is up to the teachers to decide what kind of professional development they need. No teacher who has requested professional development has been turned down this year. Teachers attend monthly districtwide math meetings and meet weekly on math objectives. They have at least four school- or districtwide meetings on science a year. In the past, teachers at Rivera received professional development through the USP, but they are no longer involved because the USP has changed the way it provides these services.

Teachers feel that there are more than enough opportunities for them to obtain professional development. They emphasize, however, that they use one another as resources as well. A school-based committee meets and decides on several in-service activities that would benefit all teachers and, monthly, a different grade level presents staff development of interest to the rest of the faculty. One teacher comments, "Our teachers are doing such a good job and we can learn from each other. We forget what we have here because we're so busy going off to some other staff development."

Teachers are satisfied with the usefulness of the professional development that they have received. In the words of one teacher, "There are some staff developments that are mandatory, but you want to go because you learn." Another comments, "I have not been to one [district sponsored] staff development and not learned." Teachers also feel that access to professional development opportunities is equitable. Says one, "Oh yes, we all have the same opportunity. It's just whether or not you choose to do it."

Teachers at Rivera are more likely to say that they feel prepared to teach to state and district math standards (63 and 67 percent, respectively) than to national math standards (50 percent). A much lower percentage report that they feel prepared to teach to district science standards (42 percent) and to state or national standards (36 percent). Well over half report feeling prepared to teach students from different socioeconomic groups (77 percent) and to overcome societal stereotypes about math/science ability and girls (65 percent), African American students (62 percent), Latino students (70 percent), and students with disabilities (70 percent). Teachers are somewhat less confident about their ability to teach recent immigrant students (52 percent).

Teachers at Rivera engage in a great deal of cross-grade articulation planning as well as within-grade coordination. They also meet with schools in their feeder pattern for alignment purposes. Ms. Baeza states that many of these meetings take place right after the SAAS is administered, although the teachers within Rivera meet once a week and report on the meeting to the principal on Fridays. Both the literacy leader and the schoolwide support teachers meet with the classroom teachers regularly around the state standards and the curriculum. The principal comments, "It's amazing that they haven't complained that their conference periods are always taken up with these meetings."

This account by the principal is supported by survey responses of teachers. Almost three-quarters of the teachers say that they interact "often" with other teachers in the school to receive or give advice or to brainstorm, and around two-thirds say that they interact with other Rivera teachers "often" in the sharing of resources and planning together. About half the teachers work on joint projects together, with much lower proportions (17 percent) responding that they team-teach "often." Teachers attribute major strong positive influences on their instruction to principal influence (75 percent), professional development (84 percent), state standards (76 percent), district standards (73 percent), district policies (73 percent), and expectations of student skills for the next grade level (84 percent).

When asked whether they think that most of the kids in class are learning what the teacher wants them to learn, students tend instead to give examples of students in their classes who are not learning math and writing in the 4th grade and spelling and reading in the 5th grade. These students, however, become excited when asked how their teacher helps them learn. They explain that they have learning partners to work with and find that helpful. They say that the teacher tells them to memorize things and tests them over and over again and they feel that it helps them to learn. When they are having problems, the teacher gives them individual attention unless she thinks that they could all benefit from the explanation. Teachers assure them that they are not the only students who have these questions. Lastly, the teacher puts the names of misbehaving students on the board, and this has improved the behavior of students.

Accountability/Evaluation System

As with most other schools in the Bolivar district, Rivera sends progress reports to parents every three weeks and report cards every six weeks. Ms. Baeza explains that she monitors progress data regularly and that if large gaps are evident among different groups of students, she questions the reason for these gaps. She gives an example of LEP students, who it seemed to her were taking a long time to transition out of bilingual education. After identifying this as a problem, she increased the emphasis on ESL for these students and made all the teachers and staff aware of the problem.

Student progress is monitored monthly, as is the progress of classes and the school as a whole. Student progress is monitored via periodic reports submitted by teachers to the principal, district-generated school-level reports on standardized tests, progress reports every three weeks, report cards every six weeks, and parent-student-teacher conferences twice a year. Measures of student progress are student in-class performance (both written and oral), grade point average, performance on minimum competency tests, and writing samples. This information is used to update the curriculum, improve instructional practices, evaluate teachers, involve parents, decide budget allocations, and make staffing decisions.

Flexibility and Autonomy

The principal states emphatically that she feels her school has been given sufficient flexibility and autonomy to provide an excellent education for its students. Like all schools in the Bolivar district, Rivera can make school-level decisions concerning instructional grouping, adoption and use of supplemental teaching materials, class size in the 5th grade (there is no 6th grade), the distribution of instructional time among subjects, the amount and type of professional development provided to teachers, the extent and type of extracurricular activities for students, and the strategies used to involve parents and the community.

The principal feels that teachers in the school have considerable influence over school policies. She comments, "I'm hoping that they feel that they have had a strong voice in it [school policy]." Over half the teachers in the school feel that they had at least partial control over the curriculum and texts they use, the assessments they use, and their daily schedule. Surprisingly, over half feel that they have no control over the content of professional development programs, in contrast with the teachers in the focus group who feel that they have total access to whatever type of professional development they need.

Instructional Time

The principal states that there are no district or school policies governing instructional time. Teachers report that math is taught five days a week, with 17 percent reporting classes of 30–45 minutes, 43 percent reporting classes of 45–60 minutes, and 33 percent reporting classes of 75–90 minutes, for an average of 68.2 minutes. In science, about one-third each (30 percent) of the teachers teach this subject twice, three, and five times a week. Half the teachers report science classes of 30–45 minutes, 31 percent report classes of 15–30 minutes, and 17 percent report classes of 45–60 minutes, with an average of 40.8 minutes per science class.

The principal reports that there are seven hours in the school day, and five full days per school week. No early dismissal days are reported in a school year of 178 days.

Opportunities for Student Participation

Although a large proportion of students is bused, the principal estimates that between 31 and 50 percent of students participate in extracurricular activities at Rivera. The school offers an impressive array of activities, including intramural and extramural sports, student government, art/music/dance/drama, and after-school math and science programs such as Family Math and Family Science. According to the principal, some students leave the school at 3:00 and return at 6:00 for activities. The school has a recreational center as well as an Olympic-size swimming pool where students can take swimming lessons. There is also a park across the street where parents and grandparents from the community walk with their children.

Because of the necessity for busing so many students, academic support programs are offered during the school day. Students, nevertheless, may stay after school to work on homework or other activities. According to the principal, if a student stays after school, it is always with parental permission, and transportation must be provided. The principal comments that she herself has taken a number of students to their homes when necessary.

Students say they are involved in several school activities, including storytelling, Odyssey of the Mind, Spelling Bee, ballet, dance, English, poem reading, soccer, basketball, volleyball, track, and football. They disagree among themselves whether they have enough time after school to do more activities because of homework requirements, but those who want to be involved in more activities, want more sports.

Support from Parents and the Community

As alluded to in sections above, parental involvement has increased this year for the first time under the new principal. The former principal was described by one staff member as "at odds with parents." Ms. Baeza has invested considerable effort in reaching out to parents, polling them about the types of activities that they want at the school, and ensuring that parents have a voice in school decisions. She describes the process:

> When I came [here] in July I didn't wait until registration time in August. I immediately had the pre-K students [and their parents] come in because I wanted to start getting a sense of families and wanted to devote more time to that because fall would have been so hectic. I introduced myself and asked parents, "What are the things you want to see here?" And they responded.

Parents suggested several activities, among them a Halloween party at the school, a cookout, an Easter outdoor activity, a Christmas program, and a talent show. Many of these activities also brought in community members and were very well attended. The principal calculates that around 70 percent of parents are active in the school.

The parent coordinator has been the unofficial coordinator for one year, but has been volunteering at the school for six years. She is in charge of 25 parent volunteers who assist the teachers, usually reading for kindergarteners and 1st graders, decorating the walls with student work, and performing other tasks to help teachers. According to the principal, the current budget clerk was the parent-home liaison, but she did not work out because she was unwilling to visit students' homes. The principal explains,

> When a child is sick I would like her to go. Well, she would like the parent to come. Sometimes that's good, but sometimes it isn't. I myself have gone to children's homes. . . . Whatever it takes! No excuses, no excuses!

She hopes to hire an official parent coordinator during the next year.

The school offers Spanish translation services for non-English-speaking parents. Some programs for parents include ESL classes, computer skills, and a women's support group of 16 sessions that includes such topics as eating healthy and managing money. The school provides free babysitting during some parent meetings. There is no parent center at the moment, and no citizenship courses are offered. School activities in place to involve parents in their children's education include Science Fair Night, SAAS family night, Math Night, and parent-teacher conferences (twice a year). The parent coordinator also sends monthly notices that provide parents with activities to do with their children at home.

The parent coordinator estimates that about 82 percent of the parents are actively involved in their child's education. She explains that after school and on weekends, the public library is full of parents and their children working on homework assignments or doing extra work.

Parents say that they feel welcome at the school because it has an open-door policy. They feel that, in general, most parents feel welcome and that parents are free to come and go as they please in their children's classrooms. They explain that they devote time in the evenings to helping their children do homework and describe how on Saturdays they go to the library to work on computers with their children or to borrow books. One woman who knows very little English comments, "When my daughter comes home from work, she helps her brothers and sisters with their homework. I make them study until she comes home. My child in kindergarten can read and although he brings me books to read to him, he reads to me."

All the parents in the focus group feel that the school is doing a good job of educating their children. They all agree that they expect their children to go to college. One woman observes, "It's more advanced this year than what it has been in the past." In response to the interviewer's comment about the increase in parent involvement this year, a parent agrees, and adds, "We have more activities than in previous years and more parents are coming to them."

The school has policies to encourage collaboration with business and industry in the community. The principal, because this is her first year and because of her focus on working with parents, has not devoted much time to developing these relationships, but the school has limited involvement with one or two local businesses and is hoping to develop more.

Why Rivera Is a Highly Effective School

Seven factors explain why Rivera is highly effective. First, the school (especially the principal) has high expectations for all students, regardless of socioeconomic background. Second, the school maintains discipline well and deals with student misbehavior quickly and effectively. Third, the principal is an effective and influential leader. Fourth, the teaching force is highly experienced and capable. Fifth, the school has an effective accountability and evaluation system. Sixth, the school uses the flexibility and autonomy granted by the district and state creatively. Seventh, parents are highly supportive of and involved in the school.

High Expectations for All Students. Ms. Baeza's determination to ensure that all children learn fuels her "no excuses" policy. This approach is a new one for the teachers at Rivera, and some are uncomfortable with it. She has insisted that teachers adapt their instructional techniques in the classroom to meet the learning needs of individual students. In the past, learning problems were addressed in after-school tutoring sessions, and it was difficult for students to attend because many were bused.

In general, teachers feel that they are responsible for the academic achievement of all children. As with other highly effective schools, students tend to be grouped by ability in reading but not in math or science. Teachers also acknowledge the benefits to learning of having students at different levels of proficiency in a classroom, and over half feel that this type of grouping is important to their view of education. They also feel that they have access to many resources for dealing with diversity. Students' responses reflect the principal's and teachers' expectations: all students in the focus groups are aware of the importance of going to college, know why they should go, and talk enthusiastically about their career plans.

Good Discipline. The discipline at Rivera is exemplary, and the principal attributes this to the fact that children have a place and a voice at the school. She also feels that the absence of behavior problems may be because there is no 6th grade. As with other highly effective schools, discipline problems are almost always handled in the classroom by the teachers, who attribute the students' good behavior to the life skills and character education classes offered by the school as well as to Rivera's small size. Teachers have telephones in their classrooms so they can communicate quickly and directly with parents; this, too, may contribute to the lack of behavior problems.

Effective Leadership. Although she has been at Rivera for less than a year, this principal seems to have exerted her influence in several critical areas in the school. For example, she has shifted the focus of school policy from benefiting teachers to serving students. In a short time, she has engineered a turnaround in parent involvement by opening up the school to parents and increasing parent activities. When the parent-home liaison expressed reluctance to visit students' homes, the principal replaced her with someone who was willing to do so. She has also worked with teachers to develop thematic units that integrate several subjects. Teachers in the focus group seem reluctant to acknowledge the principal's instructional leadership and state that it is too soon to tell whether she is an instructional leader. Nevertheless, 75 percent of teachers in the school respond that she has had a strong positive impact on their teaching.

A Capable Teaching Force. Teachers at Rivera are older, and a large percentage have more than five years of teaching experience. All are certified, and most have been teaching at Rivera for three or more years. They have received a considerable amount of professional development in mathematics and science and are satisfied with the amount and quality of the professional development offered to them. Professional development is cited as one of the most important influences on their instruction. Teachers also draw on one another as resources. A large percentage feels prepared to teach diverse groups of students, except immigrant students. They engage in considerable articulation planning, both cross-grade and within-grade. They also meet with the teachers at other schools in the feeder pattern to work on alignment.

These highly professional teachers are committed to providing quality instruction to their students. They are somewhat uncomfortable with the new direction in which the principal is taking the school, but have a "wait and see" attitude. If the principal's new policies result in increased achievement levels for students, these teachers will go along with them.

Effective Accountability/Evaluation System. The principal personally monitors student progress data regularly. If large gaps are observed among different groups of students, she looks into the reasons behind these gaps and works with teachers to address the reasons. For example, she identified a problem involving the length of time that it was taking LEP students to transition out of bilingual education and dealt with the problem by working with teachers and staff to put added emphasis on ESL instruction for these students.

Creative Use of Flexibility/Autonomy. Like the other highly effective schools in the Bolivar district, Rivera makes extensive use of supplemental materials in teaching mathematics and science. In addition, the principal encourages innovative instructional approaches such as the use of thematic units that integrate several subjects. Flexible use of instructional time supports these teaching methods.

Strong Parental Support and Involvement. Parental involvement has increased this year for the first time because of the new principal, who has made a Herculean effort to reach out to parents. About 70 percent of parents are actively involved in school activities. There is also a core group of committed parent volunteers, under the leadership of an unofficial parent coordinator, who assist teachers. The school offers translation services for non-English-speaking parents as well as programs for parents, including ESL classes, computer skills classes, and a women's support group. Parents say they feel welcome at the school because of its open-door policy.

Rufino Tamayo Elementary
A Typical School

I think that parents are afraid to come to this school.—Teacher

Rufino Tamayo Elementary School is located in the southern portion of Rios Calientes, very close to the Mexican border. This area contains a large, impoverished Latino population, many of whom are Mexican immigrants. The school's accountability rating was "recognized" in 2000–01. Tamayo has enjoyed a recognized rating since 1995–96, when it was classified as acceptable.

In 2000–01, there were 693 K–6 students at Tamayo. Most students (96.7 percent) were Latino, few were white (2.3 percent), and even fewer were African American (0.9 percent). About half (52.7 percent) were considered LEP, 10 percent were classified as requiring special education, and most (94.8 percent) were considered economically disadvantaged.[3] The school averaged a 12.4 percent mobility rate but a high attendance rate of 96.3 percent and only three disciplinary placements.

During 2000–01, there were 43 teachers. Of those, most (90.7 percent) were Latino and most (88.4 percent) were female. The average class size in K–4 was 18 students, and the average for grades 5 and 6 was 32 students.

Factors Related to Effectiveness

Several aspects of school climate and the absence of some enabling conditions contribute to Rufino Tamayo's lack of effectiveness.

School Climate

Tamayo Elementary School is located in a run-down block of concrete structures. The atmosphere is depressing, perhaps because of the dust that seems to have permeated every nook and cranny of the buildings, likely from the construction taking place nearby. Students are shabbily dressed and some have grubby faces. Upon arrival, the site visitors are informed that the principal, with whom they have made an appointment, is not in the building but that they will be able to interview the assistant principal, who has set up the site visit. The assistant principal states that the principal is leaving at the end of the school year and has been spending a lot of time on his new campus where a school is being constructed. "So that creates a strange climate." He adds, "There is a little bit of instability because of the changes that are taking place" and mentions that this principal is the second to leave the school in seven years. (Researchers were able to talk with the principal at a later date, and this case study incorporates comments from both the principal and the assistant principal.)

High Expectations for Students

The principal feels that the phrase "all children can learn" means that "every child is given the opportunity to learn and that every child is expected to do the work. . . . They should be able to reach their academic goals." When asked about their expectations that their students would attend college, teachers explain that a lot of the students at Tamayo are on welfare and their mothers do not work so they do not necessarily see the need to go to college in order to get a job. Says one teacher about students going to college, "That's our hope, but not according to the statistics." Another responds, "Most [students]? No." A third teacher is more optimistic; "All the teachers on campus push for that and we hope for that," she says.

Students, on the other hand, seem to realize that attending college will help them obtain jobs with higher salaries, and they are all very emphatic about it being important to go to college to make money. Says one, "You're not going to get anywhere if you don't go to college." Another student observes that "There are only a few jobs where you don't need to get a college degree—janitor or McDonald's." These students express the wish to support their parents when they are older, however, and feel that this might make going to college more difficult. They are all concerned about how much college costs. One student mentions saving all his birthday money for college. Asked whether they feel prepared to go to college, one student responds, "I think I will be very scared, but prepared." Another observes, "We will lose some friends." Parents seem to want their children to go to college and feel that the school is helpful in preparing them for this by introducing them to different careers. When asked about careers that interest them, students respond with a variety of jobs: psychologist, lawyer, basketball player, detective, secret service agent, wrestler, nurse, dermatologist.

Although class size in 1999–2000 in grades 1 and 2 had been 31 and 25, respectively, and above the 22-students-to-1-teacher state-imposed maximum, in 2000–01, those class sizes had been reduced to meet state requirements. When asked by the site visitor whether students are grouped by ability within the same classroom, the assistant principal acknowledges that

> In the old days we used to group students [by class] according to ability. Nowadays we don't do that any more. We put them . . . as the low, the middle, and high in the same classroom.

He goes on to explain, however, that reading classes are the exception: "With the reading program, we have children at different levels. . . . We have in some classes our resource students, so therefore you have to group them accordingly for the academics."

According to the assistant principal, the decision of how to group students is classroom-based and left to the teacher. In general, teachers speak positively about ability grouping. One teacher says, "We use a lot of cooperative learning and I have found that if you group them by ability they challenge each other and work harder." Another adds, "When you are teaching skills, it really has to be by ability grouping." Sixty-nine percent of teachers respond that they group students by academic ability; of these, 96 percent group students by ability for reading instruction, while fewer acknowledge grouping them for math or science instruction (38 and 17 percent, respectively). Over three-quarters of teachers who group say that decisions are made based on daily observation (79 percent) and standardized test scores (79 percent), while 38 percent use scores from tests they have created. Over half (56 percent) the teachers also feel that homogeneous grouping is important to their view of education, and a similar number say that they are able to implement this regularly in their classrooms.

Teachers are asked how they tailor instructional strategies to the cultural and linguistic needs of their students. Several respond that they draw on their knowledge of students' Latino background to make subjects more relevant to them. In the words of one teacher, "To make them engaged and so that they can identify with what you are teaching, it helps to know about their background. So I try to pick stories with a Hispanic background." Another comments that when teachers get their funding for books "we look for authors of books that would have topics that the kids would understand." The teachers feel that they receive a great deal of support and resources to meet the diverse needs of students. They feel that the USP has been especially helpful in assisting them in math and science as well as reading instruction. Says one teacher, "As far as resources go, they've [the USP] been incredible."

Order and Discipline

Mr. Gomez states that discipline "required some attention." In 1999–2000, the school had six incidents of vandalism and two incidents of theft on school property. The assistant principal explains, "Today children have television and a lot of things have changed. Now they're not afraid [to come to the principal's office]. So you have to find different ways of dealing with student behavior." The assistant principal, who enforces discipline on campus, states that he uses a book on classroom discipline and control and one on positive discipline in the classroom "a lot." He also shares articles on classroom management with teachers.

The main disciplinary measure at Tamayo is after-school detention for students who misbehave frequently. This is usually carried out on Fridays. Although there is a campus liaison who makes home visits to children's homes, the assistant principal explains that if a child becomes a "continuous problem," then he will call the parents in and, if necessary, make a home visit himself. The school may also make a referral to the child guidance center.

The teachers feel that students are fairly well behaved in the classroom when they are under teachers' direct control, but outside the classroom, in the words of one teacher, "that's a different story." Another teacher adds about the "bad kids," "They are very defiant. . . . They could care less if you punish them." Another supports this view, "Kids [here] don't fear discipline."

Teachers give several reasons for the behavior problems in the school. One teacher observes, "Some parents act badly in school as well and their kids see that as acceptable since their parents are doing it." Another says, "Central office acts without talking with teachers and does whatever the parents want, which sends a bad message to the parents."

Students agree that their fellow students are disruptive and not learning and "just joke around." One student says about fellow students, "Most kids are bad." Another says, "When we have substitutes, kids just go crazy and start saying bad words."

Organized Curriculum

Like all the schools in the Bolivar district (and statewide), Tamayo follows the requirements of the state standards in designing its curriculum. According to the assistant principal, "The state plays a tremendous role [in determining the curriculum]. We try to follow the state standards as much as we can." The school uses the services of a private professional development provider in math, and several teachers have gone through that training. Teachers meet as a team to determine subject area needs and, in the words of the assistant principal, "how we're going to deal with them." He comments that the campus action plan focuses on different objectives at each grade level; a focus this year is to "cover science more" because the SAAS will begin to include a science test in future years. He is uncertain about what math and science textbooks the school is using, but says that new textbooks are being used.

The assistant principal states that teachers at Tamayo generally use supplementary materials in teaching math and science. He states that they are "allowed" to use their own supplementary materials and that "sometimes people use [materials made by a private professional development provider]" as well as other programs such as *Math Your Way*. He adds, "You can't only use one program; you should be allowed to use other activities." Almost all Tamayo teachers (91 percent) use some type of supplementary materials for math instruction, with a large majority of teachers (84 percent) saying that they use their own supplementary materials and a smaller percentage (50 percent) saying that they use supplementary math materials made by other teachers. Of those who use supplementary science materials, 75 percent say that they use their own materials, while 50 percent use supplementary materials made by other teachers. Over half of all teachers (61 percent), however, say that they use no supplemental materials in teaching science.

Enabling Conditions

Enabling conditions evident at Rivera seem to be absent from Tamayo. For example, the principal is not seen by teachers as an instructional leader. Although the school has capable, committed teachers, they are dissatisfied with the principal's leadership and feel that access to professional development is inequitable. Parents express dissatisfaction with the amount and frequency of information they receive from the school on their children's academic progress. Finally, student participation in extracurricular activities is reportedly low, which the principal attributes to lack of a sports program. Parent involvement in school activities is also low, and parents do not see the school as a welcoming place.

Effective Leadership

The principal, Mr. Gomez, has had his position for four years. He will be leaving for another principalship at the end of the school year and is the second principal to leave Tamayo in seven years. According to the assistant principal (who has been at the school for seven years), the principal "spends 90 percent of his time there where they're constructing [his new] school. So, basically, I'm acting as principal here and doing whatever needs to be done."

Mr. Gomez, a Latino, holds a master's degree with specializations in art, elementary education, and educational administration. He describes himself as "very involved" in determining the curriculum and supervising teachers, "involved" in determining the time spent on academic tasks, and "somewhat involved" in setting policy on class size and grouping. He describes his leadership style as collegial and leading by consensus, but he also solicits advice from his staff, while accepting sole responsibility for final decisions.

Mr. Gomez describes his role as that of guiding "the instruction, to make sure that the instruction is going on and that teachers are teaching what is mandated by the state, which is the state standards. Also, to facilitate learning and to make sure that the children meet the objectives." The assistant principal and principal share the task of supervising teachers. According to the assistant principal, they make regular visits to the classrooms using a classroom visitation log. They also conduct walk-throughs. The assistant principal comments that the district stressed a lot of going into the classrooms and getting more involved with the programs and the curriculum. It's not like it used to be where you're just an administrator sitting in an office. Now it's more that you're an instructional leader because they want you to be able to know what is going on in the classroom.

Teachers seem to agree that the principal is not an instructional leader. According to one teacher,

> I can't count how many times the principal has said, "If you need it, ask me." However, I do not feel that he is knowledgeable about curriculum. He could not come into my room and teach my guided reading group. He couldn't tell me whether I was doing a good job or not, but that really doesn't bother me.

Another teacher mentions that when they are asked on their evaluations how effective they are, teachers know that the principal has no idea what that means, so they feel they have the right to question him. None of the teachers in the focus group feel that the principal has any influence on the way they teach. This is echoed by survey responses for all teachers, with less than half (41 percent) responding that the principal has had a strong positive impact on their instruction.

The principal cites several leaders in the school: the assistant principal, department chairpersons, team leaders, senior-level teachers, and teachers in general. According to the teachers, teachers are the primary leaders in the school, together with the literacy leader.

The principal ensures that the school's academic goals are communicated via speeches and presentations to students and staff by the principal and others; written communications that go out to parents, teachers, and staff; and through the campus action plan. He feels that the school's academic goals have a strong influence on the process of establishing the curriculum, budgets, school staffing, staff development plans, and policies on ability grouping of students.

Capable Teaching Force

Tamayo has a teaching force of 35 teachers who teach math and/or science. A great majority (32, or 91 percent) are female and 86 percent (or 30) are Latino, with 11 percent (or 4) being white and 3 percent (or 1) responding "other." One-third of the teachers are 41 to 45 years old, with the second-largest percentage (21 percent) in the 36–40 age range. Most (65 percent) have children, and only three (9 percent) live in the area surrounding Rios Calientes. Well over half (66 percent) grew up in the Rios

Calientes area, and 65 percent speak fluent Spanish. A large proportion (86 percent) holds bachelor's degrees in elementary education. Three have bachelor's degrees in a science field, three in math education, and one in science education. Twenty-six percent (9) hold master's degrees, with four in elementary education, and one each in math education, science education, administration, computer science, and medical technology. A large majority (86 percent) have had three or more years of teaching experience. One teacher is uncertified and none are emergency certified. The average amount of teaching experience is 12.5 years. Eighty-three percent have been teaching at Tamayo for three or more years, with an average time spent at the school of 11 years.

The factors that at least one-quarter of teachers considered "very important" in influencing their decisions to teach at Tamayo are that its educational philosophy reflects their own (33 percent), the professional development opportunities (30 percent), and that they were selected for the position (33 percent). Of teachers who have children, 18 percent say that their children have attended Tamayo.

In discussing the characteristics and skills that he looks for when hiring teachers, Mr. Gomez states that, "A teacher first of all needs to be a caring individual who really cares about each individual child." He also looks for flexibility, the ability to work in diverse situations and adapt to change. Motivation, willingness to learn and to give their best as far as instruction is concerned are other desired qualities, as is the ability to deliver instruction to meet the needs of individual students and to be able to work with parents and the community to meet the needs of children. The principal responds in the survey that his hiring criterion for teachers is that they be student centered. He also responds that in terms of a required math and science background and experience for hiring teachers, he looks for basic knowledge of the state standards.

The principal states that last year, 95 percent of teachers spent at least 10 or more hours on staff development focused on mathematics, and 40 percent of teachers received the equivalent hours of development in science. According to the assistant principal, teachers receive training in math instruction via a private professional development provider; the district also provides a considerable amount of professional development activities in mathematics and science, as does the USP. The teachers admit that there are a lot of different professional development resources. One teacher observes, "The principal is always willing to facilitate teachers going to a professional development activity." Teachers believe, however, that access to professional development opportunities is not equitable. They comment that the principal picks the same people over and over. They also feel that the professional development that they have received is a mixed bag in terms of usefulness. In the words of one teacher, "Sometimes they have been useful and sometimes not. Sometimes you are absent too many days from the classroom. You can fall behind—this is hard on teachers and students."

Teachers at Tamayo seem genuinely committed to students, as exemplified by their willingness to hold tutoring sessions for students who need academic assistance. According to the assistant principal, although teachers are paid to tutor two days a week, many of them offer tutoring daily without additional pay. Some of them tutor in the morning because they feel that children are more awake than in the afternoon. Saturday sessions are also conducted by the teachers.

Students say that their teachers are very helpful and understanding. On tests if there are questions the students do not understand, the teacher tells them to put a star next to the question and when the tests are returned, the teacher gives them individual help with the question. Says one student about her teacher, "She doesn't tell us the answer, but she helps us understand the answer." Unfortunately though, the students explain that when kids are misbehaving in class, the teacher gets mad and does not help anyone.

A large proportion of teachers at Tamayo feels prepared to teach to state (60 percent) and district (74 percent) math standards. On the other hand, a much smaller percentage feels prepared to teach to state (18 percent) and district (24 percent) science standards. Over half respond that they feel prepared to teach students from different socioeconomic status groups (77 percent) and recent immigrant students (69 percent), and to overcome societal stereotypes about girls and Hispanics and math and science (66 and 65 percent, respectively). Half say that they feel prepared to overcome stereotypes about African American students and students with disabilities and math and science.

A large percentage of teachers reports interacting often with other teachers at their school to obtain advice or brainstorm (71 percent) and share resources (83 percent) About half (54 percent) report interacting often with other teachers in the school to do joint projects, while smaller proportions report interacting with others often for team teaching (34 percent) or planning (46 percent).

Teachers report that the major strong positive influences on their teaching are districtwide grade-level tests (73 percent), district and state curriculum frameworks (69 and 83 percent, respectively), state and district standards (74 and 70 percent, respectively), parent expectations (79 percent), and expectations for student skills (86 percent).

Accountability/Evaluation System

The school follows the district requirement that parents receive a report of student progress every three weeks and report cards every six weeks. Parent-teacher conferences are held twice a year. When asked what the school does beyond the district requirement to monitor and report student progress, the assistant principal at Tamayo replies,

> Just constant monitoring of the students' grades and if a child is not progressing then the teacher will intervene. If the teacher is not successful in communicating with the parents, she will be brought in. It's then part of my job to call the parents in and set up a conference.

He goes on to say that all the teachers now have a telephone in the classroom to encourage their communication with parents. (Parents complain, however, that they do not feel that they are receiving sufficient information from the school if there are problems with their children's academic progress.) The principal reports that information from the monitoring process is used by the school to update the curriculum, improve instructional practices, evaluate teachers, involve parents in their children's education, make decisions regarding the budget, and make staffing decisions.

According to the principal, the school monitors student progress and the progress of classes daily. It monitors the progress of the entire school monthly. Student progress is monitored by periodic reports that teachers submit to the principal. Measures of student progress include student in-class performance, grade point average, and class assessments. The assistant principal comments that because over 90 percent of students are Latino, the school does not look at achievement/performance gaps by race or ethnicity. Neither is differential performance by sex considered an issue by the school.

Economics and social class, however, *is* an issue. As the assistant principal avers, "We are surrounded by public housing projects, and more than half of our kids come from there. You have to look at the economics." He also admits that LEP status and disability status are taken into account by the school in considering achievement gaps. He describes some attempts by the school to improve the gap due to differences in socioeconomic status among the students. Because most students who come from the nearby projects have academic problems, the school has established tutoring programs both on site and off site. One program, "Tareas," is located in one of the housing projects and run by the school counselor during after-school hours. Monday through Thursday, students are able to go to Tareas after school to do homework. The school also offers tutoring classes throughout the week after school at the school site. These sessions are run by teachers and, although the school pays for the tutoring sessions on Tuesdays and Thursdays, many teachers offer tutoring daily during the week and on Saturdays.

Flexibility and Autonomy

Both the principal and the assistant principal feel that the school has enough flexibility and autonomy to operate effectively. Additional materials and programs are used to supplement the official textbooks mandated by the state and district. The school has also been free to establish policies and practices on ability grouping, the use of instructional time, professional development, extracurricular programs for students and parents, and community involvement activities.

Mr. Gomez feels that teachers have quite a bit of influence "as far as instruction and things of that nature." He feels that much of the staff development, for example, is teacher-generated. Responding to the principal survey, Mr. Gomez says the teachers have a great deal of influence in establishing the curriculum, and moderate influence in determining content of staff development, grouping students, determining the schedule, hiring new staff, planning budgets, and acquiring educational technology. They have, in his opinion, little influence in determining professional and teaching assignments. The assistant principal observes that teacher influence is enhanced by their presence on different committees, "whether it be curriculum or discipline" that report to the campus improvement council. When queried, teachers feel that they are given as much freedom as they need. Their responses to the survey seem to indicate that they perceive themselves as having less control over the curriculum than the principal feels they have, with 49 percent responding that they have no control over the curriculum or texts and 43 percent responding that they have partial control.

Instructional Time

As with all schools in the Bolivar district, Tamayo is allowed almost total autonomy in how it apportions instructional time among subjects. According to the assistant principal, the decision on how subjects are covered is made by teachers in teacher-led grade-level meetings "to decide how much they are going to cover and what are some of the areas that they need to key into." A representative of each grade level is then appointed to give input in cross-grade-level meetings to align the coverage across grades. These decisions, however, must be justified to the district and must be keyed to the school's campus action plan.

At Tamayo, math is taught five days a week, with about one-third (31 percent) of classes lasting 75–90 minutes and about one-quarter (29 percent) lasting 45–60 minutes. On average, science is taught four days a week, with almost half of science classes (42 percent) lasting 15–30 minutes and about one-third (29 percent) lasting 30–45 minutes.

School days run seven hours for five days a week. There are no early dismissal days in the school week, and the school year is 178 days.

Opportunities for Student Participation

The principal calculates that between 31 and 50 percent of all students participate in extracurricular activities in Tamayo. He responds that the school offers intramural sports, a school newspaper/yearbook, student government, art/music/dance/drama activities, a science fair, and cheerleading. The assistant principal feels that Tamayo has a low level of student participation in extracurricular activities and attributes it to the fact that the school does not offer sports. It is one of the few elementary schools in the district, however, with a cheerleader program. The school offers some academically oriented activities such as a reading program. A Spanish-language program is also offered, as is a science fair where each child is required to compete and to have a science project. The assistant principal states that the cheerleading program is the most successful.

The school also offers extensive tutoring both at the school site and in a nearby housing project (Tareas). Students in focus groups are involved in storytelling competitions, spelling bee, band, and intramurals. They seem to enjoy these activities and express the wish for more, especially sports activities.

Support from Parents and the Community

Although the school has policies to encourage parent participation in school activities, the principal estimates that only 30 percent of parents participated regularly in school activities in school year 1999–2000. The parent coordinator, however, estimates the percentage to be between 35 and 50 percent, although teacher survey data and teacher comments suggest that this estimate is inflated. About 10 percent of parents are volunteers.

Although the school does not have a PTA, it does have a parent coordinator, who is in charge of recruiting volunteers and running outreach programs for parents. According to the parent coordinator (who has been home liaison for eight years and parent coordinator for about five years) the school offers parenting and nutrition programs, "things that will help them to be better parents." These include district-sponsored programs such as Ready to be Ready (a program that helps parents prepare preschool children for school) and a father-parenting program that is in the works cosponsored by the Child Crisis Center to help fathers participate in the lives of their children. There is also a literacy club, and parents participate in other USP-sponsored activities as well. In addition, there are ESL and citizenship classes for parents and the community. Although the parent center, which is in a mobile unit at a fair distance from the main school building, was established just a year ago, the school has sponsored parent activities for 10 years. The school sends out flyers in Spanish and English to alert parents to upcoming activities and programs.

The parent coordinator sees her role as trying to "get people to feel comfortable coming in [to the school], providing security for them, and having them know that there's something they can do here at school that will help them have a better relationship with their kids." She acknowledges that there have been difficulties in getting parents to come to school-sponsored activities, but attributes some of this to the fact that many parents are afraid to walk through the low-income housing projects adjacent to the school. The principal has provided buses on some occasions to increase the participation of parents, but this has not been entirely successful. She also mentions that a lot of parents in the community are required to attend school because of welfare requirements and that this cuts into their time.

Asked how involved parents at the school are in their children's education, the parent coordinator responds, "I think that we could have a little more personal involvement on the part of parents with their children. . . . Personally, I would like to see more parents involved." She feels that many parents do not have the ability to help their children. "They feel lost," she concludes. She also feels that parents feel intimidated because they cannot speak English and because they are single mothers on welfare and feel overwhelmed. She feels that involving parents is a high priority at the school because "If our parents don't know what's going on in school, how are we going to help our kids?"

Teachers feel that for the school as a whole, it is difficult to get parents involved and that the school is not successful at this. One teacher comments, "I think that parents are afraid to come to this school." Another observes, "They are embarrassed." A third teacher explains, "It's not a safe place for them." The most prevalent strategies used by teachers at Tamayo to involve parents are contacting parents (81 percent), open houses (78 percent), written communications (70 percent), and discussing students informally (94 percent). Over half the teachers say that no parents are involved in volunteering in their classrooms, and 61 percent say that less than 10 percent of parents go on field trips, although two-thirds say that over 50 percent of parents attend their teacher-parent conferences.

Parents who participated in the focus groups are some of the more actively involved parents in the school. Some are volunteers who help teachers in their classrooms. When asked how welcome they feel when they come to the school, however, one parent responds, "Well, sometimes it's really good and sometimes it's not. It depends on which teacher you encounter." Another parent explains, "It's just the front office that's unfriendly, but the teachers are fine." Several parents agree that teachers are helpful and willing to make time after school to talk with them. Many parents also give examples of how they help their children by monitoring their homework compliance, reading with them, and helping them with their science projects.

When asked whether they are satisfied with the information they receive from the school on their children's progress, parents express dissatisfaction. One parent observes, "Sometimes we do [get information] and sometimes we don't." Another complains,

> [The school] really should communicate a little more with us because even though we have [our kids] in the house, we don't really know how they're doing in the classroom until the third week. They say it's up to us to come and ask, but as far as them communicating with us, that doesn't happen.

Another parent adds to general agreement and laughter, "I think we would be happy with getting a report every week." Parents agree that the school seems to wait three weeks before letting them know about problems.

In general, parents feel that their children could do better than they are doing at Tamayo, although they are not very dissatisfied. They feel that the school is basically the same as other schools in the district. Says one parent, "It depends on the teacher you get, but what they learn is pretty much the same." They do seem to feel, however, that recently Tamayo has made more of an effort to reach out to parents.

In speaking of school-community collaborative efforts, the assistant principal observes that the school has a volunteer program with parents, "but not much else." He adds, however, that a Partners in Education program involves Martin's and Southwest Airlines as well as an Audie Murphy Club with the soldiers from a nearby army base mentoring students. But there does not seem to be much activity generated by these collaborative efforts, according to the assistant principal, who comments, "The ones who were here have left and new ones have come in who have just started. So they wouldn't know very much about it [collaborative efforts]."

Why Tamayo Is a Typical School

Tamayo is a typical school because it has lower student expectations, ineffective discipline, poor leadership, dissatisfied teachers, and an ineffective accountability and evaluation system. The school also fails to use the autonomy and flexibility granted by the district and state to improve instruction, and it does a poor job of involving parents and the community in school activities.

Lower Student Expectations. The principal, in explaining his view of the phrase "all children can learn," seems to imply that once students are given the opportunity to learn, the responsibility for learning is up to them. Teachers at Tamayo do not seem to feel that students could be expected to go to college because of their low socioeconomic status and the example given to them by their mothers (who, teachers claim, are on welfare). Students and their parents, nevertheless, seem to have high—albeit somewhat unrealistic—aspirations about going to college. The assistant principal acknowledges that students are grouped by ability within the classroom. Teachers, too, feel that grouping by "academic ability" is beneficial, especially in reading. Over half report that homogeneous grouping is important to their view of education. The school offers extensive opportunities for students to receive academic assistance in the form of tutoring.

Ineffective Discipline. The discipline at Tamayo is problematic and, according to the principal, "required some attention." This school reports many more acts of vandalism than most other schools in the sample. Teachers, while agreeing that students are fairly well behaved in the classroom, feel that once away from teachers' direct control, students tend to behave badly. The teachers complain about a core group of "bad kids" who do not fear discipline. Teachers attribute much of the disciplinary problems in the school to the fact that the school administration does not involve the teachers in discipline decisions and tends to side with the parents.

Poor Leadership. The principal at Tamayo, who plans to leave the school by the end of the academic year, seems to have made the transition already. According to the assistant principal, the principal is rarely at the school, preferring to spend his time supervising the construction of the school where he will be transferring in the fall. (Despite making an appointment to meet with the site visitors, he is not at the school when the visitors arrive.) The assistant principal has taken over most of the principal's responsibilities and does not seem pleased about it. The absence of the principal and the fact that the leadership of the school has changed twice in seven years make for a rather unstable environment at Tamayo. Although the principal sees himself as an instructional leader, teachers do not. They do not respect his knowledge of the curriculum or what constitutes good instruction. Few teachers in the school feel that the principal has had a strong positive impact on their instruction.

Dissatisfied Teachers. Although teachers at Tamayo are not notably less prepared than teachers in the highly effective schools, they are definitely less satisfied. Their dissatisfaction with the quality of the principal's leadership is discussed above. They also complain that although a lot of professional development resources are available, access to these opportunities is not equitable because the principal plays favorites. Teachers seem genuinely committed to their students, however, and a large proportion feel prepared to deal with diversity in the classroom— except African American students and students with disabilities. Teachers are also dissatisfied with the way the school administration handles discipline and with the low level of parent involvement (which they attribute to lack of effort on the part of the administration).

Ineffective Accountability/Evaluation System. The school does nothing in addition to complying with the district requirement for reporting on student progress. Parents complain that they do not receive sufficient and timely information from the school if there are problems with their children's academic progress.

Failure to Use Flexibility and Autonomy to Improve Instruction. Tamayo does little in addition to following the state and district mandates for curriculum, instruction, reporting procedures, and so on. In most areas where flexibility and autonomy is allowed, the school does not take advantage of the opportunities to improve the educational environment and offerings for students, although most teachers use supplementary instructional materials in math.

Poor Parent and Community Involvement. The school has a low level of parent involvement: a little under one-third of parents participate regularly in school activities. A low percentage of parents are involved in volunteer activities. Although Tamayo has a parent coordinator (but no PTA) and offers a number of parent programs, parents do not feel entirely welcome at the school. They fault the front office with being unfriendly, but say that the teachers are approachable and cooperative. Parents are also dissatisfied with the information they receive from the school on their children's progress and feel that their children could do better than they are doing at Tamayo. The school has very little involvement with the community.

Notes

1. Defeated by Demographics: Are Poor, Urban Schools Doomed to Failure?

1. The term "Latino" will be used interchangeably with "Hispanic" throughout the book.

2. Large and mid-sized city schools enroll 51 percent and 47 percent, respectively, of African American and Latino students.

3. The National Education Longitudinal Study of 1988 is a survey of a nationally representative sample of 8th graders first surveyed in spring 1988 and resurveyed through four follow-ups in 1990, 1992, 1994, and 2000. On the survey, students reported on a range of topics including school, work, home experiences, educational resources and support, educational and occupational aspirations, and other perceptions.

4. See Reynolds and Teddlie (2000); Scheerens and Bosker (1997); and Wang, Haertel, and Walberg (1993).

5. All schools tended to have above-average enrollments of English language learners, students from low-income families, and students whose parents were not high school graduates.

6. Most of these problems echo weaknesses identified by Purkey and Smith (1983).

7. For example, see Anderson and Pellicer (1998); Brookover and Lezotte (1979); Ellis (1975); Kannapel and Clements (2005); New York State Office of Education (1974); Phi Delta Kappa (1980); Snipes et al. (2002); Stringfield et al. (1993); Teddlie and Stringfield (1993); Venezky and Winfield (1979); Weber (1971); and Wilder (1977).

8. See, for example, Rothstein (2004).

9. See Fouts (2003) and Snipes et al. (2002). Fouts (2003) identifies effective practices of classrooms, schools, and districts in his review of studies of educational reform in Washington State.

10. See, for example, Bell (2001); Carter (2000); Cudeiro et al. (2005); Jesse, Davis, and Pokorny (2004); Kannapel and Clements (2005); Mid-Continent Research for Education and Learning (2005); and Ragland et al. (2002).

2. Highly Effective versus Typical Schools: How the Exception Contradicts the Rule

1. For descriptions of these pitfalls, see Purkey and Smith (1983); Rowan et al. (1983); Rosenholtz (1985); and Stringfield (1994).

2. Heneveld and Craig (1995) opt to consider contextual factors, including institutional, cultural, political, and economic influences, as exogenous factors because they feel that educators have little influence on factors outside the school.

3. All district and school names are pseudonyms.

4. Taken from the Stanford Achievement Test series 9th edition technical data report (San Antonio: Harcourt Brace Educational Measurement, 1997).

5. As noted previously, Rios Calientes comprises three very similar districts.

3. Cumberland City: Coping with Population Change

1. Data on Cumberland City, the Cumberland City school district, and participating schools were from official sources. Where naming these sources would have compromised the confidentiality of the city, the district, or the participating schools, they have not been included.

2. These quotes, and all subsequent quotes in the chapter, are taken from the Cumberland City district and cluster administrative interviews and teacher interviews.

3. Each student who did not take the test was counted in the total as having a score of 0. This made it advantageous for the school to test even the lowest-achieving students.

4. These quotes are taken from the Cumberland City School District Teacher Evaluation form, last updated January 2000.

5. The Cumberland City school district broke the SAT9 category "below basic" into three levels: below basic I, II, and III.

4. What Makes Some Cumberland City Schools Highly Effective?

1. This analysis uses data from the case studies and the teacher and principal surveys. Tests of statistically significance were performed over the teacher surveys, and results are reported only when the difference is at least at the 0.05 level. The numbers of principals and schools included in the study were too small for statistical significance testing to be performed.

2. The discussion of principals from highly effective and typical schools includes the principal from the formerly effective school (Andrew Jackson) in limited ways. She was the only principal with whom an interview could not be conducted. In addition, there was some question of the accuracy of her survey responses. The principal, who is no longer with the school, was unavailable to clarify discrepancies.

3. Across the district, approximately 12 percent of teachers have emergency certifications.

4. To increase the amount of time for professional development, individual schools can vote to "bank time." To bank time, the school day is extended by six minutes with a

vote of 75 percent of the faculty. When 2–3 hours are accumulated, the school dismisses students early and uses the time for professional development or planning.

5. "Success for All" is a comprehensive restructuring program for elementary schools based on the following principles: emphasis on prevention, early and intensive intervention, and tutoring for students with academic difficulties; incorporation of state-of-the-art curriculum and instructional methods; emphasis on the integration of phonics and meaning-focused instruction, cooperative learning, and curriculum-based assessments; writing/language arts instruction emphasizing writer's workshops; preschool/kindergarten instruction with storytelling and language development; adaptations for Spanish and English as a second language; a family support program engaging parents, community members, and integrated services; and extensive professional development throughout the elementary grades. See http://www.successforall.net/elementary/sfa.htm.

6. The Accelerated Schools Project is a schoolwide program that involves restructuring the school organization, curriculum, and instruction. Its goal is to help all students achieve their academic, social, and physical potential and perform at age-appropriate grade levels by the end of 6th grade. Dr. Henry Levin developed the program in 1986 with his colleagues at Stanford University to accelerate the achievement of at-risk students. More than 700 schools, including a network of elementary and middle schools in Illinois, have replicated the program. School staff and parents share in the decisionmaking and in the responsibility for helping students excel. Instruction builds on the strengths and cultures of students. It emphasizes interdisciplinary approaches that engage learners in real-world tasks and problem solving. See http://www.ncrel.org/sdrs/areas/issues/students/atrisk/at6lk46.htm.

5. Rios Calientes: Responding to NAFTA

1. Data on Rios Calientes as well as on the three participating districts and eight schools are from official sources. Where naming these sources might compromise the anonymity of the city, the districts, or the schools, pseudonymous data sources are cited.

2. The Rios Calientes MSA is a single-county MSA composed entirely of Rios Calientes County.

3. Taken from the Rios Calientes Economic Adjustment Strategic Plan.

4. Taken from "Borderplex Economic Outlook: 1999–2001."

5. Taken from the U.S. Bureau of Economic Analysis web site, http://www.bea.gov/index.html.

6. These names are pseudonyms.

7. Another pseudonym.

8. This quote, and all subsequent quotes in the chapter, are taken from the Rios Calientes–area district staff interviews and site-visit reports.

9. In contrast to bilingual education, which involves the use of English and another language in each class session, dual-language classes offer classes conducted exclusively in one of two languages per class, on an alternating basis.

10. The textbook with the most votes becomes the district textbook.

11. The state has three labels that can be stamped on a student's high school diploma: minimum, recommended, and distinguished.

6. What Makes Some Rios Calientes Schools Highly Effective?

1. In the sense that they have the required certifications and years of teaching experience.

2. Because the individual districts do not play a large role in determining school practice and had very similar policies, for simplicity's sake we will refer to the combination of all three as the "Rios Calientes" districts.

3. Unless noted specifically, all quantitative differences reported in teacher survey responses are statistically significant at least at the .05 level. Statistical significance was not calculated for differences found in principal survey responses because the sample size was too small for this calculation to be meaningful.

4. One exception is Mr. Cortez at Castellanos Elementary School (a typical school), who has a master's degree in linguistics and no previous experience in elementary education.

5. This difference is not statistically significant. Both types of schools have at least 95 percent of all teachers with required certification. Each group of teachers has an average 13 years of experience.

6. Differences in teacher responses regarding autonomy and control over the last three aspects of schooling—assessments, daily schedules, and professional development— are not statistically significant.

7. It is interesting to note that there are no differences by school type in terms of the percentage of teachers who reside in the Rios Calientes community (residency rates range from 84 to 91 percent overall).

8. These differences are not statistically significant.

9. The role of the district(s) as described in the previous chapter is relatively minor. The districts in this study tend to be highly decentralized at the school level with strong policy dictates at the state level.

7. Lessons Learned and What They May Mean for Educational Reform

1. In the authors' words, transformational leadership "provides intellectual direction and aims at innovating within the organization while empowering and supporting teachers as partners in decision making" (371).

2. See, for example, Ferguson (1998); Goldhaber, Brewer, and Anderson (1999); Hanushek, Kain, and Rivkin (2002); Jordan, Mendro, and Weerasinghe (1997); Sanders and Rivers (1996); and Wright, Horn, and Sanders (1997).

3. Since most district students are eligible for free- and reduced-priced lunches, including over 90 percent of the students in the study, district definitions of low income are more stringent and are based on several variables including welfare and food-stamp eligibility.

Appendix A. Sample Cumberland City Case Studies

1. Surveys were received from the principal and 40 staff, including 34 classroom teachers. The principal was interviewed, as were seven teachers, nine students, two parents,

the custodian, and three small learning community coordinators. School information found in this case study appendix has been provided primarily through these surveys, focus groups, and interviews, as well as from web sites and other documentation.

2. Cumberland City does not use eligibility for free and reduced-price lunches as a measure of low income. The city has a more stringent definition closely tied to eligibility for welfare.

3. "Success for All" is a comprehensive restructuring program for elementary schools. For more information, see note 5 in chapter 4.

4. Changes in the 2001 SSA make that year's scores not comparable to other years.

5. Normally, SAT9 scores are reported as advanced, proficient, basic, and below basic. In Cumberland City, below basic has been broken into three areas: below basic I (the lowest level), below basic II, and below basic III.

6. Surveys were received from the principal and 51 staff, of whom 48 were classroom teachers. The principal was interviewed, as were 5 teachers, 4 SLC coordinators, 6 students, 1 parent, the custodian, and the parent coordinator. School information found in this case study has been provided primarily through these surveys, focus groups, and interviews, as well as from web sites and other documentation.

7. Cumberland City does not use eligibility for free and reduced-price lunches as a measure of low income. The city has a more stringent definition closely tied to eligibility for welfare.

8. Normally, SAT9 scores are reported as advanced, proficient, basic, and below basic. In Cumberland City, below basic has been broken into three areas: below basic I (the lowest level), below basic II, and below basic III.

9. Under time banking, schools extend the school day by six minutes and bank the extra time to be used for professional development and other staff activities.

Appendix B. Sample Rios Calientes Case Studies

1. The accountability ratings were as follows: 2000–01, Recognized with additional acknowledgement in mathematics; 1999–2000, Exemplary with additional acknowledgement in reading; 1998–99, Recognized; 1997–98, Recognized; 1996–97, Acceptable; 1995–96, Acceptable.

2. The classification of economically disadvantaged is based on numbers of students eligible for free or reduced-price lunches.

3. The classification of economically disadvantaged is based on numbers of students eligible for free or reduced-price lunches.

References

Anderson, Bernice, Patricia B. Campbell, Yolanda George, Eric Jolly, Jane Butler Kahle, Nancy Kreinberg, Julio Lopez-Ferrao, and Gwendolyn Taylor. 1998. *Infusing Equity into Systemic Reform: An Implementation Scheme.* Arlington, VA: National Science Foundation.

Anderson, Lorin W., and Leonard O. Pellicer. 1998. "Toward an Understanding of Unusually Successful Programs for Economically Disadvantaged Students." *Journal of Education for Students Placed at Risk* 3(3): 237–63.

Baron, Rueben, David H. Tom, and Harris M. Cooper. 1985. "Social Class, Race and Teacher Expectations." In *Teacher Expectancies,* edited by J. B. Dusek (251–69). Hillsdale, NJ: Lawrence Erlbaum.

Bell, Jennifer A. 2001. "High-Performing, High-Poverty Schools Are Distinguished by Their Strength of Leadership and Their Understanding of How Children Learn." *Leadership* 31(1): 8–11.

Brookover, Wilbur B., and Lawrence W. Lezotte. 1979. *Changes in School Characteristics Coincident with Changes in Student Achievement.* East Lansing: College of Urban Development, Michigan State University.

Brookover, Wilbur B., Charles Beady, Patricia Flood, John Schweitzer, and Joe Wisenbaker. 1979. *School Social Systems and Student Achievement: Schools Can Make a Difference.* New York: Praeger.

Brophy, Jere E., and Thomas L. Good. 1986. "Teacher Behavior and Student Achievement." In *Handbook of Research on Teaching, 3rd edition,* edited by Merlin C. Wittrock (328–75). New York: MacMillan.

Campbell, Patricia B., Joseph Harris, and Norman Webb. 1998. *What Works for Whom? A Research Agenda to Inform Systemic Reform Efforts to Improve Mathematics and Science Achievement for All Students.* Groton, MA: Campbell-Kibler Associates, Inc.

Carnoy, Martin, and Susanna Loeb. 2002. "Does External Accountability Affect Student Outcomes? A Cross-State Analysis." *Educational Evaluation and Policy Analysis* 24(4): 305–31.

Carter, Samuel C. 2000. *No Excuses: Lessons from 21 High-Performing, High-Poverty Schools.* Washington, DC: The Heritage Foundation.

Casserly, Michael. 2005. *Beating the Odds: A City-by-City Analysis of Student Performance and Achievement Gaps on State Assessments.* Washington, DC: Council of the Great City Schools.

Charles A. Dana Center. 1999. *Hope for Urban Education: A Study of Nine High-Performing, High-Poverty Urban Elementary Schools.* Austin: Charles A. Dana Center, University of Texas at Austin.

Clewell, Beatriz Chu, Michael Puma, and Sharon McKay. 2005. "Does It Matter If My Teacher Looks Like Me? The Impact of Teacher Race and Ethnicity on Student Academic Achievement." Paper presented at a Presidential-Invited Session of the American Educational Research Association 2005 Annual Meeting, Montreal, Quebec, April 14.

Coleman, James S., Ernest Q. Campbell, Carol J. Hobson, James McPartland, Alexander M. Mood, Frederic D. Weinfeld, and Robert L. York. 1966. *Equality of Educational Opportunity.* Washington, DC: U.S. Department of Health, Education, and Welfare.

Creemers, Bert, Rob de Jong, F. Javier Murillo, Pentti Nikkanen, Jaap Scheerens, Louise Stoll, and Felicity Wikeley. 2001. *A Framework for School Improvement.* Groningen, The Netherlands: GION, Institute for Educational Research, University of Groningen.

Cudeiro, Amalia, Joe Palumbo, Jan Leight, and Jeff Nelsen. 2005. "Six Schools that Make a Difference." *Leadership* 35(2): 18–19.

Darling-Hammond, Linda. 2000. "Teacher Quality and Student Achievement: A Review of State Policy Evidence." *Education Policy Analysis Archives* 8(1).

Dee, Thomas S. 2001. "Teachers, Race, and Student Achievement in a Randomized Experiment." Working Paper 8,432. Cambridge, MA: National Bureau of Economic Research.

Edmonds, Ronald R. 1979. "Effective Schools for the Urban Poor." *Educational Leadership* 37(1): 15–27.

Education Trust. 1999. *Dispelling the Myth: High-Poverty Schools Exceeding Expectations.* Washington, DC: Education Trust.

Education Week. 2003. "To Close the Gap, Quality Counts: Executive Summary." Quality Counts Issue. *Education Week* 22(17): 7.

Ellis, Allan B. 1975. *Success and Failure: A Summary of Findings and Recommendations for Improving Elementary Reading in Massachusetts City Schools.* Waterton, MA: Educational Research Corporation.

Ferguson, Ronald F. 1991. "Paying for Public Education: New Evidence on How and Why Money Matters." *Harvard Journal on Legislation* 28(2): 465–98.

———. 1998. "Can Schools Narrow the Black-White Test Score Gap?" In *The Black-White Test Score Gap,* edited by Christopher Jencks and Meredith Phillips (318–74). Washington, DC: Brookings Institution Press.

———. 2003. "Teachers' Perception and Expectations and the Black-White Test Score Gap." *Urban Education* 38(4): 460–507.

Fouts, Jeffrey T. 2003. *A Decade of Reform: A Summary of Research Finding on Classroom, School, and District Effectiveness in Washington State.* Education Resources Information Center (ERIC) Clearinghouse Document ED482631. Lynnwood, WA: Washington School Research Center, Seattle Pacific University.

Goldhaber, Daniel, and Emily Anthony. 2003. *Teacher Quality and Student Achievement.* ERIC Clearinghouse Document ED477271. New York: ERIC Clearinghouse on Urban Education, Teachers College, Columbia University.

Goldhaber, Daniel, Dominic J. Brewer, and Deborah Anderson. 1999. "A Three-Way Error Components Analysis of Educational Productivity." *Education Economics* 7(3): 199–208.

Good, Thomas L., and Jere E. Brophy. 1986. "School Effects." In *Handbook of Research on Teaching, 3rd edition,* edited by Merlin C. Wittrock (570–602). New York: Macmillan.

Grissmer, David, Ann Flanagan, and Stephanie Williamson. 1998. "Why Did the Black-White Score Gap Narrow in the 1970s and 1980s?" In *The Black-White Test Score Gap,* edited by Christopher Jencks and Meredith Phillips (182–226). Washington, DC: Brookings Institution Press.

Hanushek, Eric A. 1992. "The Trade-Off between Child Quantity and Quality." *Journal of Political Economy* 100(1): 84–117.

Hanushek, Eric A., John F. Kain, and Steven G. Rivkin. 2002. "Inferring Program Effects for Special Populations: Does Special Education Raise Achievement for Students with Disabilities?" *Review of Economics and Statistics* 84(4): 584–99.

Hedges, Larry V., and Amy Nowell. 1998. "Black-White Test Score Convergence since 1965." In *The Black-White Test Score Gap,* edited by Christopher Jencks and Meredith Phillips (149–81). Washington, DC: Brookings Institution Press.

Heneveld, Ward, and Helen Craig. 1995. "A Framework for Using Qualitative Research to Inform Policymakers and Empower Practitioners: Lessons from Madagascar." Paper presented at the annual meeting of the International Congress for School Effectiveness and Improvement, Leeuwarden, Netherlands, January.

Hoover-Dempsey, Kathleen V., and Howard M. Sandler. 1995. "Parental Involvement in Children's Education: Why Does It Make a Difference?" *Teachers College Record* 97(2): 310–31.

Jencks, Christopher, and Meredith Phillips, eds. 1998. *The Black-White Test Score Gap.* Washington, DC: Brookings Institution Press.

Jencks, Christopher, Marshall Smith, Henry Acland, Mary Jo Bane, David Cohen, Herbert Gintis, Barbara Heyns, and Stephan Michelson. 1972. *Inequality: A Reassessment of the Effect of Family and Schooling in America.* New York: Basic Books, Inc.

Jesse, Dan, Alan Davis, and Nancy Pokorny. 2004. "High-Achieving Middle Schools for Latino Students in Poverty." *Journal of Education for Students Placed at Risk* 9(1): 23–45.

Jeynes, William H. 2003. "A Meta-Analysis: The Effects of Parent Involvement on Minority Children's Academic Achievement." *Education and Urban Society* 35(2): 202–18.

Jordan, Heather R., Robert Mendro, and Dash Weerasinghe. 1997. "Teacher Effects on Longitudinal Student Achievement." Paper presented at the National Evaluation Institute, Indianapolis, July.

Jussim, Lee, Jacquelynne Eccles, and Stephanie Madon. 1996. "Social Perception, Social Stereotypes, and Teacher Expectations: Accuracy and the Quest for the Powerful Self-Fulfilling Prophecy." *Advances in Experimental Social Psychology* 28: 281–387.

Kannapel, Patricia J., and Stephen K. Clements, with Diana Taylor and Terry Hibpshman. 2005. *Inside the Black Box of High-Performing High-Poverty Schools.* Lexington, KY: Prichard Committee for Academic Excellence.

Klitgaard, Richard E., and George R. Hall. 1975. "Are There Unusually Effective Schools?" *Journal of Human Resources* 10(1): 90–106.

Lee, Valerie, Xianglei Chen, and Becky A. Smerdon. 1996. *The Influence of School Climate on Gender Differences in the Achievement and Engagement of Young Adolescents.* Washington, DC: American Association of University Women Education Foundation.

Marks, Helen M., and Susan M. Printy. 2003. "Principal Leadership and School Performance: An Integration of Transformational and Instructional Leadership." *Educational Administration Quarterly* 39(3): 370–97.

Marzano, Robert J. 2003. *What Works in Schools: Translating Research into Action.* Alexandria, VA: Association for Supervision and Curriculum Development.

Mid-Continent Research for Education and Learning. 2005. *Final Report: High Needs Schools—What Does It Take to Beat the Odds?* Regional Educational Laboratory. Denver, CO: Mid-Continent Research for Education and Learning.

Murnane, Richard J. 1975. *The Impact of School Resources on the Learning of Inner-City Children.* Cambridge, MA: Balinger Publishing Company.

National Center for Educational Accountability. 2006. *Just for the Kids, Best Practice Studies and Institutes: Findings from 20 States.* Austin, TX: National Center for Educational Accountability.

National Council of Teachers of Mathematics. 1991. *Professional Standards for Teaching Mathematics.* Reston, VA: National Council of Teachers of Mathematics.

National Institute of Justice. 2004. *Toward Safe and Orderly Schools—The National Study of Delinquency Prevention in Schools.* Washington, DC: National Institute of Justice.

New York State Office of Education Performance Review. 1974. *School Factors Influencing Reading Achievement: A Performance Review.* Albany: New York State Office of Education Performance Review.

O'Day, Jennifer A., and Marshall S. Smith. 1993. "Systemic Reform and Educational Opportunity." In *Designing Coherent Education Policy: Improving the System,* edited by S. Fuhrman (250–312). New York: Jossey-Bass.

Perie, Marianne, Wendy S. Grigg, and Gloria S. Dion. 2005. *The Nation's Report Card: Mathematics 2005.* NCES 2006-453. Washington, DC: U.S. Department of Education, Institute of Education Sciences, National Center for Education Statistics.

Phi Delta Kappa. 1980. *Why Do Some Urban Schools Succeed?* Bloomington, IN: Phi Delta Kappa.

Purkey, Stewart C., and Marshall S. Smith. 1983. "Effective Schools: A Review." *The Elementary School Journal* 83(4): 426–52.

Ragland, Mary A., Betsy Clubine, Deborah Constable, and Pamela A. Smith. 2002. *Expecting Success: A Study of Five High-Performing, High-Poverty Schools.* ERIC Document ED468010. Washington, DC: Council of Chief State School Officers.

Reynolds, David, and Charles Teddlie. 2000. "The Processes of School Effectiveness." In *The International Handbook of School Effectiveness Research,* edited by Charles Teddlie and David Reynolds (134–59). New York: Falmer Press.

Reynolds, David, Bert Creemers, Sam Stringfield, Charles Teddlie, and Gene Schaffer, eds. 2002. *World Class Schools: International Perspectives on School Effectiveness.* New York: RoutledgeFalmer.

Rosenholtz, Susan J. 1985. "Effective Schools: Interpreting the Evidence." *American Journal of Education* 93(3): 352–88.

Rothstein, Richard. 2004. *Class and Schools: Using Social, Economic, and Educational Reform to Close the Black-White Achievement Gap.* Washington, DC: Economic Policy Institute.

Rowan, Brian, Steven T. Bossert, and David C. Dwyer. 1983. "Research on Effective Schools: A Cautionary Note." *Educational Researcher* 12(4): 24–31.

Sammons, Pam, Josh Hillman, and Peter Mortimore. 1995. *Key Characteristics of Effective Schools: A Review of School Effectiveness Research.* ERIC Document ED389826. London: International School Effectiveness and Improvement Centre, University of London.

Sanders, William L., and June C. Rivers. 1996. *Cumulative and Residual Effects of Teachers on Future Student Academic Achievement: Research Progress Report.* Knoxville: Value-Added Research and Assessment Center, University of Tennessee.

Scheerens, Jaap, and Roel J. Bosker. 1997. *The Foundations of Educational Effectiveness.* New York: Elsevier.

Smith, Marshall S., and Jennifer A. O'Day. 1991. "Systemic School Reform." In *The Politics of Curriculum and Testing,* edited by Susan H. Fuhrman and Betty Malen (233–67). Bristol, PA: Falmer Press.

Snipes, Jason, Fred Doolittle, and Corinne Herlihy. 2002. *Foundations for Success: Case Studies of How Urban School Systems Improve Student Achievement.* Washington, DC: Council of Great City Schools.

Stringfield, Sam. 1994. "Outlier Studies of School Effectiveness." In *Advances in School Effectiveness Research and Practice,* edited by David Reynolds, Bert P. M. Creemers, Pamela S. Nesselrodt, Eugene C. Shaffer, Sam Stringfield, and Charles Teddlie (73–83). Oxford: Pergamon.

Stringfield, Sam, Linda Winfield, Mary Ann Millsap, Michael J. Puma, Beth Gamse, and Bonnie Randall. 1993. *Urban and Suburban/Rural Special Strategies for Educating Disadvantaged Children: First Year Report.* Washington, DC: U.S. Department of Education.

Teddlie, Charles. 1994. "The Integration of Classroom and School Process Data in School Effects Research." In *Advances in School Effectiveness Research and Practice,* edited by David Reynolds, Bert P. M. Creemers, Pamela S. Nesselrodt, Eugene C. Shaffer, Sam Stringfield, and Charles Teddlie (111–32). Oxford: Pergamon.

Teddlie, Charles, and Samuel Stringfield. 1993. *Schools Make a Difference: Lessons Learned from a 10-Year Study of School Effects.* New York: Teachers College Press.

U.S. Department of Education. National Center for Education Statistics. 2003. *Status and Trends in the Education of Hispanics.* Washington, DC: U.S. Department of Education, National Center for Education Statistics.

Venezky, Richard L., and Linda F. Winfield. 1979. *Schools That Succeed Beyond Expectations in Reading.* Technical Report 1. Newark: Department of Educational Studies, University of Delaware.

Wang, Margaret C., Geneva D. Haertel, and Herbert J. Walberg. 1993. "Toward a Knowledge Base for School Learning." *Review of Educational Research* 63(3): 249–94.

Waters, Tim, Robert J. Marzano, and Brian McNulty. 2003. *Balanced Leadership: What 30 Years of Research Tells Us about the Effect of Leadership on Student Achievement.* Aurora, IL: Mid-Continent Research for Education and Learning.

Weber, George. 1971. *Inner-City Children Can Be Taught to Read: Four Successful Schools.* CBE Occasional Paper 18. Washington, DC: Council for Basic Education.

Weinstein, Rhonda S. 1985. "Student Mediation of Classroom Expectancy Effects." In *Teacher Expectancies,* edited by Jerome B. Dusek (329–50). Hillsdale, NJ: Lawrence Erlbaum.

White, Kerry A. 1999. "High-Poverty Schools Score Big on Kentucky Assessment." *Education Week* 18(34): 18, 20.

Wilder, Gita. 1977. "Five Exemplary Reading Programs." In *Cognition, Curriculum, and Comprehension,* edited by J. T. Guthrie (57–68). Newark, DE: International Reading Association.

Williams, Luther. 1998. *The Urban Systemic Initiatives (USI) Program of the National Science Foundation: A Summary Update.* Arlington, VA: National Science Foundation.

Williams, Trish, Michael Kirst, and Edward Haertel. 2005. *Similar Students, Different Results: Why Do Some Schools Do Better?* Mountain View, CA: EdSource.

Wright, Paul, Sandra Horn, and William L. Sanders. 1997. "Teacher and Classroom Context Effects on Student Achievement: Implications for Teacher Evaluation." *Journal of Personnel Evaluation in Education* 11: 57–67.

Young, Deidra J. 1997. "A Multilevel Analysis of Science and Mathematics Achievement." Paper presented at the annual meeting of the American Educational Research Association, Chicago, March.

Zigarelli, Michael A. 1996. "An Empirical Test of Conclusions from Effective Schools Research." *Journal of Educational Research* 90: 103–10.

About the Authors

Beatriz Chu Clewell is a principal research associate and director of the Program for Evaluation and Equity Research at the Urban Institute in Washington, D.C. During her 25-year professional career, she has conducted research on factors that influence positive educational outcomes for girls and women, minority students, limited English proficient and immigrant students, and low-income students. She is a coauthor of the book *Breaking the Barriers: Helping Female and Minority Students Succeed in Mathematics and Science*, as well as several book chapters and journal articles.

A recipient of the Distinguished Scholar Award from the American Educational Research Association, Dr. Clewell was born and raised in the Republic of Panama. She has taught at both the middle school and university levels in Honduras and Venezuela and credits her middle-school teaching experiences with inspiring in her a lifelong interest in the education of low-income children. She holds a B.A. in English literature and an M.S. and Ph.D. in educational policy, planning, and analysis from Florida State University.

Patricia B. Campbell is president of Campbell-Kibler Associates, Inc., in Groton, Massachusetts. Dr. Campbell has been involved in educational research and evaluation with a focus on science, technology, engineering, and mathematics education and issues of race/ethnicity, gender, and disability since the mid-1970s. A former professor of research, measurement, and statistics at Georgia State University, she has written more than 100 publications, including cowriting *The AAUW Report: How Schools Shortchange Girls*. Her varied professional activities include conducting educational evaluation and research training in South Africa and Uganda and serving as an expert witness in the sex discrimination case brought against the Citadel.

Dr. Campbell received the Betty Vetter Research Award from Women in Engineering Programs & Advocates Network and the Willystine Goodsell Award from the American Educational Research Association. She holds a B.S. in mathematics from LeMoyne College, an M.S. in instructional technology from Syracuse University, and a Ph.D. in teacher education, also from Syracuse University.

Lesley Perlman is the deputy director of the Center for Khmer Studies, a nonprofit nongovernmental organization based in Siem Reap, Cambodia, that works to rebuild the higher education sector in Cambodia and offers fellowship and research programs for foreign and Cambodian scholars and researchers. She previously worked as the senior research associate at Campbell-Kibler Associates, conducting research and evaluation for five years in educational projects examining gender and race equity in mathematics and science. Ms. Perlman cowrote *Upping the Numbers: Using Research-Based Decision Making to Increase Diversity in the Quantitative Disciplines and Engagement, Capacity and Continuity: A Trilogy for Student Success*, as well as other publications. She holds a B.S. in biology and women's studies from Boston College and an M.A. in sustainable international development from Brandeis University.

Index